A GUIDE TO

EFFECTIVE
MANAGEMENT

Practical Applications from Behavioral Science

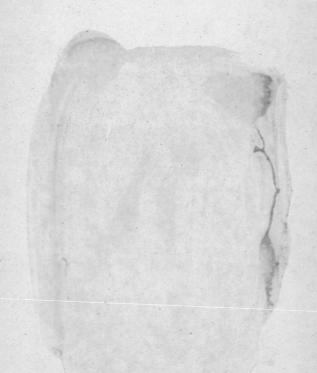

A GUIDE TO

EFFECTIVE MANAGEMENT

Practical Applications from Behavioral Science

LESLIE E. THIS · Project Associates, Inc.

ADDISON-WESLEY PUBLISHING COMPANY

Reading, Massachusetts · Menlo Park, California
London · Amsterdam · Don Mills, Ontario · Sydney

ISBN 0-201-07559-8

BCDEFGHIJ-CO-798765

No person is "self-made"—more than he realizes, he has been fashioned by all with whom he has interfaced. This book is dedicated to those persons who have significantly contributed to the development of the author:

- My wife, Delight, whose intuitive use of most of the management processes in a microsetting—our family—opened to me many avenues of exploration and application in the macrosetting—the organization.

- The 5000 managers with whom the author has worked, representing approximately 100,000 years of recent managerial practice, and who helped us abstract their learnings from that vast practice.

- Gordon L. Lippitt, whose remarkable diagnostic and analytical talents and fully "sharing" friendship have been particularly impactful.

Preface

Every manager, supervisor, staff specialist, or organizational leader has two primary job objectives—to achieve maximum production and at the same time provide for maximum employee job satisfaction. Often, the manager feels that these are two completely incompatible goals.

Since 1900 three major approaches have been identified in the search for a balanced answer:

1. From shortly before the turn of this century until about 1940, the major emphasis was: "Get the work out—no matter what you do to people." This is oversimplified, and not all organizations bought the philosophy, but most were oriented in this direction. Employees were a physical resource to be manipulated and interchanged as was any other resource. Scientific management was in full sway. Human-engineering experts with stop watches, clipboards, and slide rules studied the best ways to get the most from man/machine interfaces. If the human resource wore out early or broke down, there was always another human unit waiting to take his or her place. American enterprise made great progress

under this system, and related to its time was an understandable evolutionary phase.

2. About 1940, with American attention turning to the need for the increased production required by World War II, a new philosophy began to emerge. Usually, it was stated as: "Management is the art of getting work done through others." Increasingly, we became aware that two organizations existed side by side in the enterprise:

a) The mechanistic organization—organization charts, classification systems, functional and program statements, job descriptions, wage and salary systems, etc. —usually referred to as the "formal system."

b) The people side of the enterprise—feelings, ambitions, social needs, emotions, loyalty, ego and self-actualization needs, etc. This is normally referred to as the "informal system."

Organizations became acutely aware of how the informal organization could, and often did, not only modify the formal system, but often defeat the objectives of the formal system. A great deal of interest and research was directed toward the study of the informal system. At first, this trend took the form of a pseudo, naive approach—"Smile at the employee in the morning, and he'll bust a gut for you all day." Later, the approach became much more sophisticated, as the behavioral scientist and organizational leaders recognized that they were dealing with a very complex set of forces.

3. About 1968 the literature increasingly began to reflect still another philosophy: "Management is the art of developing people through their work." A number of forces brought this about: the questioning of traditional organizational values by the young, a more highly educated work force, the search for life's meaning, changing values, more open confrontation in our society, affluence—the list goes on and on.

The manager and organization increasingly turned to the behavioral scientist to ask: "What do you know about people in the work place? How can we more effectively motivate employees?

How should we structure and organize them? How can we improve decision-making? How can we improve teamwork and reduce vested interests and empire building?"

There was no lack of response. Management and training consultant firms sprang up like mushrooms. Academic professors spent more time consulting than teaching. Every piece of limited research was reported out, systems often developed around it, and concepts and models spewed through the country. When the organizational manager asked, "But how do you apply the concept or model?" he was generally told, "I was paid to explain it, not to apply it. That's your problem."

This book makes no pretense of covering all the processes or concerns of managers. It does not provide a systematic, integrated way of looking at the manager, the manager's job, or the organization. Rather, the chapter content reflects the major content areas and managerial concerns with which organizations have increasingly asked the author to deal during the past three years. Similarly, no attempt has been made to cover, or identify, all of the research within the content areas selected for study.

We consider that many of the managers in organizations are behavioral experts, even though they are not affiliated with the academic world or do not hold advanced degrees issued by it. The author has attempted to ferret through the academic research, look at organizational programs and approaches derived from this research, ask other consultants what they have discovered works in the content area under inquiry, and inquire of organizational managers what they have found to be useful guidelines and techniques. These guidelines have been identified, where they exist, and are reported in the chapter discussions.

In such an approach, it is inevitable that the inquirer will also develop some notions about useful guidelines. It is also understood that what to the inquirer is objective and descriptive may, to another observer, be out and out bias, prejudice, faulty observation, or misdirected application. It may also be seen as nonscientific and nonprofessional. Each observer of organizational phenomena, however, must hammer out a personal framework that makes sense of observed fragments of behavior. By seeing how the world looks to different persons, perhaps we shall all be moved a bit closer to seeing and understanding organizational reality.

To manage effectively, a manager must be knowledgeable and skillful in these areas:

- Have an understanding of self and how one's personal behavior affects others, as well as an understanding of the dynamics of other people and of groups.

- Have some understanding of what an organization is all about—its purpose, developmental stages, and the common problems occurring within the organization at a given stage of development.

- Have an understanding of the management processes through which the manager gets the organizational work done—delegation, decision-making, and communication.

The chapter discussions are concerned with selected portions of each of these three major areas. On occasion, the reader may be tempted to say of certain guidelines, "But everybody knows that." It is the deep conviction of the author, and of most effective managers with whom he has worked, that it is not usually the malfunctioning of the macrosystem in organizations that creates most organizational problems, but the neglect or failure of managers and others to do the simple things "everybody knows they should do."

For example, the owner of a small company, with 25 employees, does not have to set up complex systems to get a job done. The manager is in direct contact with all employees and knows them very well. The relationship is direct: owner to nonsupervisory worker. In a large organization, however, the president is not in direct contact with the nonsupervisory worker, and it is not unusual for the president to be eight echelons removed. The organization introduces all kinds of macrosystems to secure the same kinds of objectives and results desired by the owner of a small company. The organization introduces complex systems for recruitment, training, wage and salary administration, promotions, requisition of supplies, inventory controls, motivation models, operations research, "zero defects," management analysis, computerized programs—the list goes on and on. Yet, the objectives are identical for both types of organizations. However, now the managers have to contend with systems, programs, directives, manuals, standard operating procedures, coordinative meetings, etc. The manager can soon make the mistake of servicing the mechanism and the structure—and in so doing forget what the structure and mechanics exist to accomplish.

Two other items should be clarified. First, the term "manager" is used throughout, since it does not seem appropriate to continue to say: "manager, supervisor, administrator, leader, staff specialist." Everyone, at every level, "manages" time, resources, outputs, structure, and methodology, and the term "manager" best conveys the sense of these multiple functions. Second, it is always awkward to find a term that includes both male and female. Terms such as "manager" and other terms and pronouns in the masculine gender are to be understood as including both male and female.

McLean, Virginia   L.E.T.
September 1974

Contents

9

OVERCOMING RESISTANCE TO CHANGE 185

10

OFTEN, ORGANIZATIONAL MEDIA ARE THE MESSAGES ... 205

11

**SELECTING AN ORGANIZATIONAL STRUCTURE
FOR MAXIMUM RESULTS** 221

Coping with the Multiple, Changing Roles of the Manager

1

"Jim, I may need you to work late tonight to get out that Fairfax report."

"Mr. Bronstad, could you show me what you want done on that Chicago survey?"

"Mr. Bronstad, I'm calling you to remind you of our PTA Executive Committee meeting tonight."

"Mr. Bronstad, Mr. Robertson called to say you have been appointed as a member of the new Inventory Control Task Force."

"Daddy, don't forget my birthday party tonight."

"Jim. About that meeting of our professional society tonight you are to chair. . . ."

"Mr. Bronstad, I need to see you about some advice on a personal problem."

Sound familiar? Most readers will say, "There, but for the name, go I." Each day we are called on to behave appropriately in many different roles—wife, husband, parent, friend, counselor, decision maker, boss, subordinate, peer, small-group member, advocate, planner, teacher, etc., etc., etc. As we assume more responsible jobs, we find that the number of organizational roles multiplies. Some of the roles remain constant; new ones are added; in some we feel uncomfortable or unskilled; some of the roles may even be in conflict.

How can a manager deal effectively with these multiple role demands? Where are helpful guidelines? Social science has explored this area, and while much more research is needed and being accomplished, certain helpful findings have emerged.

CHARACTERISTICS OF ORGANIZATIONS

Bigness

We begin by looking at the nature of organizations and are struck by their "bigness." The large-scale, rationalized, formalized, efficient organization is a major reality of our time. In this bigness, certain factors stand out:

2. *Specialization.* So specialized are we that recently we have had demands in Congress for investigating committees to investigate investigating committees. With specialization comes increased roles.

2. *Division of knowledge and labor.* This process has been accelerated ever since the beginning of the Industrial Revolution. Its impact on organizations coincides with the general practitioner giving way to the specialist.

3. *Coordination, synthesis, and synergism.* With bigness comes separateness, and with separateness comes the need for coordination and integration. We find that this must be done if we are ever to turn out a unit of production or give service to a single community member.

If this list partially describes the effect of bigness, what happens to the employee who inhabits such organizations? Much has been written recently to describe these impacts. Employees feel isolated, powerless, and sense that their destinies are shaped by impersonal forces. More and more emphasis is put on efficiency and rationality, but the more emphasis is applied, the more ephemeral efficiency and rationality become. Employees begin to put a high value on conformity. (Even in newly created organizations, one sees this phenomenon. Once "rebellious" individuals create a group and an organization, the "organizational demands" temper much of their initial fervor, and they, too, begin to serve the organizational requirements.) Employees speak of the "bureaucratized man." The demands of organizations are seen as incompatible and antimaturing. The roles to be played are seen as many, often vague, and frequently in conflict. Most managers feel that they can, at best, find their way through the maze of demands only through "flying by the seats of their pants."

Many managers are unwilling to live by such precarious guides. "Surely," they say, "there must be guidelines emerging out of all the experience of so many managers and from the research in the field." Their search for guides is heightened by such practical considerations as:

- The single largest block of one's "awake" hours is spent in one's job.

- Increasingly, employees are demanding that their organizational life be complementary and congruent with their total life.

- Unwillingness to permit organizations and their management solely to define the roles and role postures of employees.

- A search for integrity among the roles one plays on and off the job.

- A search for roles that are dynamic and proactive rather than traditional and reactive.

As we indicated earlier, managers are troubled by the multiplication and formalization of roles not only within the organization, but also within the family and the community. These roles can never, of course, be divorced from a study of people's roles in an organization. However, we will direct our major attention to the roles within organizations. This focus does not in any way imply that family and community roles are less important or that they do not materially contribute to the difficulties inherent in organizational roles.

System of Relationships

We come now to one other consideration about organizations, their essence. Basically, an "organization" may be defined as the search for regularity, standardization, and predictability in people's relationship with one another. These relationships may, of course, be formal or informal.

How do we define a "role" within an organization, family, or community? Role may be defined in terms of my position and the expectations I and others have about that position. A "position" locates me in a system of work and social relationships. Your organization has a set of such positions, and you occupy one of those positions. A position may be thought of in several ways:

1. *Function*—what a person does in his job.

2. *How a person relates to others*—for example, a supervisor and a subordinate.

3. *How a person ranks hierarchically*—at the top is the president; at the bottom is probably the night cleaning staff. Somewhere in between is you.

These are ways in which we define the position each employee occupies. In addition, each of the positions has a number of roles the incumbent is expected to play when occupying that position. Sometimes these roles are known and public; sometimes they are vague and ill-defined. They may or may not be reduced to writing. They may be formal or informal. Some are inherent in the job; others develop because of the personality of the employee occupying the position.

Some of the roles that go with a position are waiting—like clothes in a closet—for an employee to "put on." For example, Calvin Coolidge went to church one Sunday morning. His wife was not feeling well and did not accompany him. Upon his return from church, Mr. Coolidge (well known for his uncommunicativeness) sat in a chair and began to read the Sunday paper. His wife waited a bit, then asked, "What did the minister preach on today?" There was a pause. "Sin," Mr. Coolidge replied. "And what did he have to say about sin?" There was another pause. "He's against it."

This example illustrates a ministerial role and the inherent values that go with it. No minister could come out for sin, for he has only one basic role in respect to sin—to be against it. Similarly, every job we occupy has its ready-made quota of roles all defined and waiting for us to put them on—roles of supervisor, big boss, little boss, chairman of the staff picnic committee, consultant, decision maker, instructor, night coverage worker, delegator, controller, lunch hour worker, etc., etc., etc. Sometimes these roles and the trappings that go with them are quite comfortable. At other times, the roles are quite new, and new job incumbents find the trappings unfamiliar, uncomfortable, chafing, and at times almost intolerable.

As we learn to assume the roles expected of us, we find ourselves raising many questions and encountering many problems. Frequently we are confronted with the problem of how, as the holder of this job, we should interact with others. "What should I do? What should I not do?" It is at this point that the manager frequently seeks counsel —and makes a peculiar discovery. If one asks one's boss, one gets one set of things to do and not to do; if one asks one's subordinates, one gets another set; and, if one asks one's peers, one gets yet a third set.

Observers have frequently been fascinated in watching middle-management persons step into the lower echelons of top management. For months afterwards they are quite lonely. The advice of top management seems unattainable; that of lower management too confining; and that of peers too accommodating to social pressures or the expediency of the moment. The manager expresses it like this: "In my last job, I only supervised ten people. We knew one another quite well. I knew all about their families. We often ate or had coffee together, entertained frequently, played sports together. Now I have 100 employees for whom I am responsible. How can I know each of them personally? Should I even try? What happens to their relationship with their immediate supervisor if I try to know them? How can I stay 'one of the gang' and still be 'big boss' to them? Are these roles compatible? Should they be compatible? How aloof must I become? What do I do with information I know about my former peers that is undesirable from the organization's standpoint but which was shared with me on a 'buddy' basis before I got this job? What's different about my relationships with my former peers? What is different about my supervisory function?" Anyone who has watched a manager in this dilemma seek out answers to these kinds of questions knows that the paraphernalia of a new role can be most galling.

As we find working answers, or accept the solutions of others, we find that the answers or solutions become evaluative standards. The behavior we display, the way we "play the role," becomes the way we apply the standards to our job, our roles, and those who inherit the role. Further, others do the same thing—this is what others use in interpreting to themselves and to others what we do, or should do, in our jobs.

As we examine the expectations we and others have of the roles we play in a given position, we find that for each role we ask a number of questions. One question has to do with behavior. What should I do in this role; what should I not do? Obviously, this question has to do mostly with appropriate behavior, but very frequently ethical and value judgments are also involved. Usually such questioning ends with our defining for ourselves, consistent with organizational philosophy, something like, "In this role it is appropriate that I conduct myself this way."

Another question has to do with priorities. What ought I to do or what must I do? This almost becomes a rank-ordering of the aspects of the roles that are important and to what degree. Hopefully, this ensures, in a busy schedule, that those expectations in the role that are most crucial are met before lesser expectations are met.

Still another question is, "Who are the expecters and what right do they have to expect this or that from me?" For any position, the number of expecters are legion. Most of them are legitimate expecters. In my position the organization makes clear that I am there to meet certain expectations. However, my manager must always be on guard for the legitimate expecters who bring illegitimate expectations or for staff with expectations that should be met elsewhere in the organization. This is particularly likely to happen if the manager enjoys some good degree of staff acceptance and gains a reputation for being a good administrator. If one is near the top of the echelon, staff may begin to hail one as the Messiah and build up expectations that are not only inappropriate, but may well jeopardize one's efforts to accomplish legitimate expectations.

Another question often asked is, "Who are the recipients of what I am expected to do?" It is well to sort the targets out carefully. This is true from two standpoints. First, if one is to meet a group's expectations effectively, one must know a great deal about the group and why they expect what they do. Such a study will reveal many leads as to the best way to meet expectations, a way that is most readily acceptable in terms of the standards, values, personalities, and insights of the group concerned. Second, it is sometimes found that in meeting the expectations of what seems to be the primary target group, one is really meeting the expectations of another, apparently secondary, group that may really be the primary group. For example, in the area of grievances, it may appear that the employees are the primary group whose expectations are to be met and that one's role in this area is defined by the employee group. However, one may soon learn that some expectations, in terms of both behavior and appropriate decisions, stem from management and that the primary target to satisfy is not the employee group, but management.

One may ask the question, "What can I, as a job occupant, expect from others as against my obligation?" "What, in short, are my rights? Do I have any? If so, what are they?"

In every role, people not only have the right of certain expectations from me, but they are also in a role, and their role should encompass certain expectations from them on my part. This is a two-way street, and managers will do well to be sure that not only are staff helped to know what they can expect of managers, but also that there is another ingredient—what managers can expect of staff. When being appraised, for example, a subordinate has a right to expect help from the manager. However, the subordinate does not have the right to an expectation that says, in effect, "Here I am, sitting like a sponge. Now fill me up with an evaluation of my performance, directions in which I should move, how I can qualify for promotion; tell me my aptitudes, and point me in the direction of the fuller life."

The manager has a right to expect that a subordinate come to such an appraisal conference with the kind of preparation and frame of mind that indicates: "I have determined that this is the kind of vocation I like and want to pursue. I have been sharing with you my need for help, and you have been helping me. As I see my performance now, these are the areas in which I believe I need help, and these are the ways in which I think you and the organization can help me. In addition, here are some things I can, should, and am doing on my own to improve my performance and potential. I'd like to review all of this with you and see how it checks out so that both the organization and I can gain by my continual improvement."

There is one last question a manager might well raise about

expectations, namely, attributes as distinguished from behavior ("What I should be as against what I should do"). One of a manager's greatest powers is the power of example. Most managers tend to scoff at the idea of their behavior influencing employees, but managerial behavior has a tremendous impact on subordinates. It isn't enough to say, "Do as I say, not as I do." The subordinate can counter with, "What you are speaks so loudly that I can't hear what you are saying."

As you gain experience in the managerial area, you will find that you can learn a great deal about the head of a unit or department by simply observing the work patterns, behavior, attitudes, and work performance of the employees in that unit or department. This power of example, unfortunately, works just as effectively for undesirable behavior as for desirable behavior. Managers must continually examine their assumptions, feelings, and image of their position so that they are congruent with their behavior. If they aren't, staff members soon learn which set of expectations to meet—the spoken or the behavioral.

As managers look at their various roles within and outside an organization, they find that to work effectively in these roles they must understand themselves and their roles. A human being is a very complex organism and behaves in response to many forces from within and outside the organization.

All individuals perceive their environment in their own way. Each of us is unique in our values, our feelings, and our interpretation of what we see and experience. This is true because these parts of us are shaped through the many experiences we have had up to this point in life, and for no two of us have the experiences been identical. No two of us seeing the same scene, the same incident, or the same work role will see the identical thing. This accounts for different actions in response to the same stimulus; each of us takes what seems to us fitting action in terms of what we have perceived. The manager and the subordinate never will "see" an incident or interpersonal transaction the same way.

This phenomenon is well illustrated in a film frequently used in training programs, *The Eye of the Beholder.* Another example is found when a family prepares to spend a weekend in their country cabin. As they leave their suburban home, the sky is threatening, and the family fears that rain will spoil their weekend. Upon arrival in the country, they talk with two farm neighbors. It has not rained for five weeks, crops are parched, and the farmers look at the clouds and pray it will rain. The reality—threatening skies—is identical for both the family and the farmers. However, the family sees the reality as a weekend spoiler, whereas the farmers see the reality as a hoped-for blessing. Similarly, in organization life, one often encounters a reorganization effort. Management sees it as desirable, a better way of working more economically, efficiently, etc., whereas the employees affected may see it as a disastrous threat to security, present relationships, efficiency, and may even view it as antiunion or antihumane.

Individuals are influenced by their environment. For most of us, people are the most important part of our environment, and therefore we tend to be influenced most by people. We are continually assessing our environment and the people who comprise that environment, and such perceptions are both accurate and inaccurate. As one strives for final answers—final positions—one gradually learns that this is never possible. Because I feel and because I experience, I am never the exact same person on any two consecutive days. The act of reading a book has an impact on the reader—perhaps considerable, perhaps negligible—but it has an impact. Add up all the impacts of this day, and you will not be the same person tomorrow that you were this morning.

Other examples of this generalization are seen in my awareness that I do not behave the same way in church as I do in a nightclub, in the presence of my boss and in the presence of my subordinates, in a crowd and when I am alone, in the environment of a courtroom versus a dinner party, in an appraisal setting versus a training activity in a classroom. I do respond to my environment—the people and physical aspects of any particular environment.

Individuals also influence their environment. In some situations I have a great deal of authority, and my influence is quite noticeable. I can influence by persuasion, by setting expectations, by rationality. Much of our life is spent in organizations as "change agents." Draw back from your desk some time and reflect on the activities of a single day; you'll be amazed at the time you have spent in attempting to change something or some bodies. Much of organizational life is a process of attempting to change behavior, change markets, change buying patterns, change ways of working, change ways of thinking about things, influencing others; in short, an effort to influence the environment.

An individual becomes a part of the environment of others. To every person I met today, I was a part of that person's environment. To some degree I was one of the forces changing that person, making an impact on that person; therefore, what the person becomes tomorrow is partly a result of my contacts with that person today. I may, officially in my job, limit or release the creative potential of others. I live in a variety of environments, and in each environment I have a role and an influence.

This is often a difficult concept for people to grasp. In police officer training, for example, one of the toughest tasks is helping the young officer understand that as he approaches a person or group, their reaction, response, and behavior is in part a function of how the officer reacts, responds, and behaves. By the same token, managers find it hard to accept that as they describe the behavior of subordinates, they often are telling a great deal about themselves. This is the way their subordinate—these subordinates—behave with *me,* as their manager, behaving as I do. If they had a different manager, or if I behaved differently, their behavior would, at least to some degree, be different.

Just as it is difficult to separate us from our environment, so, too, it is hard to separate individuals from their jobs. A job is a person in action, and to a large degree an employee makes a job. We have all heard it said of a given position, "That isn't the way that office operated before Brown got in there." And it wasn't. Brown brings something peculiar to the job that wasn't there before. In this, of course, lies danger, but in this also lie many strengths. The right person in an ill-defined or ill-located job can make a significant contribution.

But the reverse is also true; no person completely makes a job or is free to play a self-defined organizational role. A number of limitations and expectations are built into most jobs and the roles we step into. Seldom are we ever complete masters of our organizational fate. Our actions are not determined by ourselves alone; rather, they are affected by a whole host of other people who have their own expectations of us. We can visualize these other influences in four categories, and we will illustrate this concept by using one role—that of being "boss."

What accounts for the present way you are behaving in the role of a boss? First, you are influenced by factors inside yourself—how you think the role should be played. This might take the form of "Let them know who's in charge. Carry a big stick. Give orders and don't tolerate any questioning. Be tough—ruthless. Get the job done; that's what really counts." Or, it could be at the other extreme. "Be democratic and group-oriented. Involve subordinates in decision-making and planning. Be human-relations conscious. Share the leadership function." In part, these internal influences derive from your early programming—from parents, school, church, basic personality pattern, etc. But, seldom are you free to behave the way "I really would like to play the role of boss."

Second, the way you play the role is modified by the expectations of significant others:

- Your subordinates and their expectations of how a boss should behave
- Your peers
- Your own boss
- Your profession
- Your religion
- Your spouse
- Your children
- Your union and union rules

A third factor influencing your action is your own organization and how it believes the role should be played. Most organizations have policies, directives, and regulations that detail the desired "boss" behavior in their organization.

Fourth, society also lays down some rules and guidelines. No longer can a boss use cruel treatment or punishment. Equal-employment laws circumscribe "boss" behavior.

Out of all these inputs each of us finally fashions what, for us, is the best way to play the role of "boss." However, it should be noted that in organizational life, roles for the manager may come and go; they may be fairly permanent, but periodically be stressed or underplayed, or they may remain fairly constant. Emerging roles will, of course, vary with organizations, profession, function, geography, and current societal concerns. Among those rules frequently mentioned in recent months have been:

- Human behavior engineer
- Ecology expert
- Minority group/women's rights legal expert
- Job restructurer
- Union interpreter
- Consumer specialist
- Internal consultant
- Change agent
- Advocate
- Instructor
- Continuing student
- Team member
- Social responsibility leader

One of the questions that often troubles managers is, "But, if I play many roles in the course of a day, how do people ever see or know the real me; and how do I know the real 'others' whom I meet?" A few guidelines can be helpful here:

1. Casual meetings or short exposure to another person can be misleading. We see that person in only one role. Judgment should be withheld until we see the person in several roles and can begin to abstract the centrality in that person. This is why we often dislike a person initially, but after knowing him awhile, say, "I found out that Joe's really a good guy." What we are saying is, "When I saw Joe in one role, I didn't like him, but when I saw his behavior in several roles, I liked the totality of him."

2. There should be congruence in all our roles and role behavior. Carl Rogers refers to this as "authenticity."

3. A person can play a role inappropriately, with contrived behavior. This is what we mean when we say that someone is overacting or "putting on a show." In response to such behavior, we might say "Act your age" or "Be yourself." For example, how does one play the role of job applicant? One may overact or underact and be eliminated from further consideration.

All this, even for the best of managers, is not easy. What a person does on a job is complex. The forces are many. The demands are confusing. The better person one is, the more responsibility one assumes, and the more complex is the job. A person needs a way of sorting out the demands, a way of thinking about the job, a way of bringing some order into the confusion without oversimplifying the realities.

Frequently, we have trouble in sorting out the demands in relation to our jobs. Many different people expect different things from us, and sometimes their expectations conflict. In the examples cited at the beginning of the chapter, it would be difficult for our Mr. Bronstad to meet the expectations of his daughter, the church, his work organization, and the PTA—all on the same night. Even worse, sometimes the values of these other people and organizations are in conflict with our values.

This matter of value conflict can be a crucial one for the manager. If the conflict for time demands is hard, the conflict between values systems can be traumatic. Often, the conflict is easily reconciled because some values I don't place too high, and these I can accommodate. For example, I hold the comfort value of dress to be sport clothes. My organization holds different values on dress; it requires a business suit and tie.

But I have other values, like providing for my family, getting ahead in the organization, tenure, and security. Although there is a conflict here, I don't have much trouble sublimating my comfort-dress value to these other values, and I wear a suit and tie.

But what happens in a situation when one of two employees must be released? One is young and single and does a measurably better job than the other. The other employee is older, will have trouble finding work, has a large family, but does a noticeably less efficient job. Which employee shall I release? The organization value system says one thing; my personal set of values about how to treat people, responsibility for the family, and a host of other values say something else. How do I now conduct myself? How do I handle this conflict in roles?

Unfortunately, there is no reference volume to which we can turn which lists all of the values in life and rank-orders them so that we can see which value has the highest priority and should be selected to apply in a given situation. One learns that values may be relative—that they may apply with different force, depending on the situation. We have the value that it is good to be a law-abiding citizen. We have another value that says it is good to save a human life. Should we come across an accident on a lonely road in a 30 mph posted zone, and if the victim is bleeding to death and we can't stop the flow of blood, our two values of being a law-abiding citizen and saving human life come into conflict. In this instance we will reorder the ranking of the value of being a law-abiding citizen as it relates to the speed limit.

Many such conflicts in values come in the expectations of others toward us in our multiple organizational roles. There are no hard and fixed rules to guide us. Each manager must ferret out the answer for himself. Generally, one probably tries to apply the value or values which will serve the greatest good of the greatest number over the longest period of time. Sometimes we may have to ask to be released from an organizational role because we can't accept the value conflicts in expectations. If enough of our values, particularly those which rank quite high in our own value system, are continually in conflict with organizational values or the expectations of others, we probably will resolve the conflict by resigning and identifying with an organization whose value system coincides more closely with ours.

As we try to learn what roles we must play and how best to behave in the various roles, we must be allowed some flexibility to try out different ways of playing a given role so that we can find the best behavior for that role. This means that we must be willing to do some experimentation and that the organization must permit some experimentation. Not to provide for such flexibility means that organizational roles become stereotyped, traditionalized, and perfunctorily performed in ways that are no longer effective or desirable.

Some of the keys to improving managerial role behavior are:

1. Watch the results. What role behavior seems to stimulate constructive responses in other people and in myself? For I, too, will respond to my behavior.

2. I am helped if I have a sense of security and am able to "trust" my environment.

3. I am also helped if I have a sense of adequacy—the feeling that I am able to influence my environment.

4. It helps if I can remember that people who have expectations of me also will be helped if I can contribute to their sense of security and adequacy.

5. I can continually look for cues as to the effect of my role behavior—both positive and negative.

6. I can realize that role demands change and periodically review the behavior that seems most desirable.

7. I can be open to feedback and consciously experiment with new role behavior in order to improve my performance and effectiveness.

How Organizations are Attempting to Motivate Today's Employees

2

Every manager must be concerned with two major organizational demands: (1) maximum quality production from the staff assigned to the manager, and (2) maximum individual job satisfaction for the staff assigned to the manager. At times these seem to be irreconcilable demands. In the manager's efforts to find answers, too frequently he swings from one extreme to the other. Organizations also frequently make this same error. Sometimes production is stressed, particularly in emergencies, recessions, and periods of profit squeezes. The manager becomes a close-controlling, hard task master—"all work and no play." The other extreme is to place emphasis on pseudohuman relations and to run a "happy shop." Everyone is having a good time, but little work is being accomplished.[1]

Managers, organizations, and societies have coped for milleniums with this problem. In the past, the issue was relatively simple, because for the most part, organizations did not have large numbers of employees. Another factor was that, until recently, no nation had a surplus of output, so it was evident to the worker that he worked, or else starved. The techniques most commonly employed to handle employees were:

1. *Slavery.* If you owned a person, you had a right to say what was to be done and how it was to be done.

2. *Serfdom.* The landowner "tied" the peasant to his land by supplying housing, a portion of the crops, seed, military and police protection, and an unwritten understanding that he would provide for the tenant in years of poor crops. Modifications of this system were to be seen in the United States in the tenant farmer and sharecropper system and in the practice of certain industries, notably lumber and coal mining, where the company owned the company housing and the company store.

Most organizations, and managers, tend to think that the concept of serfdom is something that is years behind us. However, a good case can be made that this is not so. For example, how do organizations today attempt to "tie" the employee to the organization? They do it with increasingly more attractive sick-leave benefits, annual-leave increases, retirement plans, bonus plans, salary increments based on tenure, etc. These can be viewed as an attempt to make continued employment so attractive that the employee cannot quit. Says the employee, "I would like to leave and go to another employer—or start up a business of my own. But when I think of the benefits I now have, and am working toward, I realize that I cannot afford to leave."

3. *Apprenticeship.* The normal pattern here was for the artisan to take one or more apprentices for periods of from three to five years. Usually, the apprentice was given little or no pay, but did receive board and room and was taught a skill, craft, or trade. The apprentice could then go out on his own as an individual entrepreneur. Remnants of this system are to be seen today in some crafts, guilds, and trades.

4. *Individual ownership.* Most of our early products were produced by the individual farmer, miller, wheelwright, merchant, cobbler, carpenter, etc.

At the turn of this century, with the introduction of labor-saving machinery and the phenomenon of large masses of workers working under one roof, none of these techniques seemed to be useful as motivational techniques. The motivational model that was developed under scientific management, early in the 1900s, was financial remuneration. The assumption was that workers wanted money above all else and would do anything for money. To secure production and to motivate workers was a matter of manipulating their financial pay. When workers' behavior was in the right direction, management held out additional financial carrots. When their behavior was not in the right direction, management threatened to reduce their pay, in the expectation that the workers would modify their behavior.

This system has come under heavy attack in the past 20 years, although it should also be noted that the United States made tremendous gains under this system. Placed in the context of history, it was a significant development. In recent years there has been an increasing realization that a person does not work only for money. We now talk about things like "psychic pay." We hear of the "revolt of the blue-collar worker." Women and minority groups are demanding more than traditional work roles.

Slowly, subtly, the meaning of work has undergone significant changes, and this has had far-reaching implications on employee motivation. It is beyond the scope of this chapter to indicate the many changes and their implications. A nontechnical explanation of many of these factors can be found in a recently published report of a special task force to the Secretary of Health, Education, and Welfare, entitled *Work In America.*[2]

The manager who looks at this kaleidoscopic, changing pattern of dynamics is often at a loss as to how to motivate his workers. He knows the problems all too well. In 1972 I became interested in whether changes in employee work habits and job behavior were fairly constant among different industries and businesses and whether or not they tended to differ in various parts of the nation. A survey was made of 1000 supervisors and managers attending management and supervisory development seminars, conferences, and workshops. These people came from 23 organizations from all parts of the United States. About one-third were supervisors of office personnel and represented business, industry, government, and nonprofit organizations. The responses were surprisingly constant. Either managers and supervisors all have the same set of biases, or there are some very noticeable, constant changes. Following are some of the results of this survey (the responses are rank-ordered).

A. What changes in the meaning of work and employee motivation have you observed in the past seven years among wage, hourly, and blue-collar workers?

1. Less pride in workmanship.
2. Menial work is "not in."
3. Less loyalty to the organization.
4. Those with long seniority are not motivated, and you can't touch them.
5. They are less dependent on the employer and look to the government to meet their needs.
6. More independent because of other wage earners in the family.
7. Less concern for quality, waste, housekeeping.
8. More awareness to the job, company, community, and society.
9. More mature, sophisticated, and educated.
10. Don't want overtime.
11. More grievances about work environment.
12. Work is not as great a part of their life as it once was.
13. Less responsive to authority.
14. Unionization has leveled out performance between and among grades.
15. Want more control over their destiny.

B. What changes in the meaning of work and employee motivation have you observed in the past seven years among technical and professional workers?

1. Impatient with the future—want to "get there fast."
2. Less company loyalty.
3. Resist regimentation.
4. Work is less central in their lives.
5. Want challenge in their assignments.

6. Less respect for authority.

7. Want to know the effect of their work.

8. Are more confident in their abilities.

9. Demand to be independent of the company in selection and expression of social values.

10. More open questioning of corporate objectives, philosophy, actions, and methods.

11. Want freedom to perform.

12. Want job enrichment.

13. More questioning.

14. Participate more in community activities.

15. More concerned with individual personnel record than with performance (noted almost exclusively by governmental employees).

C. What changes in the meaning of work and employee motivation have you observed within yourself in the past seven years?

1. It is less fun to work.

2. Loss of power.

3. They have changed the ground rules on how to handle a job and how to supervise.

4. Great deal of challenge in the job.

5. More concern with people and interpersonal relationships.

6. More concerned with environment.

7. Less confidence in my ability to do the job.

8. Less authoritative.

9. I am less resistant to change.

10. I am a greater risk taker because I don't fear retaliation as I once did.

11. More questioning.

12. I get involved in more participative decision-making.

13. Aware the company exists for employees as well as for profits.

14. Loss of direct, individual praise; receive more group rewards.

15. Question my value to the organization.

(It can be assumed that not all the changes that supervisors and managers note in the work force are necessarily negative or undesirable. It can be further assumed that supervisors and managers will often tend to resist even those changes they might personally feel are positive, though their organization may not agree. Based on these assumptions, we then asked the supervisors and managers):

D. Why do you think supervisors and managers tend to resist most of these changes?

1. It is not what I thought the job would be.

2. It seems to say that what we've done in the past was not good enough.

3. Fear of the unknown.

4. They're crapping all over everything we hold dear.

5. It negates my values, and I honestly feel the new values are wrong.

6. I am jealous, because I didn't have it so good when I was younger.

7. I am losing authority, but am still being held accountable.

8. Less predictable results.

9. There is an implied threat that I must move with the changes, or I won't be around.

10. I'm losing control, and it makes my job harder.

APPROACHES TO MOTIVATION

How, then, can the manager find guidelines to assist him as a motivator of employees? Research in this area has been fairly prolific in the past 20 years. Frequently, an organization will select one research approach and build a motivational system or motivational emphasis from it. This is probably a mistake. No one yet fully knows or understands employee motivation. Although each researcher is adding to our incomplete knowledge, we still don't know all the facets of what motivates employees. Therefore, the manager is probably better advised to use what seems applicable and useful from all the approaches.

Looking at the research and at the organizational motivational systems built on that research, one finds that the various approaches range from those in which the motivational stimulus is considered to be "outside" the employee, to those in which the motivational stimulus is considered to be "inside" the employee. Seven fairly discrete approaches can be identified. Although this description of motivational approaches is oversimplified and the approaches are not mutually exclusive, this oversimplification seems justified in order to assist the manager in sorting out and understanding the differences and specific focus he will find in the many books and articles he reads about motivation.

External Motivational Stimuli

Habit (stimulus-response approach)

One way to secure the behavior we desire is to control the person's response to a stimulus. If the desired response is insisted upon and rewarded each time the stimulus is presented, the person will ultimately adopt that response, without thinking every time the stimulus occurs. This approach is used a great deal in military training: the drill sergeant puts the recruits through the same response to a command over and over until the time comes when the recruit hears the command and automatically and unthinkingly gives the proper response. This approach is also used extensively in child training, driver-education training, and safety training.

Habit is a major way we cope effectively with our complex life. We train ourselves to follow desired habit patterns. Probably close to 85 percent of our behavior is dictated by habit. Those who doubt this have only to observe themselves in the morning for a half hour. The ritual begins with the ringing of the alarm clock: the alarm rings, we get up, and stumble into the bathroom; the ritual of the next half hour probably has not varied for ten years.

The supervisor uses this approach when he says, "Get the employee started right (coming to work on time, leaving on time, proper work habits), and the odds are fairly strong the employee will continue the behavior." Any time a group begins to work together for the first time, they will establish work, behavior, and interaction patterns within 72 hours that will continue for months and often years. This is why, in new plant start-ups, some organizations assemble the key staff months before the new plant opens. They attempt both to think through the work and interaction patterns they want to have in the new plant and to design ways they can have these patterns initiated the morning the plant opens. The manager should be aware of this dynamic and should (in a new organization, reorganization, or other situation in which employees are beginning to work together for the first time) take special pains to ensure that the initial behavior, interaction, and work patterns are those that should continue to operate.

One of the major researchers in this area is B. F. Skinner.[3] He holds that any behavior we desire can be had by identifying and defining the desired behavior, setting up a system of immediate feedback, and rewarding the person for progress in the direction of the desired behavior. His position is that most of us have much less free choice than we imagine—that most of our behavior and values have been preprogrammed in us through our society, parents, schools, churches, work associates, friends, etc.

Little was heard of this approach in work organizations until about 1970, when a host of training programs, in and out of organizations, based on this concept suddenly began to arise. In practice, the technique appears to be almost too simple:

1. Make the performance targets very clear.

2. Give immediate feedback to the employee about how he/she is doing.

3. Reward the employee for behavior that is in the right direction.

Often, the reward is simply verbal. It can, of course, take other forms, such as financial. Emery Air Freight Corporation is probably the best-known organization which has used this approach.[4] A manager is well advised to become familiar with this approach, since the literature and training programs are increasingly giving attention to it. Some organizations think that the approach is too oversimplified for the dynamics in today's work force. Few question that the approach will work—at least for a while. The major question relates to what group in the organization shall have the right to identify and specify the behavior that all employees shall follow.

Psychological/biological/cultural approach

This is the same dynamic as operates in the "habit" approach. However, in this instance the bonding between the stimulus and the response was forged so long ago that one can no longer identify where or when the bonding occurred. The behavior of members of groups, especially as they relate to the work place, are now so identifiable in the presence of certain work stimuli that we are willing to generalize: "This is how these people will behave in the work place." Often, the groups identified with this work behavior are racial, but this is certainly not totally true.

For example, how would you respond if asked for words to describe a German worker? Usually, one gets words and phrases like "craftsman," "skilled," "industrious," "takes orders," "follows directions," "hard-working," etc. Now, how would you respond if asked for words to describe a Chinese worker? A black worker? A woman? An Irish worker? A Mexican worker? A resident of Appalachia? These are examples of this approach. The members of the group have, presumably, adopted certain behaviors in the presence of work stimuli that make the individual members ideally suited to certain kinds of work.

To illustrate further:

- Where, until recent years, did the Navy almost invariably go to recruit cabin and mess boys?

- To what group does an organization look when recruiting a clerical worker?

- When we think of a top salesman, what racial group do we think of? *141 483*

- Besides the economic and tax considerations, what causes a plant to move into the south or rural areas?
- Where does your own organization recruit its middle-level managers? Supervisors? Top management?

This is not an approach that can be developed; it takes years, if not generations, to develop these behaviors and perceptions. However, the manager should be aware that many organizations unconsciously use this approach in filling a specific job or a class of jobs. This is not to say that there is no validity in the concept. On the contrary, much of B. F. Skinner's research indicates that the phenomenon is a reality. The manager may find this approach useful in matching an employee to a job. On the other hand, the manager must be aware of overgeneralizations in this area. For example, women and minorities are particularly sensitive to this "typing" and "generalization." It is at this type of generalization that much recent social and work-employment legislation has been directed. Certain employment practices based on such perceptions, and often prejudices, are now illegal. However, this approach still affects many individual managers—often in very subtle ways.

Human-engineering approach

This approach says, "Manipulate the environment so that the environment suggests the appropriate behavior." The placing of ash trays in a conference room is a good example. The message to participants, upon noticing the ash trays, is "I may smoke, and here is where the ashes should be placed." No one has to tell the participants the rules; rather, the rules are suggested by manipulating the environment—in this instance, the ash trays.

Another example of this approach is the use of colors to produce a mood or to suggest a particular environment. On production floors, where activity of a physical nature is desired, colors are often quite vivid. Up in the management offices, where contemplation, reflection, planning, and concept-building are desired, the colors are more subdued and quiet. Similarly, most of us have learned to associate "red" with flammables or danger; "yellow" with caution; "green" with go-ahead. Some organizations use music in the same way: loud and lively where activity is desired; quiet and mood-creating where mental activity is desired. Lines on highways are interpreted fairly universally; broken stripes for passing, and solid lines for a no-passing zone. Other examples of this technique are the use of painted footsteps to indicate the proper path to follow to reach an objective; the use of numbers in stores to determine who is entitled to be waited on next; the use of ropes to indicate areas that are off-limits, etc.

One of the most interesting applications of this approach was discovered by a large chain of short-order restaurants.[5] The chain became aware of problems between cooks and waitresses. A team of behavioral scientists was brought in to study the dynamics: after the waitress (a woman) took the order from the customer, she gave the order to the cook (normally a male). Males, the researchers concluded, do not like to take orders from women, and this was the subconscious root of the problem. After several remedial actions had been suggested, it was finally decided to have the waitress place her order sheet on a spindle placed on the counter top. In this situation, the cook apparently saw himself taking an order from an impersonal object (the spindle) rather than from a woman. Variations of this device can be seen in most restaurants today. In more recent years it has been discovered that the problem can be alleviated if the waitress uses a telephone; apparently the cook sees himself as taking an order from an impersonal object—the telephone.

A Forest Service supervisor reported on a problem he faced which was solved by use of this approach. "We were working out in the field. We started work at eight in the morning. When I became supervisor, I faced a real problem. Every morning, exactly at eight, employee "A" would start up a noisy generator. Ten feet away, employee "B" would pick up a phone that was fastened under a protective hood on a tree, to give instructions to a work crew 20 miles away. Employee "B" found it difficult to converse by phone with a noisy generator pounding away only a few feet from him. I pleaded with them to take turns, to have consideration for each other, to practice good human relations. Finally, one day they got into a fist fight. Only then did it occur to me how simple the solution was. I simply relocated the phone 100 feet away on another tree. Now "A" could start his generator and "B" could make his phone call without the noise. I didn't have to conduct a course in human relations; I simply manipulated the environment to keep these two out of each other's hair."

Another supervisor commented, "I was responsible for 20 machines. It was our practice to place the entire day's work to be machined at each machine station before starting time. You could see the operators look at that pile of work to be machined before they could go home. Usually, it was 15 minutes past start-up time before they picked up the first piece to begin machining it. Then I decided to try something. I put only ⅓ of the work to be machined by the machine in the morning. Now, the operators know there are going to be two more piles that same size placed at the machine before the day is over. But, the smaller pile looks accomplishable. By five minutes after start-up time, all operators now have started machining their first piece."

Hospitals have learned that patients recuperate faster when in social contact with other patients. By simply rearranging the position of beds and chairs on a ward, they have increased patient interaction by 100 percent and thereby facilitated patients' recovery. One architect discovered that by using a central garbage disposal, as contrasted with individual garbage disposals within individual apartments, tenant interaction was increased by a factor of 80 percent; tenants made these contacts while meeting at the central garbage disposal.

Most managers, however, have not begun to look at their operation and ask, "How can I manipulate the work environment to suggest proper work behavior and proper work habits?" In this regard, one other approach should also be mentioned here, i.e., shaping employee behavior through organizational structure, though this also has direct application to the process of organization. One of the foremost proponents of this approach is Robert N. Ford of AT&T.[6] Those who take this approach say that too often our technique for changing employee behavior was to place them in a training program, in which we first tried to change their attitudes, then their values, and then hoped this would translate into changed performance and behavior back on the job. These researchers and practitioners say there is a faster way: change the organizational structure so it calls for a certain kind of behavior; if one behaves in that given way long enough, one will come to believe that the behavior is good and will accept the value underlying that behavior.

Every family has its own structure of behavior called for and rewarded. A child brought up in a permissive family structure is sure that it is a good format. The child who was sternly disciplined is just as positive that to "spare the rod and spoil the child" is a laudable concept and value. A simple organizational example is the person from national headquarters who is transferred to a regional field facility. If the employee stays there six months and returns to national headquarters, the odds are strong that by coffee break of the first day back at headquarters, at least three of the employee's former peers will have commented, "What's happened to you? You sound like one of the heathen west of the Mississippi." The reverse will be true if a regional employee is transferred to national headquarters. Only then, the comment will be, "What's happened to you? You sound like one of the egg-heads at the Marble palace."

There is much to be said for this concept. Instead of preaching participative management and trying to sell the staff on its merits, a faster way often is to set up a structure that demands that employees function in a participative manner: participation in planning and decision-making; group interaction; open communication. If employees stay in this structure a while, usually two to five years, they will acquire the values of this behavior. The key here is not only to see that a structure is created that calls for the desired behavior, but also to insist that the behavior desired is actually practiced. Otherwise, the behavior of the old structure will be carried over to the new structure.

Economic-man approach

It is not necessary to discuss this approach at length. Every manager is very familiar with it. It is the major approach, even today, used to motivate and influence the behavior of employees. When the employee's work behavior is in the right direction, hold out financial inducements—in-grade increases; merit increases; hope of promotion; payment for cost-saving or more efficient work procedure suggestions. When the employee's work behavior is not in the direction wanted, do the reverse—withhold an in-grade or a merit increase; say you won't recommend for promotion; give leave without pay; demote; and, if the behavior is bad enough, threaten to take away all money by firing the employee.

Probably 95 percent of the techniques made available by the organization to managers to motivate subordinates have to do with money. A cursory examination of personnel and supervisory policies, procedures, and manuals will support this statement. Money is still a most important motivator. Few researchers would challenge this fact. It is, normally, a more potent motivator at the lower pay grades and when the economy presents an "employer's market." But the manager should never downgrade the importance of money as a continuing motivator.

Internal Motivational Stimuli

Achievement motivation approach

Most of the research in this approach has been done by David McClelland and his associates.[7] Principal here is the concept that all men and women have "X" amount of need to achieve. High achievers are not high risk-takers. For instance, they do not like games of chance, which cannot be influenced. They like to have a job challenge them; if the job goal is reached, they can feel they really accomplished something significant. On the other hand, they don't want unattainable goals.

This need to achieve can be determined, through various testing techniques, for individuals, organizations, and nations. Persons who have a high need to achieve need only to know the goals and to receive feedback about how they are doing. They supply their own motivation to work toward the goals. Such persons will work as diligently on a small task as on a much more significant task, because they don't like to fail. As a result, they are much in demand by PTA's and other community organizations.

Managers, supervisors, and professionals generally have a fairly high degree of the need to achieve. Under this condition, organizations will tend to use such programs as the Robert Blake "grid" program and "management by objectives" as a key way to maximize motivation of their staff. The basic assumption is that the motivation is there. What is needed is a clear definition of the goals so that the motivational energy of the employees is properly channeled.

Interestingly, McClelland's research has apparently not had as great an impact in the United States as it has had in other countries, notably Mexico, and Central and South America. Earlier, McClelland and his associates seemed to feel that the amount of achievement need was a "given" in people and was not subject to much change.

In recent years this concept seems to have changed, and now McClelland and his associates offer training programs designed to increase the "need to achieve" level of participants.

Job enrichment

The researcher most frequently connected with this approach is Frederick Herzberg,[8] whose research indicates that the items that make for poor motivation and job dissatisfaction on the job tend to be unrelated to the work itself. Herzberg terms these "job dissatisfyers," and they include:

- Interpersonal relations with peers, subordinates, and boss
- Technical supervision
- Company policies and regulations
- Working conditions
- Training opportunities
- Job security
- Pay

Herzberg termed the items that make for good motivation and job satisfaction "job satisfyers," and they include:

- A sense of achievement
- Recognition
- The work itself
- A sense of responsibility
- Opportunity for advancement

One critical distinction between the job satisfyers and job dissatisfyers is that job satisfaction and effective motivation will not result from the correction of job dissatisfyers. Even when these items are done well, we are at a zero point; job satisfaction and motivation stem only from the job satisfyers.

Initially, in attempting to restructure jobs so that the job satisfyers could be met, organizations engaged in what was called job enlargement; that is, responsibilities and duties at a horizontal level were added to the job being restructured. Also, job rotation was often utilized. But more and more evidence indicated that job enrichment must also look to expand job responsibilities in a vertical manner—more responsibility and complexity.

It should be noted that many jobs in organizations were defined and structured around the beginning of this century, in the hey-day of "scientific management." This made sense: the average worker's education was less than one year of grade school, and the influx of immigrants often created a real language barrier. There were, of course, the additional considerations of job specialization and breaking a job down to its most simple parts. Today, we are dealing with an affluent society and a mobile, well-educated work force; this has created both a context in which the meaning of work is changing and a desire among employees for self-actualization. Many organizations are taking another look at the structure of work and asking, "How can we make this job more complete, challenging, and capable of using the total abilities of the worker?" Unions, too, have recently become interested in the structure of jobs and organizations, and there is a fair amount of evidence that this may well be one of the next areas about which they will negotiate with management and organizations. The so-called "revolt of the blue-collar worker" is to be understood in this light. It should also be emphasized that some of these same dynamics and demands are beginning to emerge from clerical workers.

A number of organizations are beginning to experiment with the restructuring of jobs, notably Volvo, SAAB, Bell Telephone, and Gaines. The experimentation is so widespread that it is difficult to attempt a listing of companies so engaged, as many experimenting with the concept have not been reported in the literature. Some of the common denominators of this approach seem to be:

1. Letting employees do more of the complete job; for instance, permitting an employee to build an entire radio rather than a single component.

2. Working in teams. The team often selects its leader or rotates the leadership role. Often, when there is a vacancy in the team, the team interviews and hires the replacement.

3. Remuneration is based on how many of the critical skills and knowledges an employee learns and possesses.

5. Quality control becomes one of the functions of the team or individual.

This approach is not without its cautions and traps, however. For example, there is so much room for improvement in job redesign that it is fairly easy for initial attempts to show positive results—sometimes dramatic results—in such areas as production, efficiency, quality, and cost reductions. However, it has not yet been proved that job enrichment can accomplish a job more economically and efficiently than an assembly-line approach can. It may well be that a single industry cannot introduce job restructuring on a large scale without being penalized. The entire industry may need to elect to go the job-enrichment route. It may well be that one of the trade-offs society will have to accept is that services and products will need to cost more in order to provide for increased job satisfaction of employees.

Another possible drawback is that under job enrichment, an employee will perform at a level higher than that for which he is currently being paid. He will be content with this state of affairs for about six months, but inevitably, he begins to ask, "If I am performing at this higher level, why should I not be paid at this higher level?" Job enrichment may have the ultimate effect of creating a much narrower range of organizational echelons, with a narrowing of pay differential between echelons. This trend is already noticeable in project-type and professional-type organizations.

Organizations and managers will often find, as they attempt job restructuring, that all the elements that should be built into a job for more meaning do not lie within the province and sphere of influence of a single department or manager; part of the job may lie outside the manager's influence. Thus, to engage in significant job restructuring may mean that the effort must be approached on an organizationwide basis rather than on a departmental basis or by a single manager.

Despite all these problems, the route of job restructuring is currently quite popular in organizations and seems to hold much promise. Some guidelines for the manager in this area are:

1. Take a good look at the jobs in your sphere of influence. How can you build more fullness and meaning into them by restructuring the job?

2. Involve employees, appropriate to their level, in setting objectives, planning, and decision-making.

3. Informal group membership has a vital meaning to employees. Your work group has many of the aspects of an informal group, so make sure it is a satisfying one. In the last three surveys the author has made within organizations, the following question was asked on a questionnaire, "What do you like most about your job?" In all three organizations, heading the list was the voluntary response "the association of the people with whom I work."

4. If you can't make the job itself self-fulfilling, then work on the hygiene factors or job dissatisfyers. But realize that this is only a temporary measure.

Self-motivation approach

This is the approach that has almost solely been taught in most of the courses, conferences, and workshops in motivation for the past 15 years. The several researchers most frequently identified with this approach are Rensis Likert, Saul Gellerman, Chris Argyris, Warren Bennis, and probably Frederick Herzberg. The research and writings of these men have two principal findings:

1. The best-motivated worker is the self-motivated worker.

2. Real motivation stems from the work that people do.

All of these researchers base their work on that of two previous researchers—Douglas McGregor and Abraham Maslow.

Douglas McGregor.[9] McGregor pointed out that managers and organizations hold a set of assumptions about people in the work place. He identified two of these assumptions sets and placed them at opposite ends of a continuum. One set he termed "Theory X"; the other he termed "Theory Y." Among Theory "X" assumptions are: (1) people do not want to work; (2) people will not work unless forced to do so; (3) people do not want to take on responsibility; (4)

creativity is narrowly distributed in the work population; (5) people must be closely supervised; (6) people want money above all else, etc. Theory "Y" assumptions are the reverse of these.

McGregor noted that although people often behaved in a way that supported Theory "X" assumptions, they behaved in that fashion because that is where they perceived the rewards to be. However, it was his feeling that this was not basically the worker's nature; rather, if the manager would treat the worker according to Theory "Y" assumptions, the manager and organization would be amazed at the results. In recent years, many researchers have recognized that Theory "X" behavior may be so ingrained in many workers that it would be exceedingly difficult, if not impossible, to expect them to change within their remaining work career.

Abraham Maslow. [10] Maslow is particularly remembered by most managers, from their reading and attendance at management development programs, for his concept of a "hierarchy of man's needs." These are most popularly depicted as:

1. Physiological needs
2. Safety or security needs
3. Social needs
4. Ego needs
5. Self-actualization needs

Few managers or training personnel are aware, however, that Maslow also identified two higher needs—cognitive needs and aesthetic needs. It was not this umbrella listing, however, that made Maslow's work significant. Rather, it was the three corollaries that were drawn from his studies:

1. Man's needs tend to be met in the indicated order.

2. A man will sacrifice, or risk losing, a higher-level need in order to hold on to, or to regain, a lower-level need. That is, if an employee is in danger of losing his job, he doesn't care if the organization meets his social, ego, or self-actualization needs; he wants to be sure his security and physiological needs are going to be met.

3. Once a need has been met, it no longer tends to act as an immediate motivator. Maslow has been often misinterpreted here as saying, "Once a need has been met, it no longer motivates." This is not true. Of course, setting a second dinner before me will not motivate me to eat as did the first dinner, but that does not mean I am through with hunger. I am temporarily sated, but five hours from now that second dinner will motivate me quite strongly. Many managers and training personnel interpreted this corollary as meaning that money is not a motivator, but as Herzberg has very pointedly observed, "When you give a man a raise he is temporarily not unhappy, but I can assure you he is going to become very unhappy again with his remuneration."

For managers who accept this approach, the emphasis in motivation is on meeting the employees' higher job needs—social needs, ego needs, and self-actualization needs. These managers also recognize that real motivation is to be found in the work people do. If the job is not intrinsically satisfying and challenging, then no motivation can occur. This is why such managers also pay a good deal of attention to the concept of job restructuring.

Some useful guidelines to help implement this approach are:

1. When recruiting employees, don't "oversell" the job. Stress the undesirable job aspects, as well as the desirable ones. If the job is not intrinsically meaningful, the manager will soon have a most unhappy employee on his hands.

2. When recruiting to fill a vacancy, it is generally best to take a lesser qualified applicant who likes the job in preference to a well-qualified applicant who does not like the job. You can teach an employee the skills needed to do a job, but you cannot teach an employee to like a job. Of course, you are not going to take a high school graduate if the job calls for a Ph.D. The general rule is, "If the skills or knowledge can be taught within a six-month period, take the lesser qualified applicant who likes the job."

3. Take a hard look at the qualifications needed in the jobs in your sphere of influence. Don't ask for overqualified people unless you have good opportunities for upward mobility. Too many job specifications call for skills, capabilities, and knowledge that simply are not

needed in the job. When an employee possesses skills, knowledges, talents, and capabilities not demanded in the job, you have a candidate ripe for all kinds of job dissatisfaction and morale and motivational problems.

GUIDELINES FOR EFFECTIVE EMPLOYEE MOTIVATION

We have now discussed all the major motivational models being researched today. Based on these avenues of research exploration, organizations and managers build organizational motivational systems and models. How can a manager decide which is best, which model to use, and how to find his way through the maze of conflicting advice and counsel? Managers who seem to do a good job of effectively motivating their employees generally suggest the following guidelines:

1. You have a number of motivational models to help you. Be flexible in their use. Don't lock yourself into any one single approach. Pick and choose from each. Some employees will respond to one approach; some, to another. There is no substitution for knowing your employees individually and knowing what approach will be most effective with each. It is also critical that whatever approach used is natural for you, the manager. To behave otherwise is to step out of "role" and to appear to the employees to be contrived and playing games.

2. Motivation is highly individualistic. What turns one employee on will leave another employee cold.

3. Motivation changes. What effectively motivates an employee today may not do so tomorrow. Provide for this in organization placement policies. Few organizations will permit an employee to change career ladders without pointedly questioning the employee's stability. In order to change career ladders, the employee too often has to leave the organization and to begin the new career in another organization.

4. Remember that all employees are not ready for a high level of self-actualization. Some are dependent; some like control; some like repetitive work; and some don't want responsibility. Don't attempt

a single-thrust approach, such as participative management; it can badly frighten and immobilize some employees. The key here is flexibility in management and motivational style.

5. Most employees want to work in an organization that is socially significant and is responsive to influence from within. This trend has increasingly been noted in the past five years, and it may or may not continue. For the moment, however, there is good pay-off in helping employees understand how the organization and the job the employee is doing contribute to social responsibility and to the solution of some of our nation's social problems.

6. Be aware that within the constraints of time and energy available to you, there are some employees whom you cannot motivate toward your organization's objectives. There is a time to fire an employee without feeling guilty that you were unable to motivate that employee. Yes, there is a motivational problem, but the problem is within the employee. Often, the best thing the manager can do is to say to an employee, "Friend, it is probable that you can be motivated, but not with me as your manager and you in this job in this organization." You will be surprised how often the discharged employee will contact you later and say, "The best thing that ever happened to me was to have you make me face up to reality. I was never happier than I am in my present job." The answer is not in passing the employee on, each six months, to a different manager, hoping that someone will find the magic motivational key. Ultimately, the employee has so much seniority that he or she is eligible for the presidency.

7. Last, many employees respond most favorably to recognition and positive "stroking." This is implied heavily in both the behavior modification approach and in the self-motivation model. For a full discussion and suggestions for implementing this concept, you are encouraged to become familiar with the concept of "stroking."[11]

NOTES

1.
Probably the most thorough study of the concerns and interrelatedness of productivity, morale, and employee job satisfaction is to be found in the research of Rensis Likert. The best known of Dr. Likert's books setting out this research is *New Patterns of Management*, New York: McGraw-Hill, 1961.

A later book that generalizes and amplifies his earlier research is his *The Human Organization: Its Management and Value,* New York: McGraw-Hill, 1967.

2.

Work in America. Report of a Special Task Force to the Secretary of Health, Education, and Welfare, Cambridge, Mass.: MIT Press, 1973. The report, which has an excellent bibliography, examines employee job dissatisfaction, problems of American workers, health problems, the changing meaning of work, and current efforts to redesign jobs.

3.

For a more complete understanding of Skinner's research and some of the major implications he sees in its implementation, see B. F. Skinner, *Beyond Freedom and Dignity,* New York: Alfred A. Knopf, 1971.

4.

A full explanation of this approach is contained in two publications put out by Emery Air Freight Corp., System Performance Department, Wilton, Conn. 06897. One publication is called "Positive Reinforcement"; the other, "Feedback Systems." The publications outline the program as used in Emery Freight and contain a step-by-step procedure for initiating the system in another organization.

5.

A short report of this study and generalizations from it are discussed in the article by Elias H. Porter, "The Parable of the Spindle," *Harvard Business Review,* May–June 1962.

6.

A recent article discussing the experience of AT&T with this concept is an article by Robert N. Ford, "Job Enrichment Lessons from AT&T," *Harvard Business Review,* January-February 1973.

7.

Probably the best work to set out the concepts of achievement motivation is an earlier book by David C. McClelland, J. W. Atkinson, R. A. Clark, and E. L. Lowell, *The Achievement Motive,* New York: Appleton-Century-Crofts, 1953.

8.

Two books here will give the initial concepts of job enrichment and some of the later refinements: Frederick Herzberg, B. Mausner, and B. Snyderman, *The Motivation to Work,* New York: John Wiley, 1959; and Frederick Herzberg, *Work and the Nature of Man,* Cleveland, Ohio: World Publishing, 1966.

9.

A complete description of Theory "X" and Theory "Y" is to be found in Douglas M. McGregor, *The Human Side of Enterprise,* New York: McGraw-Hill, 1960. A later volume that expands on these concepts and deals with implications of the research for the manager is to be found in Douglas McGregor, *The Professional Manager,* New York: McGraw-Hill, 1967.

10.

Maslow's concepts are probably best set forth in his book *Motivation and Personality,* 2d ed., New York: Harper & Row, 1970. For a brief and quite readable treatise on the researchers in the self-motivational school, see Harold M. F. Rush, *Behavioral Science Concepts and Management Application,* Personnel Policy Study No. 216, New York: National Industrial Conference Board, 1969.

11.

Muriel James and Dorothy Jongeward, *Born to Win,* Reading, Mass.: Addison-Wesley, 1973. In a very readable style, the authors examine man's need for "stroking"—reinforcement of behavioral change when it is in the right direction and the need for reinforcement of one's self-image. Strokes can, of course, also be of a negative nature. Managers and supervisors who ask "When should I encourage and reward, how often, and how?" will find this book of great value.

Work Groups and the Territorial Imperative

3

One of the major concerns of many organizations and managers is the reality of empire-building and vested interests. Says the typical manager plagued with this problem, "How do you get staff to see and work for the big picture and organizational objectives? Honestly, my departments fight each other harder than they fight the competition. Each is scrapping for the largest possible share of personnel, budget, equipment, facilities, and other resources. A disproportionate share of our organizational energy and time is directed toward these nonproductive goals."

This concern is quite legitimate. In our structuring of organizations, we use two major tools: job specialization and division of labor. Both of these contribute toward tunnel vision and isolation of interests and perspective. So much does this get ingrained into managers, supervisors, and professionals, that top managers report that the two most difficult abilities to find in personnel being considered for promotion are the ability "to see the big picture" and the ability to conceptualize.

Today's organizations are so constructed that the whole is dependent on the parts. If one part is dysfunctional, the entire organization is in danger of collapse or serious malfunctioning. Most of the major decisions and plans made by organizations no longer are made by a single decision-maker or planner; rather, they are made by a group or are intergroup decisions and plans. The need to improve intra- and intergroup decision-making, planning, and functioning is a critical one. Most training programs currently conducted by organizational resources or offered by outside resources focus heavily on team building, teamwork, group decision-making, and effective membership. (Most of these concerns are the primary focus of organization development programs. This will be considered in some depth in Chapter 7, "The Manager's Role in Organization Development.")

A curious observation can be made here. Despite the fact that there is much concern about vested interests and the need to obtain more effective organizational teamwork, a difficult question for managers and training personnel to answer is, "Assuming the manager and the manager's unit had good teamwork, what would the unit look like and what would be happening?" At first most managers draw a blank. Upon reflection, they will identify the following kinds of behaviors that they believe reflect effective organizational and departmental teamwork:

- Staff people volunteer suggestions for work improvement.

- Problem-solving, decision-making, and planning are concerned with and consider total organizational goals and objectives.

- Staff members volunteer to help one another and other units when these persons or units have an emergency, overload, or backlog.

- Staff feel that their personal work/career goals are quite compatible with organizational goals.

- Staff freely share openly and honestly information with one another, even if this information is adverse.

- Staff voluntarily seek out the manager for assistance with their problems. The relation of manager to staff is more that of a coach and consultant than that of a boss-subordinate relationship.

- Staff accept and set high standards of performance and quality of work.

- Staff exercise a large amount of self-control. They do what needs to be done without waiting to be told.

- Staff have minimum concern for doing only what "their job description says they are responsible for doing."

- There are a low number of grievances.

- Decisions, plans, and operational actions are seldom made and then revised because it turns out they were made on the basis of inadequate or erroneous information.

- Employees volunteer to work late, work overtime, or work outside their assigned task areas in order to get a job done.

THE DYNAMICS OF GROUP PROCESSES

How does one get to this desirable way of working? A great deal of study has gone into exploring the dynamics of intragroup and intergroup processes that make for effective or ineffective teamwork. These studies have taken three major directions.

Relationship Between Task and Maintenance Functions in a Group

Every group, as it works on the task assigned to it, will find that the group always works at two levels. The first is the *task level*. At this level are the skills that must be present for the group to handle whatever task or problem brought them together. Many skills have been identified, but six of the most common ones are:

1. *Initiating.* Someone must initiate ideas, information, solutions, etc.

2. *Information- or opinion-seeking.* Someone must ask for facts, ideas, suggestions, and feelings.

3. *Information- or opinion-giving.* If someone asks for information, others will normally supply information or give their opinion. It is interesting that in most groups, three times more people respond to requests for information than will ask for information.

4. *Clarifying or elaborating.* One or more persons in the group will ask that some idea presented be made more clear.

5. *Summarizing.* Periodically, during the group discussion and particularly toward the end of the meeting, one or more persons will

attempt to summarize what the group has discussed and where they are at that moment.

6. *Consensus-testing.* One or more persons will test to see if the group is ready to make a total group decision or agreement.

A group also works at a second, or *maintenance,* level. Too often, group members focus solely on the task skills to get a group task accomplished. If the group is meeting only once, or if the group task is of an emergency nature with a short time limit, this is understandable. Normally, however, to be effective the members of a group must feel like working on the task. The members must feel accepted by other members; they must feel that the group is aware of each member's comfort needs and that members are being considerate of one another. To accomplish these ends, a group will find that it needs members who have group maintenance skills, the six most common ones being:

1. *Encouraging.* Members smile at one another, nod approvingly, pat a member on the back, and otherwise encourage continued participation in the group.

2. *Expressing group feelings.* This is the ability to sense group feeling and mood and to express this so the group can deal with it, e.g., "I sense we're all tired and need a break."

3. *Harmonizing.* This is the skill of attempting to reconcile disagreements—to "pour oil on troubled waters."

4. *Compromising.* When two ideas are in conflict, someone may show how the two ideas can be changed a bit to be acceptable to both parties.

5. *Gate-keeping.* This is the skill of sensing when others are not getting the opportunity to participate because of more aggressive, verbal members. When one member has the floor, another member keeps the gate open so a more quiet member can participate—"We haven't heard from Sybil yet."

6. *Setting standards.* Shall the group work at a shallow depth; will it level; face "gut" issues?

The group leader does not have to supply all these skills. In participative, well-functioning groups the members sense when one or more needed skills are not being provided and will step in to supply them. The leader's role is to see that all appropriate skills are being provided.

Not everyone is equally adept at these skills. Most frequently each of us will find we tend to supply either task skills or maintenance skills. But even when one tends to most frequently provide task skills, for example, one will often employ perhaps only three of the specific skills; for example, one might almost always initiate ideas and act as a summarizer.

There is no judgment as to which skills are most vital. The answer is to be found in balance. The manager should be aware of these two levels at which a group operates and ensure that there is a balance between task skills and maintenance skills in the group. For example, if the group members are particularly task-centered, the manager might occasionally put one or two members on the group who do not possess much technical knowledge needed to solve the task or problem, but who are very much oriented to providing maintenance skills.

Individual Roles in Groups

Most managers will find that they have one basic role they assume when they are a member of a group. Part of this is undoubtedly due to their basic personality structure, but much of it is related to the concept of roles (see Chapter 1). Being a member of a group is a role every manager must play, and each manager develops a behavior that he believes will make him most effective in that role. Sometimes, the way the manager plays the role is, of course, the most effective way he can participate as an effective group member. More often, the manager will find that he can improve his performance as a member of a group.

Many observers and students of group behavior have identified a large number of stereotyped roles managers play in groups. All of us exhibit some of these behaviors at different times, and this may be quite appropriate. What we are concerned about is the individual whose behavior in groups is predictable and falls within the labeled stereotypes. Some of the common group roles that have been identified are the joke teller, the play-boy, the religious fanatic, the silent member, the angry member, the skeptic, the "we tried that before," the mouse, the stickler for protocol and Roberts Rules of Order, the sex twister, the philosopher, the "here's how we did it at good old Conglomerate," etc., etc.

One listing of three basic roles and orientations managers take within groups has been found to be quite helpful. These are common roles and stances taken particularly by managers in work-organization groups. These three roles are:

1. *The "confronter."* This person's way of behaving in groups is to face each issue and problem squarely. If the group task is difficult, the "confronter" is ready to go to work on it. If conflict arises, this type of person does not run away from the conflict, but attempts to face it and cope with it. Usually, the "confronter" is very task-oriented.

2. *The "objective thinker."* This person has an overwhelming respect for facts, data, and logical thinking. "What do the facts say? What did our last report show? Where can we get figures to tell us exactly how much we lost? Let's get the latest computer printout." People are secondary to facts. The "objective thinker" wants to keep feelings and emotions out of the discussion. The decision will be made entirely on the data, with little or no concern for the human factors involved.

3. *The "friendly helper."* This person is heavily oriented toward the maintenance skills and is uncomfortable with the "objective thinker" and, to a lesser degree, with the "confronter." Rather, the "friendly helper" is concerned with feelings and emotions and with the effect of the group's decision or plan on other people.

No one of these three basic roles is more valuable to a group than the other two. The manager should strive to see that all three orientations are present in continuing work groups, since each has a valuable contribution and tends to balance the others, thus contributing to the best possible group product. Few of us individually have the flexibility to play all three roles equally effectively and will normally feel more comfortable with only one of the roles. Managers should, of course, try to improve their total group performance so that they are not too "skewed." However, the real key is to play the role the way one feels most comfortable with, but also being sure that the group composition provides for the presence of all three orientations.

Characteristics of Groups

Small groups have been the target of concentrated study for the past 20 years, and these studies have isolated the common characteristics most groups possess. The characteristics are constant, and almost every group, particularly those which have an on-going life, will have these identifiable facets. However, how each characteristic looks within specific groups will vary from one end of a continuum to the other. On most of the characteristics, a group can be judged as being mature, immature, or at some point between these extremes. It therefore follows that every group has its own personality and is unique. No two groups are ever the same. Indeed, considering the external inputs that occur between group meetings, no group convening today is the same group it was the last time it met. This is why the manager needs to allow time at the beginning of each group meeting for the maintenance function and for people to assess the dynamics and changes that have occurred since last they met.

The manager should periodically diagnose his work groups along the dimensions listed on the following pages and, with the involvement of the group members, determine how the group can improve its performance. A number of checklists are available for this purpose, and most training offices can supply them to the interested manager. However, the manager can simply use this listing of group characteristics and ask his group to reflect on "How are we doing along this dimension?" More characteristics can be found described in the literature than are listed below. However, these are the most critical ones that affect effective group functioning.

Group background

Every group has a different membership. Each member brings a different background, and out of these diverse backgrounds comes the group's personality. The backgrounds brought to the group may either enrich or block the group's problem-solving ability. Among the factors in individual backgrounds that will affect the group's functioning are the following.

1. Whether or not all the members come from the same work organization

2. The sex make-up of the group

3. Whether or not all the members are from the same part of the country

4. Whether or not the members have worked together before

5. The degree of similarity of the members' economic and title status

6. The members' previous experience in meetings and groups

7. The extent of the members' age differential

8. The degree of similarity of the members' job tenure.

These kinds of background factors will affect how the group can function. For example, to put inexperienced with experienced people can be frustrating and nonproductive to both and thus significantly affect the group product. The manager might consider this dynamic of group background in his or her own work unit. When a vacancy occurs, the manager should ask, "What kind of a background would it be desirable to add to my work group? An experienced person? Inexperienced? Young? More mature? Woman? Research-oriented? Dynamic? Creative? Minority-group member?"

Group participation pattern

Here, we are concerned with the volume and direction of the communication. How much does the leader talk? Who talks how much? Who talks after whom? Who is silent? Do only "status people" talk? To whom are questions addressed? Every group will develop a participation pattern which may or may not be the most effective pattern. For example, in hospital settings, it is still not unusual to find that the doctor speaks, then the head nurse, then the nurse. This pattern is never violated. Or, in a business firm, the manager speaks, then the most senior department head, then the next senior department head, and so on. However, significant contributions in a group normally do not follow hierarchical ranking.

Group communication pattern

The focus here is on the quality of the communication. Are real issues being identified, or are people talking around the issue? Are there semantic problems? Are people trying to impress one another with their technical vocabularies and concepts? Are group members seemingly addressing the problem, but in reality addressing some status person who is present?

Group communication can occur at both the verbal and nonverbal level. The manager needs to become familiar with reading nonverbal communication—facial expressions, posture, changing coloration of skin, fidgeting, etc.

Group cohesion

This may be defined as "the attractiveness of a group to its members" and can range from almost total absence to so much that it becomes sticky and exclusive. Cohesion can partially be assessed by listening to recurring remarks ("They're a great bunch"; "Oh, my God, not that bunch again.") and by observing whether group members relate after the meeting or whether they go their own way as individuals.

The manager will notice an interesting thing about group cohesion. Although a group may be very noncohesive, an external threat to the group almost invariably causes it to cohere. This can be observed in news stories about a husband beating his wife. A "good samaritan" comes to her rescue, only to find both of them turning on him. Police are well aware of this phenomenon when they receive calls for help in domestic brawls. Managers sometimes use this dynamic by conjuring up possible threats in order to cohere their group, e.g., "I hear rumors that if we don't improve production, we may be taken over by the home office."

Group atmosphere

Group atmosphere is often defined as the "climate of the group." It can range from being cold to warm; from hostile to accepting; and from relaxed to stiff and formal. You can also observe this when you visit someone's home for the first time. In some homes you immediately feel comfortable and relaxed; in others, you are uncomfortable and stiff during the entire visit. If you visit one unit in an organization, you may find that people are relaxed, busy, talking, and someone asks if he can help you. But if you visit another unit, you find that no one talks, people are engrossed in their own tasks, and no one offers to assist you. Your reaction in such a unit is likely to be, "What a cold place. I wouldn't want to work here."

Subgroupings

In the past, subgroupings were often felt to be dysfunctional. We now know, however, that subgrouping is an effective way for a large group to get its task done. One way to understand an organizational chart is to view it as the way the organization believes subgroupings can be most effective.

Of course, subgroupings are affected by such matters as seating arrangements, friends, function, woman-man, issues, likes and dislikes of others, etc. As long as subgroups form and reform around issues, subissues, and tasks to be accomplished, subgrouping is normally quite effective. Subgroups become inappropriate, however, if they become permanent groups and the members stick together and think and act as a bloc. Such a group has now become a clique, and these almost invariably are disruptive.

Group standards and/or norms

A group standard or norm is a guide to the group members as to what is appropriate conduct and behavior in and out of the group. Group standards always operate at two levels—explicit and implicit.

Explicit standards or norms. These are the behavioral guides which are made public either in writing or verbally. Explicit standards are found in policies, manuals, procedures, and rules.

Implicit standards or norms. These are not explicit; the group simply adopts them, often unconsciously. Few managers take the time to look at the implicit norms adopted by their work groups to determine if they are consistent with the explicit norms or even whether they are desirable. By contrast, new employees spend a lot of time learning these implicit norms. For example, the sign on the production floor may say explicitly, "No Smoking"; however, the employees may modify this explicit norm with an implicit norm: "No smoking when the supervisor is around." Or, "You may smoke in this hallway, and even the supervisor won't say anything to you." Another explicit standard may be that the work day begins at 8:00 A.M. The manager makes quite a verbal point to the employees of coming to work on time. The employees obey, but replace this explicit norm with an implicit one: "You have to punch in by 8:00 A.M., but there's nothing that says you have to begin work then." Therefore, work begins at 8:20, or it may even be understood that employees can go to the cafeteria and have breakfast before beginning to work.

Public and private goals

Almost every group that is created is given a task, problem, or goal to be accomplished. Usually, the group's purpose is stated in writing and is often shared with the group members in advance of the meeting. This is the public goal. But the manager will find that the statement of a public goal is not always easy to set forth. Often, a group will spend much time working on a vague goal, coming up with good, but nongoal-directed, work. The manager should always spend some time stating and clarifying the public goal or task to be sure that all members agree on it and understand what is expected of them.

A more subtle aspect of goals is that most group members bring to a group meeting one or more private goals they expect to have met. These are called "hidden agendas." Most frequently, the group members will not identify these publicly. However, they will judge the group and meeting as being effective to the degree that not only the public, but also their individual, private goals are met. For example, an outside resource person is engaged by a major appliance manufacturer to provide a day's session on the subject of planning at the company's home office in Chicago. Attending the meeting are 60 middle managers from all over the United States. The resource person and the company training director spend much time drawing up a set of public objectives and goals for the day's work, and this is sent to the participants in advance of the meeting. If the resource person believes, as he begins the day's work, that the reason these 60 persons are seated before him is their overriding interest in the subject of planning or his ability as a resource person, he is badly deluded. Ask the participants, over a drink at the end of the day, "What really caused you to attend this meeting?" The answers are, "I'd attend anything to get away from the job for the day"; "I need to have this program noted on my personnel record to be eligible for promotion"; "I have a girl friend in Chicago. Where else could you get a company to pay for the trip to see her?" (Try to schedule an evening meeting and see how that participant will rate the program in terms of its meeting its objectives!); "I wanted to visit a couple of people at headquarters and make some Brownie points," etc., etc.

In the organization, members attending meetings are instructed by their boss about how to vote and what position to take on the public goals or issue or decision. The members cannot share this with the other members, but their group behavior and input and actions are heavily affected by this hidden agenda. Therefore, the manager must be alert to hidden agendas that are shared by a number of group members. Once the manager has identified or suspected these hidden agendas, he will need to decide whether to "flush them out" and deal with them publicly, or whether the nature of the hidden agenda will not permit making them public; in either case, the hidden agenda will affect the manager's conduct of the meeting.

Group member/group leader behavior

Here, we are concerned with whether the group leader completely controls the group, whether the group controls the group leader, or whether there is a sharing of the group leadership. There is no right or wrong answer. The key is whether a single pattern has emerged and whether or not it would be more desirable for the pattern to be flexible and adapted to each meeting's purpose.

Decision-making process

Are the decisions made by the group; by the leader; jointly? Does the group identify in advance what process will be followed for making decisions? The end of a meeting is no time to decide whether the decision must be unanimous, needs a two-thirds majority vote, a simple majority vote, or will be made by the leader. Are decisions arrived at by consensus, or is the vote always according to Roberts Rules of Order? Normally, the more formal the decision-making procedure in work groups, the more the manager can suspect mistrust and lack of open communication.

Toleration of individual differences

Quite often, in the early stages of a group, the members will tolerate little deviation from norms established by the group. The more meaningful the group is to the members, the more this will be true. However, as a group matures, the members find they can work together quite effectively and still tolerate great extremes in dress, personalities, violations of norms, values, and biases.

Ability to handle conflict

Most groups will develop a single, repetitive response to conflict. There are four common response patterns.

Fight. Unfortunately, this often leads to cliques; the subgroup or clique will remain constant and fight with other subgroups over every issue that emerges.

Flight. The group cannot tolerate conflict and will flee from it. The group will move to another, less threatening topic; someone will tell a joke and the issue is dropped; the group will take a break, adjourn, or adopt a compromise that all know is not workable.

Deny. The group will deny that there is any conflict and therefore silence the dissenters, for to do otherwise would be to threaten the group's cohesion. This response can be identified in such comments as "Come on now, we're all one big happy family. Right?"; "Remember, we're all partners in this fine old organization. I love you all."; and "We're really a great bunch, huh? We may have our little old differences, but we really stick together."

Cope. The issue is brought to the surface and identified, data are obtained, and the group resolves the issue before moving on to the next item on the agenda.

Structure adequate to the purpose of the group

Too often, structure precedes function. The group conveners set up a group chairman, vice-chairman, recording secretary, social secretary, master at arms, etc. Then the group tries to force the group's task and organization into this predetermined structure. But instead, the group should define its work and then consciously ask, "What kind of structure will best enable us to get this job done?"

Ability of the group to identify and use its resources

The identification of group resources is not easy. In our culture it is not considered polite to reveal one's strengths and capabilities. There is the further reality that if one's strength is known, one may get an additional assignment. Group members should feel encouraged to freely and openly announce the skills, knowledge, experience, and capabilities they have which will enable the group to get its job done. It is amazing how often managers do not know the capabilities of their staff. Staff members are assumed to have the same capabilities and interests they had when recruited. Organizations find it extremely difficult to recognize that staff people are continually growing, enlarging their experience base, and changing their interests. In addition, they often have capabilities that are not required to be identified by the job specifications and which are therefore unsuspected by the manager or the organization.

Once the resources in the group are recognized, the talents of the members should be appropriately used to meet the group's goals. This may well mean that a very junior member occupying a lower echelon is the best-qualified group member to take on a significant group task.

GROUP PRESSURE AND INDIVIDUAL IDENTITY

We have commented upon the tremendous emphasis today on effective team-building and teamwork. It is recognized that this is an area of concern, and rightfully so, for both the manager and the organization. The trick seems to be posed in the question, "How does a group member function as an effective member of a group and, at the same time, retain his individual identity and high values?" Most behavioral scientists do not sufficiently appreciate the subtle and immense pressures that groups can exert on their members. If membership in the group happens to be highly desirable, then this pressure of group conformity and group thinking can be particularly dangerous.

One of the few who have looked in depth at this danger is Irving L. Janis.[1] Some of the major pitfalls he identifies that can occur when a group becomes too cohesive are the following:

1. An illusion of invulnerability
2. Collective efforts to rationalize in order to discount warnings
3. An unquestioned belief in the group's inherent morality
4. Stereotyped views of rivals and enemies as too evil to warrant genuine attempts at negotiation
5. Direct pressure on any member who expresses strong arguments against any of the group's stereotypes, illusions, or commitments
6. Self-censorship of deviations from the apparent group consensus
7. A shared illusion of unanimity concerning judgments conforming to the majority view
8. The emergence of self-appointed mindguards—members who protect the group from adverse information.

What can managers do to insure, insofar as possible, that they are effective group members but, at the same time, do not lose their identity as individuals or fall victim to "group-think"? Managers who have confronted this issue suggest three broad categories of guidelines.

1. As a member of a group:
   a) When you have pertinent knowledge, ideas, or experiences, express them.
   b) Really listen and try to comprehend what others are saying.
   c) Realize that there is seldom one right plan, decision, answer, or approach. Know when to dig in and bleed and die—and when not to.
   d) When you have feelings that are pertinent, let the group know.
   e) Make an effort to comprehend and understand the total organization, its goals, its interrelatedness, and let your actions be decided by the total good.

    f) Know when to make group decisions and when to make individual decisions.

    g) Focus on the job and job performance in the group and not on individual personalities, looks, dress, values, etc.

    h) Have an overriding goal to which you can wholeheartedly dedicate yourself.

    i) Cope with—don't dodge—conflict within the group.

    j) Be concerned primarily with setting objectives—not the means for reaching those objectives.

2. As an individual:

    a) You cannot command trust within a group; you earn it.

    b) You can trust another person and not be open; similarly, you can be open with a person and not trust him.

    c) Never compromise a value that ranks very high in your value system.

    d) If the way the group action was arrived at was made public, and if your part in it was completely known, could you explain it to your wife, husband, children, and significant other close persons and know they would fully approve?

3. As a leader:

    a) Appoint a devil's advocate. This person is to take the opposite side and to find weaknesses in the group decision or plan. Sometimes, the use of "role reversal" can be employed for the same purpose.

    b) Encourage openness in the discussion. Solicit full information. Don't be punitive, and don't permit members to engage in punitive behavior.

    c) Bring in an impartial third party to evaluate the decision or plan. Some organizations use a "process observer" for a similar purpose.

    d) When appointing the members of the group, be sure to include "objective thinkers" and "tough battlers."

e) After the decision or plan is made, encourage the group to play out the scenario that will result. Can the group live with it?

f) Use secret balloting. If several members have not gone along with the emerging decision or plan, encourage the group to secure additional data as to why the plan or decision does not have full support.

g) Often, the leader's "antennae" will indicate that some members are hesitant and have reservations but are not expressing them. Check with these members in private to determine the reasons for their reservations.

The Territorial Imperative

In attempting to understand fully the dynamics behind empire-building and vested interests, it has struck this author that one avenue of exploration that seems to have the possibility of helping us more fully understand these realities has been largely ignored. This is the concept of the "territorial imperative."[2] For years this author has been impressed with the observation that in any relationship, personal or organizational, there is always competition, conflict, and the drive by one person or organization to ultimately assert domination and superior authority. Within oneself there is the conflict between the ego and the superego—"What I must do vs. what I would really like to do." Among children, one will ultimately emerge as a dominant leader. Between husband and wife, despite protestations of equality, one or the other will almost invariably occupy the dominant role. Place two people in an office, and one of them will emerge dominant. Let two agencies or organizations enter the same field in a particular geographical location, and one will emerge as superior, even though both will protest that they are equal and share the client load and responsibility.

Borroughs and towns will fight to maintain their local identity when all facts and data and reality argue for merger and consolidation. School districts fight to the bitter end to maintain their separate identity. The states fight the national government. Local and regional offices and divisions fight their national office and national headquarters. Departments and units within a local organization fight their top management for identity and independence.

The territorial imperative approach really poses the question, "What does being a manager have in common with birds, apes, seals, eels, salmon, and beetles?" The answer seems to be man's need, like that of all other living creatures, to own and to defend a piece of territory—something that is peculiarly one's own. Initially, the work in this field was done on birds; later, it was expanded to other species, such as mammals, fish, and insects. Early researchers thought that the concept of territory was related to the need for an adequate food supply. Increasingly, however, the evidence indicates that this is not so.

What does territory offer?

1. Territory that is peculiarly one's own

2. Security in possessing that territory

3. Excitement in the defense of the territory. One of the fascinating discoveries of the research is the apparent fact that no species can tolerate boredom and therefore goes to great extremes to avoid it. This might offer a most fertile field to explore in terms of organizations' concern with worker boredom.

Types of territory

Each researcher will differ in the kinds of territory that are identified. Most, however, would agree on at least three different types.

Individual space territory. This is sometimes called "life space" or a "space bubble." This is a piece of territory that each of us carries around with us and is accorded to us by other members of our species. This individual space is apparent in birds sitting on a telephone wire. They are equitably spaced. Each has its own space bubble.

For humans, this space bubble is a piece of territory about three feet in diameter, but it varies with races and different parts of a country. You can test this by observing the spacing of seats in any public area, such as a restaurant or movie house. Or, observe yourself in a line of people; invariably, you will not move closer than about

18 inches to the person in front of you. To do so is to invite a turned head and a disapproving look. Observe the distance you stand when talking to another person. (It is interesting to note here that we will give a person of higher status a larger space bubble. We will not stand as close to the president of the company as we will to an associate.) Observe how uncomfortable we feel in the middle seat when traveling coach on an airplane. Someone is always thrusting an elbow or leg into "our space." Up in first class, we don't feel uncomfortable; we have our three-foot space bubble. (The author is aware that on occasion we invite others to violate our bubble; if we did not, the species could not be propagated.)

Area space. All members of a species will "stake out" a territory that is "theirs." Many mammals do this through combining a pungent scent with urine and urinating around the parameters of their territory. Man is, of course, more subtle. He does it by meets and bounds, with pictures, with fences, etc. This can be seen in man's tremendous drive to own a home and lot. After that is accomplished, he wants a piece of land in the mountains, in a rural area, or on a beach— somewhere he can go and let the soil run through his fingers and exclaim, "This is mine." Women apparently do not have quite the same driving need to own the territory; like females of other species, she desires the man who owns a lot of territory. Further evidence can be seen in examples such as the following: unless the training staff intervenes, participants in a training group will normally be sitting in the same seats on Friday afternoon that they occupied on Monday morning; in a company parking lot, employees will stake out "their" space; children will create their own spaces in the house and yard; the kitchen is mother's territory; ships have "officers' country."

In the work organization, a typist or secretary will draw an imaginary line around her desk that outlines "her territory." Even though she is not using it, she will not permit another employee to place a desk, cabinet, or table in "her space." It has been observed that engineers and scientists not only define their work space, but they also want a wall around it. The higher you go in an organization, the more space you get. If you doubt this, simply look at the square footage allowed different echelons. In the government, the General

Services Administration (GSA) at one time had this reduced to a formula that was followed by agencies: a clerical worker got 100 square feet; a clerical supervisor got 125; a supervisor got 150; a branch chief got 175; and a lab worker got 275. (We once pointed out to GSA that a dead person gets 6 times 4 feet, or 24 square feet, which indicated that a clerical worker is only four times as active as a dead person.)

Further exploration will reveal that humans, in organizations, do as any other species do. The fittest get the more desirable spaces. Organizations will vary in how they define desirable spaces; in general, however, the most coveted spaces (in descending order) are corner rooms, rooms next to corner rooms, rooms with windows, a given floor (usually the top floor has more status), rooms facing the front of the building, rooms facing the back of the building and, finally, desk space (in the interior of the building) surrounded by corridors and no windows.

Psychological space. We do not, of course, know whether or not other species have this territorial need. Some day we may communicate with porpoises (which now seems a distinct possibility) and may learn if this need exists for them. A personal psychological space is that part of one's life that is one's own, and no other person or organization has a right to invade it without the person's permission. It is this psychological space that a person is defending by resisting or objecting to polygraph tests, school questionnaires inquiring into parental sex habits and other personal information, the sharing of personal data by public and governmental organizations without the individual's express permission, being placed on lists sold to other vendors simply because one bought a specific product or service, or being requested to answer various questions that appear on census forms.

Similarly, this concept of psychological space is a factor in some of the dynamics in management-labor negotiations, e.g., management resists unions' interfering in what they consider to be "management prerogatives." In so doing, management is in effect saying, "This is my territory. You have no right to intrude, and we will resist and defend that territory." This same phenomenon operates in jurisdictional fights between unions as to which has the right to install what and where and when.

THE TERRITORIAL IMPERATIVE IN WORK ORGANIZATIONS

Man no longer stakes out a territory in a jungle and defends it. However, the territorial need remains—it is too deeply ingrained and imbedded in man to be eradicated in a few generations. So, man continues to have this drive for territory. Subtly, probably quite unconsciously, man has substituted the territories in the work organization for the literal territory he once owned. Managers speak of "my staff, my office, my budget, my facilities, my plant, my resources." These have now become man's territory and he will, as any species will, not only defend it, but also attempt to improve his territory by wresting a more desirable territory from another person.

It is intriguing to observe the language we use to describe aspects of work organizations and our roles in those organizations and to relate this terminology to the territorial imperative concept.

- When one makes a lot of money, we say, "He made a killing."
- When trying to get the best of an opponent, we say, "I'm setting him up for the kill." We also say in such situations, "I'm going to trap her."
- We "get his hide."
- We go on the "warpath."
- We refer to our pay checks as "bringing home the bacon."
- The competition threatens "our territory."
- When going to the organization, we say, "I'm going down to the jungle."
- We create a "circle" of friends.
- We "go to the heart" of a matter.
- We refer to our bosses as "Chief."

Further, it should be remembered that a man and his job are hard to separate. This can be seen in such surnames as Millwright, Carpenter, Fisher, Turner, Cook, etc. It is almost impossible to introduce one person to another without including the person's occupation, title, or profession. David G. Moore commented on this when he noted:

The problems of relationship are enhanced by the strong personal identification which employees make with their own occupations. A job is more than a function: to the individual, it is a sense of purpose, a set of interests, a way of life, a value system, above all, a personal identity.

When you attack my job—you attack me.

When you hinder my work, you thwart my interests.

When you push your own values at my expense, you become my enemy.

When you fail to understand my interests and values, you are perverse, deliberately obstinate, intellectually stupid, and possibly even morally incompetent.[3]

The implications of all of this are not quite clear at the moment. Few researchers have undertaken the task of relating the concept of the territorial imperative to the work organization. One clear implication, however, is that when discussing an issue involving the "territory" of two persons, the discussion should be moved into a neutral territory!

The territorial imperative is both a blessing and a curse to organizations. It is a blessing in that it is doubtful that people will ever work as hard for a group or organization as they will for themselves or for something they feel is theirs. For example:

- American farmers far outproduce their Communist counterparts, even discounting the better equipment, methods, and farming knowledge of the Americans.

- The author remembers a cab driver in Pittsburgh who commented during a ride, "Hear that noise? Hear that rattle? Hear that rough motor? Mister, until six months ago this cab was assigned to me. I took care of it like it was my own. Then they made me share it with two other drivers. None of us take care of it now."

- Public utilities have learned to assign a line truck to a specific crew. The crew then care for it and keep it in good repair.

- The military finally learned to encourage crews to consider assigned equipment as "my truck," "my ship," "my tank," "my plane," "my gun."

- Cars assigned to a motor pool are poorly cared for; those assigned to individuals tend to be kept in top shape.

- Tools drawn from a central pool by workers are routinely found in poor condition. But if the tools are assigned to an individual worker, they are generally well maintained.

In short, people in organizations will work harder and more efficiently if they feel that "this is *my* part of the action."

The territorial imperative is also a curse, however, to organizations. It explains in part the phenomenon behind "empire-building" and "vested interest." The terminology of much of the behavior we observe in the organization is analogous to the hunter besting a beast:

- The salesman has to "beat" the customer.

- The department head has to "beat" the other departments.

- The fun is in the struggle and battle.

- Talk of efficiency and economy is simply not heard.

Taking Advantage of the Territorial Imperative in Organizations

How can the manager use the insight provided by the concept of the territorial imperative in coping with the phenomena of vested interests and empire-building? Managers suggest the following approaches:

1. First, if you recognize what is probably operating, at least in part, you can laugh at yourself and realize what you are doing. Certainly, you can say, "I am not going to be ruled by my genes and preprogramming as an emerging mammal. I am a creature who also possesses thought and reason, and this I will assert over my genes."

2. When it is necessary to take territory, real or psychic, from a subordinate, realize that at the "gut" level, it hurts the person losing territory. Even if the person realizes that the change means more efficiency, productivity, or economy, it hurts and hurts badly.

3. Too often, we take away territory and attempt to compensate with a larger title, such as "Vice-President in Charge of Special Programs," and act as if no one will notice what has happened. This is nonsense. The person losing territory knows what has happened, as do those associated with the person. Despite surface amenities, they will treat the person, at the "gut" level, as an animal who has lost territory and is headed toward the outward periphery of the lesser organizational spaces.

4. Probably the best solution in such a situation is for the manager to help the employee who has lost territory, real, psychic, or psychological, to face the fact. The manager should also help the employee see that the new territory being assigned is the best possible for that individual—that the new territory is desirable and that the employee will be better able to defend it. Normally, an employee should be willing to give up 100,000 acres in west Texas for 10 acres in downtown Dallas.

NOTES

1.

Irving L. Janis, "Groupthink," *Psychology Today,* November 1971. In this article, Mr. Janis examines several recent governmental decisions made by close groups within the political administration in power and analyzes some of the dynamics that made for ineffective and possibly erroneous decisions. For a more detailed treatment on this subject, see Irving L. Janis, *Victims of Group Think: A Psychological Study of Foreign-Policy Decisions and Fiascoes,* Boston: Houghton Mifflin, 1972.

2.

For those readers interested in exploring this subject in more detail, the following books may be helpful (bibliographies in each of these books will suggest more reading for exploring this content in more depth): Robert Ardrey, *African Genesis,* New York: Atheneum, 1961; Robert Ardrey, *The Social Contract,* New York: Atheneum, 1970; Robert Ardrey, *The Territorial Imperative,* New York: Dell, 1966; Raymond Aron, *Progress and Disillusion,* New York: New American Library, A Mentor Book, 1968; Edward T. Hall, *The Hidden Dimension,* New York: Doubleday (Anchor Book), 1969; Edward T. Hall, *The Silent Language,* Greenwich, Conn.: Fawcett, 1965; Clyde Kluckhohn, *Mirror For Man,* Greenwich, Conn.: Fawcett, 1967; Gay Gaer Luce,

Body Time, New York: Bantam, 1971; Desmond Morris, *The Naked Ape,* New York: Dell, 1969; J. B. Priestley, *Man and Time,* New York: Dell, 1968; B. F. Skinner, *Beyond Freedom and Dignity,* New York: Alfred A. Knopf, 1971; Robert Sommer, *Personal Space,* Englewood Cliffs, N.J.: Prentice-Hall, 1969; Gordon R. Taylor, *The Biological Time Bomb,* New York: Signet, 1968.

3.
David G. Moore, "The Human Relations Approach," in Sidney Mailick and Edward H. Van Ness, eds., *Concepts and Issues in Administrative Behavior,* Englewood Cliffs, N.J.: Prentice-Hall, 1962, p. 195. Reprinted by permission.

How the Manager Can Reduce Organizational Communication Misfires

4

One of your major roles and functions as a manager is your ability to solve problems within your sphere of influence and responsibility. You should look at your organization as a mechanism for both solving problems and planning. Within your organization, whether it is a business, a government agency, or a volunteer group, units and individuals are solving problems and planning within narrow limits. For example, one employee is concerned with sales, another with accounting procedures, another with training, etc.

Knowledge workers constitute the largest single bloc of workers in America today. These workers traffic in an extensive amount of knowledge in a very limited field. The identification of this knowledge and skill in applying it is one of the major purposes of job descriptions and employee qualification applications. If the organization had its way, it would hire employees who already possessed all the information they needed to solve the problems, accomplish the planning, and handle the operational requirements in a job.

Once you understand this fully, you will never look at your in-box in quite the same way again. Your in-box is your umbilical cord to your future in the organization and your career. If you were totally cut off from the flow of information from within and outside your organization, within a period of a few weeks you would have such a faulty record of bad decisions and plans that your job would be in jeopardy. Therefore, you should recognize that your company needs a communication system to carry information to you and all employees within your organization so that you and they can make efficient, accurate decisions and plans that reflect the best information available at the moment.

However, communication also serves another, very subtle purpose in an organization, and this purpose is seldom fully understood by managers. One of the ways by which you gauge your importance within an organization, by which you receive some status and ego buildup, is the kind of information you are entitled to possess and how quickly you receive it. This relates particularly to secret, confidential, and sensitive information. If, after having had access to this type of information, you are then refused it, you feel that you have lost caste and status. What is more, you also "lose caste" in the eyes of your fellow managers and the people under you. Often, the people in your unit have no trouble perceiving a reorganization as more efficient and economical. What your people resent is that they are being cut off from information to which they once were entitled and have thereby lost *status*. Seldom will any of your people openly talk about their resentment. Status is a subtle dynamic, but it operates much more frequently and strongly than a manager realizes. The possession of information can also be used as part of a reward and punishment system. When you cut off information, you "punish" the worker under you.

When you think of "organizational communications," you may think of only one system—the formal system of memos, directives, letters, and manuals. Actually, there are several systems of communication within an organization. Each has its own "membership" and carries a different kind of information. This chapter will describe four of the common systems (the "grapevine" is often described as a separate system, but this discussion will consider the grapevine as part of the "informal" system).

You can get a fairly good idea of who is in your various communication systems by duplicating and completing the analysis chart shown in Table 4–1. Take a few minutes and jot down, in the first column, the name of all the persons with whom you have talked or corresponded within the past ten days. In the next column, indicate

Table 4-1 Contact analysis chart

Persons with whom I discussed my organization, subunit, or something related to my job (within last ten days).	Who initiated the contact?		Person was in:			
	I did	Other person	Formal communication system	Work-relationships system	Informal communication system	External communication system

whether you, or the person communicated with, initiated the communication. That is all you need to do now. As each of the communication systems is discussed, review the list of persons communicated with and place a check mark opposite that person's name in the column headed by the system identification (formal, work relationships, etc.). When you have completed the chart, and all persons in the first column have a check mark under one of the systems, you will have a fairly good idea about which people are in the various systems of all the people who communicate with you.

FORMAL COMMUNICATION SYSTEM

The first communication system we will discuss is the formal communication system; this is the one that most employees know very well and consider to be the only communication system within the organization. The formal system carries official correspondence, manuals, directives, policies, regulations, etc., and is composed of your chain of command—your boss and those above him—and your subordinates.

The Problem of Distortion

One of the assumptions we make about the formal communication system is that it can transmit information with little or no dilution or distortion. However, anyone who has worked in an organization longer than one week knows that this idea is a fool's paradise. Information in this system is subject to serious distortion. What is more critical for the manager, information passed to higher echelons is subject to more dilution and distortion than is information transmitted downward. One reason for this is that management normally has more channels available to transmit information downward than subordinates have channels available to submit information upward. The manager can use directives, call staff meetings, request the employee to visit his office, use the company house publication, post notices on the bulletin board, request his superior to give him information, etc. The employee is limited to fewer channels—going through his boss or using grievance procedures. To do otherwise is to be accused of by-passing the boss.

We can get some idea of how serious the distortion and dilution factor is by reviewing a study done by the Lewis Corporation around 1960. The study, which dealt with verbal communication, has been replicated a number of times in other organizations, with similar results. The study found that if the president attempted to transmit a verbal communication or statement to nonsupervisory workers: vice-presidents understood 67% of what president meant to communicate; general supervisors understood 56%; plant managers understood 40%; foremen understood 30%; and nonsupervisory workers understood 20%. In other words, if a verbal communication passes through four echelons, about 80% of the initial communication will be lost, diluted, or distorted. Managers should therefore understand that if a communication passes verbally through only one person, the problem is not whether this communication might be distorted, but rather, *how much* distortion has occurred.

What accounts for the distortion? Many organizations have looked at this problem, and the villain most frequently identified is "inappropriate filtering" of communication. Note the *"inappropriate"* nature of the filtering. Filtering information is a very proper function of a manager; he is not expected to transmit all information received from higher to lower echelons. Nor is he expected to take the mass of operating data he receives and transmit it willy-nilly to his superiors. Rather, the manager is expected to read, digest, analyze, abstract, and summarize such information. The problem, however, is that in doing this, he may inappropriately filter the information he receives.

The question often arises, "But is not, then, the way to handle this problem by putting everything in written form?" Another question raised is, "Is written communication subject to the same amount of distortion?" A similar study looking at this distortion phenomenon related to written communication may have been made, but the author is unaware of it. Organizational managers have been queried on this, as have other organizational communication consultants. The general view is that written communication is, of course, also subject to dilution, distortion, and loss, but probably not to the same degree as verbal communication. For example, consider the ways in which written communication can be filtered.

- The manager receives information and files it or throws it in the wastebasket. This effectively kills that piece of information for the manager's subordinates.

- The manager simply routes it—or places it in the files.

- The manager says, "I have been told to read this to you." As an employee, I know he means, "I have done my job. Now go ahead with business as usual."

- The manager's tone of voice or facial expression tells me how he reacts to the information and how I should respond to it.

What are the most frequently encountered inappropriate filters? Interestingly enough, they tend to differ for information coming down and for information going up. The following seem to be the most common inappropriate filters for downward communication:

1. *Selective or inattentive listening.* Ralph Nichols' studies have made us painfully aware that most of us are very inefficient listeners.[1] You can easily test this, after a staff meeting, by having coffee with some of your peers who attended the same meeting and asking, "What did you understand as having been said, and what is wanted?"

2. *Manager's perceptions.* The manager is always affected by what he thinks his subordinates ought to know or what he thinks they want to hear. Management may think something should be disseminated, but the manager may not give that item the same priority or may not think it should be transmitted. Or, he may decide that employees should know the content, but not take the trouble to route it or discuss it because the staff couldn't care less about that piece of information.

3. *The reputation or credibility of the source of information.* If the manager either doesn't like or has professional disagreements with a superior, he may find it very difficult to transmit information received from that source.

4. *Adding information to the message received.* Although the manager may have something he wants to communicate to subordinates, he may feel that he does not have enough weight or status to get the

behavior, action, or results he wants. Therefore, he adds his message to the one received, hoping that the status of higher echelons will carry his message through.

5. *Subordinates overreact to messages from above.* Many managers comment, "It has gotten so that I am afraid to open my mouth in my organization. My slightest expression of interest or approval is taken as a signal for 'full steam ahead' on this matter. Similarly, if I ask a question for clarification, it is taken as a signal that I am not interested and want to kill the project under discussion."

6. *Value system and the resultant personal biases.* A clear example of the effect a person's value system and the resultant personal biases and prejudices can have on a communication has been observed within the past ten years in federal organizations. Departmental sources have issued many directives about integration, employment of women, appointment of women to executive positions, employment of the hardcore, employment of minority groups, ecological and environmental concerns, etc. It is fascinating to observe that the actions taken with regard to the information or directive depend on whether or not the values implied in the directives "jibe" with those of the subordinate manager.

7. *Problem of operational priorities.* Says the manager, "Of course I would like to share this information with subordinates, but we are so busy, there simply is not time to hold a staff meeting to pass on the information."

8. *Feelings of the moment.* Most communication experts agree that probably the strongest single filter is the influence of the feeling of the moment by those who have received the information. It is not by accident that, when it is important to us to receive an affirmative reply, we stop by the desk of the boss's secretary and ask, "How is the old man feeling this morning?" Depending on the answer, we make a judgment about whether or not to attempt to communicate with "the old man." Our response to information and communication has a lot to do with how we are feeling at that moment. It would be intriguing to review organizational decisions, many of a very significant nature, to determine the degree to which the decision was influenced by heavy drinking the previous night; fights with spouses,

children, peers, and subordinates; headaches; upset stomachs; frustrated sex fulfillment; or a bad stomach ache or constipation.

The most common filters for upward communication seem to be the following:

1. *Inability to differentiate between major and minor complaints.* Many bosses say, "It is the nature of employees to gripe and complain. This data is simply a gripe and and should not be reported." Often, of course, this is true. Employees do complain and gripe. This is one of the things people removed from the work force for long periods state that they miss. The navy says, "A griping ship is a happy ship." Mental health practitioners support this view, because griping is a good way to get rid of frustrations. Too often, however, the manager cannot distinguish between a healthful complaint ("Why don't they use styrofoam cups so the coffee won't taste of wax?") and one of substance ("I don't have a place to work" or "I haven't been paid for nine weeks").

2. *Volume of communication.* When the manager is swamped with information and messages from below, everything tends to get downgraded.

3. *Disguising the message.* Will this item make my boss mad or make me or my unit look bad? If the answer is "yes," the subordinate will tend to delete the information entirely, bury it in footnotes, place it at the end of a long report, or to handle it in such a way as to cause the manager to come out "smelling like a rose." For example, one manager reported, "In fiscal year 'X' our field unit accomplished what let's call a Unit A. This caught the attention, favorably, of headquarters which, for fiscal year 'Y,' set our field unit a quota of four Unit A's. At the end of fiscal year 'Y,' we had accomplished only two units." How can the field office report this accomplishment in such a way as to be in line for a superior-service award? We all know how to do it. We report, "During fiscal year 'Y,' we doubled our accomplishment over fiscal year 'X.' Or, "We had a 100% increase in . . . " Unless headquarters management is on the ball and inquires what the quota was, we end up with an award for outstanding performance. Managers get to be past masters in learning how to read such information reports.

4. *Anticipating the reaction to the message.* "The boss wouldn't be interested in this, so why report it?" We spend much time figuring out our boss, top management, and the organization's current interest or interests in order to slant our information to conform to this perception. Of course, this can be legitimate, but it can also winnow out some very critical information.

5. *Hoping for the best.* Maybe things will work out. If they do, I'm home free. If they don't, I'll worry about it at that time. "But," says management, "under this condition, by the time we get the problem or information, so much time has elapsed and positions have become so polarized that it is impossible to ferret out fact from fantasy, and we haven't a chance to reconcile or solve the problem."

6. *Acknowledging others' idiosyncrasies.* The necessity to write up information within prescribed formats, on required forms, or according to the whims of the signer may also act as a filter. The problem here is that the information may not fit the form or format, and the real purpose is therefore lost, buried, or changed to meet the semantics, form, or style required.

7. *Inaccurate perceptions.* Probably the most frequently occurring filter is the assumption by subordinates that managers don't really want accurate information or data about how things actually are going, but simply assurance that all is going well. Ask any subordinate how things are going, and he'll normally respond "fine" or "great," on the assumption that the manager doesn't really want the actual information—he wants assurance that all is well. Most field persons say of visiting male headquarters personnel, "They don't want the facts. Just fix them up with a good room in a good hotel, a round of golf at the best course, good meals, some female compansionship—and they're happy and consider it a great field trip and will report your office is doing a great job."

Enhancing the Formal Communication System

How do you correct inappropriate filtering and protect against other communication "traps" in the formal system? When this question is posed to managers, they most frequently mention the following techniques.

1. Differentiate between approval needs and information needs. A form is developed to secure approval for some action or item. Only three signatures are required. The form is set up in this fashion. However, one by one other persons realize either that they are slightly affected or that their ego demands they be "in the know." One by one these names are added to the form until, within two or three years, 12 signatures are required for approval of that action or item. With the additional signatures required, it now takes two to four months to get the action or item, because at least two of the people are on extended field trips, ill, or so busy they haven't got to the bottom of their in-box, where the form is gathering mold. The answer is to review all such approval documents and take off all names except those actually needed for approval. Additional copies of the document can be made and sent as information copies to the other nine or ten persons. If they have comments or objections, they can make their feelings known.

2. Most managers, when issuing an order or instruction to an individual or group, will do so and then ask, "Do you understand?" Almost inevitably, the reply is "yes," even though the employee or group has not the foggiest idea what is really wanted; the employee who says he does not understand is indicating either that he was not listening well or that the boss is not a very good explainer. Also, such an employee, in a group context, assumes that everyone else except himself understands. In a group setting, a good technique is to *say* if you do not understand. At least 40 percent of the others in the group will thank you, because they didn't understand either. If you are the boss in this situation, you can correct the problem with a simple twist of the question. Instead of merely asking whether everyone understands, say something like, "Would you tell me, in your own words, what you understand is wanted?" Or, you might ask, "Would you tell me how you are going to go about accomplishing this task?" As the individual or group gives feedback, the boss can quickly test whether or not his task or request was understood. Some managers estimate that one-fourth of the difficulties in communication could be eliminated with this technique.

3. When you take an action, make a decision, or undertake a planning activity, take 15 seconds and ask yourself, "Who else's job in

the organization is affected by this action, decision, or plan?" Then inform that person or group.

4. It has already been noted that any verbal communication passing through only one person will have some distortion. Often, the distortion does not materially change the request or assigned task. Obviously, it is not being suggested that every verbal request received through another person be checked with the originator. The request may be so low-level that a distortion in it will not matter very much. However, if the consequences of a verbal communication received through another person are extremely high, or if the commitment of resources is highly significant, it is desirable to check back with the originator. Four out of five times, had the manager worked on the communication received, he will be performing on the request in a way that is not wanted or desired. This will probably not be done in the instance of more than one out of 15 verbal requests. If your boss is sensitive about your checking personally with the originator, request your boss to check the portions of the communication you think are questionable. Usually, the boss will be glad to do so, for the boss, too, has a great deal at stake.

5. If you ask for recurring reports or information, be sure that those who supply the information know that the information is being read and used in some way to influence operations or the organization. One of the fastest ways to ensure sterile reports is to provide no feedback to those supplying the information on what is being done with the data.

6. If several people are involved in a discussion resulting in operational agreements, write up a memorandum of understanding and send it to those who attended the meeting. You will be surprised how often your understanding is not fully shared by others and needs to be clarified. You will also find that people's memory is quite unreliable; with the passage of several weeks, few who attended the meeting can remember what exactly was agreed upon.

7. Locate for yourself good sources of information—persons or written sources. Persons who have a consistent record for providing reliable information are jewels; if they can interpret the consequences of the information, they are even more valuable. Some providers of

information do no filtering or screening whatever; others have a personal goal and will filter the information; others will distort the information; and still others will give you highly selective information, so you seldom get all the facts.

8. Your method of handling unpleasant information has a lot to do with whether or not its source will remain an open channel. If an employee provides you with critical but unpleasant information, and you storm, rave, curse, rant, and otherwise belittle him, especially in the presence of others, you are almost guaranteeing that you will receive no further unpleasant information from that employee. If at any time in the future he has such data, he will say to himself, as he holds it back, "remember the last time."

9. One of the ways subordinates can punish a boss is to deliberately withhold information. Your decisions, plans, and operational actions are only as good as the data you possess. Employees know this. The possession of information is power. The manager needs to do everything possible to establish a climate of trust and openness so that the information flow from subordinates is maximum.

10. When looking for information for planning or decision-making, most of us go only to friendly sources. This is often a tragic mistake. Normally your friends will tell you only what they think you want to hear. It is extremely difficult for subordinates and peers to level with you. Therefore, also seek information from unfriendly sources. These sources have data and information you need as you fashion your decision or plan. Better to have it now and modify your decision or plan than to proceed with only friendly information and have the unfavorable information later emerge and scuttle your decision or plan.

11. Too often, someone in the "Duplicating" or "Directives" office makes the decision about what directives, manuals, policies, regulations, etc., should be sent to what managers and units. Sometimes, the decision is made (since it is so difficult to determine who is interested in what) to send everyone everything. Generally, except in small organizations, this tends to downgrade all communications distributed. A number of organizations have found it useful to send a listing of all communications published regularly to all managers and to let them indicate the ones that they would like to receive on

a regular basis. The user is, after all, the best judge of what is and is not helpful or essential.

WORK RELATIONSHIPS SYSTEM

The second system to be found in organizational communications is the "work relationships" system. The people in this system are all in the organization; however, they are outside the manager's formal chain of command. They do not include the manager's boss or subordinates, but can be above, below, across, or diagonal from him. They are the people with whom the manager communicates because they are critical in getting his job done, but they are outside his formal chain of command. For example, suppose the manager wants income tax forms. He knows that Personnel Service stocks them as a convenience for employees. If the manager wants to check if they are available, he doesn't ask his boss if he can contact Personnel Service; rather, he visits them or phones them to ask if the forms are available. No one is offended; no chain of command prerogatives have been violated.

Most organizations understand this system and encourage it. For most employees, it is probably true that most of their communication and contacts to accomplish their job occurs outside their normal chain of command. Unfortunately, however, many employees do not understand this and feel guilty when they use the system. At best, there are occasions when employees are not sure which system to use. Managers should take pains to ensure that employees understand the system and understand when to use the formal system and when to use the work relationships system.

Let's explore the work relationships system further. It can best be understood by sketching how we usually get introduced to it. When someone joins a new organization or a new, major unit within the organization, the new employee is given a desk, an organization chart, functional statements, job descriptions, policies, directives, etc., and told, "Familiarize yourself with who we are, what we do, to whom we relate, and the procedures we follow." Depending on how critically he is needed, the new employee may stay in such limbo for two days or six months.

Finally, he is given a job assignment. As he tries to accomplish it, he finds that he needs something. He consults the voluminous documents and charts he has been given, but can't quite figure out who is responsible for the thing he needs. Finally, he gets a clue that it is "Y" office and calls or visits that person or office to make known his request. The person contacted looks quizzical and inquires, "What made you think we did that?" The employee brings out whatever document or directive gave him this clue. The person contacted examines it, looks amused or surprised, and comments, "Well, I'll be damned, I'd forgotten we ever said we did that." Or, "We used to do that, but in the last reorganization it was taken away from us." The employee inquires who performs that function now. Says the contacted person, "I don't really know, but why don't you see Jane down in the mail room?" You can't figure out, for the life of you, what Jane has to do with that item, but you see her. Sure enough, Jane handles the item for you.

If the new employee's peers accept him, they'll watch him struggle in this fashion for a while; then they'll say in effect, "Look, Joe, we like you. We think you're going to be o.k. We'd like to see you get along and make out well. Look, Joe, let us tell you how this outfit really works."

Now they will in effect tell the employee to forget the organization chart and the functional statements he was given, and they'll sketch out a whole new organizational chart and set of functional statements. They'll explain who in the organization is going places and who is on the way down or arrested in their position; who makes things happen and who doesn't; who are the booze-heads; old-time employees with good data and contacts; who is holding what position because he knows what on whom or who owes him a debt; who is on the way out; who is in disfavor; who are the fair-haired boys and girls. The functional statement or organization chart says see the director? Forget him! His assistant—or his secretary or some other person—runs that shop. They'll tell the new employee who moves things, who kills things, and which people, if they are for him or approve the item, are the kiss of death.

The employee now possesses a whole new organizational system —and it works. And, if he has to bet, he should never bet on the formal system, but rather on the work relationships system. One of the ways the work relationships system network succeeds, if there is a showdown with the formal system, is to say to management, "O.k., we'll work through your system—the formal system." But working through the formal system doesn't get the job done. And, what's

Table 4-2   Potentially confusing organizational situations.

Situation	Employee should use: Formal communication system	Work relationships system
1. There appears to be no policy or regulation covering the action required.	————	————
2. An employee's request of another unit or person will call for a sizeable commitment of time.	————	————
3. An employee needs routine technical data from another unit.	————	————
4. An employee wants to test out an idea with someone else.	————	————
5. In working with someone in another unit, an employee becomes aware that the other person is stealing company property (excess of $100).	————	————
6. An employee's boss won't give approval to work on a problem with someone in another unit, but the employee thinks it is critical to do so.	————	————
7. An employee needs some supplies or equipment immediately, but to go through the formal system will take three days.	————	————
8. An employee knows that his boss won't forward his idea to another unit.	————	————

Note: There are no "right" or "wrong" answers. Each organization will use different guides. What is critical is that subordinates understand what, in their organization, is the correct guideline to follow in these and other situations.

more, you can't touch the members of the work relationships system. Everything they are doing has a rule, policy, or regulation in the formal system that says "This is how the employee should work." Any group of employees can grind an organization to a halt within three weeks if they follow to the letter the organization's policies, regulations, rules, and manuals. Of course, however, the work relationships system can also be abused. Managers need to be fully conscious of the two systems—formal and work relationships—and help their subordinates understand when they are free to work in the work relationships system and when they must work within the formal system.

Table 4–2 lists some of the situations that arise within organizations that often confuse subordinates. Put an "X" in the appropriate column to show which system the employee should use in each of the following situations.

INFORMAL SYSTEM

The third system of communication within organizations is the informal system. The membership of the manager's informal system are persons within the organization. However, the manager does not need to communicate with them in order to get his job done. The primary reason he communicates and associates and relates to people in his informal system is because "these are my kind of people." He likes and can trust them; their values are his values. He can level with them, cry on their shoulder, tell them his frustrations—and they won't violate his confidence. They'll usually agree with the manager. They'll certainly give him love and understanding.

The basis for such associations can be many:

- Same age group
- Same church or clubs
- Same profession and professional society
- Same car pool
- Accounting service vs. the travelers
- Production people vs. sales people

- Union vs. nonunion
- Managers vs. nonsupervisory personnel
- Same university
- Wives know one another
- Same sex
- Functional work or units
- "They ring my chimes"
- "Good vibes"

These informal groups are critical to us all. We all have membership in one or more such groups in the organization. In the past, organizations tended to discourage these groups; they felt that such groups worked at odds with the organization's purposes. Today, there is an increasing awareness that such groups cannot be outlawed, that they meet a basic need of us all, and that if their values are those of the organization, they can be a tremendous asset.

An interesting thing about informal groups is that they tend to form across peer lines. Seldom do they include one's boss or subordinates. This will not hold true, however, if the work unit consists of about 12 people or less. Then, the amenities of social courtesy take over. One of the reasons the informal group is composed of peers is that some of the major topics of discussion in informal groups are one's boss and one's subordinates.

This phenomenon of informal groups is a difficult one for beginning supervisors to understand. A nonsupervisory worker who becomes supervisor is immediately faced with the problem of how to continue to relate with former peers. A common mistake newly promoted supervisors make is to say, "Nothing has changed. I'm still good old Joe. We'll play cards, drink, and talk as we've always done." Then, one day, when he walks across the cafeteria floor to join his old buddies for a cup of coffee, they stop talking when he gets within 20 feet of them. After three such experiences, the new supervisor realizes that something has changed. In addition, there are other subtle differences; something he says in jest is picked up as factual. Now he *knows* that something has changed. Every time an employee takes a promotion, he faces this problem: "How do I break my membership in informal groups at the level I am leaving and establish membership in informal groups at the level I am entering?"

Membership in informal groups is particularly difficult for the head of an organization. With whom does the president relate in an informal group? It is not by accident that the navy says, "The captain eats alone." About the only person the captain can relate to is the chief engineer, and this is often unsatisfactory. Therefore, heads of organizations usually look outside the organization for informal group membership. They form the "Presidents' Club." It has often been observed that district or regional managers will form telephone networks with other district or regional managers in the organization. Another technique is to form an informal group with other heads of similar organizations in a city or region.

One dynamic that many managers do not understand is that a reorganization or change of locations will frequently bring about employee resistance. What the employee or employees are resisting is often not the change itself; they accept the change or reorganization or move as more efficient or economical. What they are resisting is that the reorganization is breaking up their membership in informal groups: "You're breaking up my car pool," "You're breaking up my coffee drinking group," or, "You're breaking up my poker or bridge or pinochle group." Reorganization that minimizes disruption of existing informal groups is normally advisable and will often help reduce resistance to change. It is true, of course, that if the informal groups are working to the detriment of the organization, it may be advisable to break up these groups.

Informal groups often are the real policy makers in an organization. Their meaning to employees is so high that if they must choose between violating the organization or the informal group, they will choose to violate the organization almost every time. The manager can test this by reflecting on the last policy or regulation issued by his organization. The odds are strong that before implementing the policy or regulation, he called one or more of the members of his group and said, "Hey, can we have a cup of coffee?" Over the cup of coffee he asked, "You folks see that regulation issued yesterday?" What the members of his informal group decide they are going to do with that policy or regulation has a lot to do with how the manager will implement it.

One manager said, "I saw this clearly last year. In my organization I am both a resource person and a board member. There were three other resource persons in the city who were in my informal group. We met to eat once a month. These fellows meant a lot to me personally and professionally. I liked them. We talked at dinner about what all informal groups talk about: we were underpaid, underloved, underappreciated; what was wrong with our boss and the organization; how we got more help from one another than from the organization, etc., etc. Two weeks later I'm sitting in a board meeting. Some of the items coming up for discussion and decision were some of the same matters we had discussed in my informal group two weeks earlier at dinner. I was never so aware in my life how my voting as a board member was influenced by my membership in that informal group. I was not going to vote in a way that would jeopardize my standing or acceptance in my informal group; the informal group heavily influenced my voting, even though efficiency or organizational economy indicated that I should have voted otherwise."

If the work standards, values, and commitment in the informal group are consistent and in harmony with organizational goals and objectives, the organization can get commitment and production it could not dare ask in normal performance standards. If not, the organization will suffer every time.

This phenomenon can be observed in every work group. The informal group can police its members continually; the manager cannot. A member of an informal group who does not follow the rules, values, and standards of the informal group faces ostracism, and few people can tolerate such exclusion. Organizations are going to have to learn more about the importance of these groups and how they might be better used in organizations.

Occasionally, it occurs to an organization that if these informal groups, and especially their leaders, are so important, then it should take special pains and measures to be sure they are well informed on organizational matters. However, in three instances we know of, when the informal leaders were briefed in formal meetings on organizational matters, the informal leaders lost their leadership position; they were now seen as part of the organization and management. Similarly, it sometimes occurs to organizations that informal leaders would make good supervisory candidates. Most organizations report that this is not true, however. Apparently, informal leaders work and operate best and most efficiently outside the formal system. When they are made part of the formal system, they cannot work effectively within the necessary restraints.

Informal groups are a reality, and they are extremely critical in determining what and how policies, procedures, and regulations are implemented. It should be obvious that the information carried in this system is extremely frank and open and is not carried through the formal or work relationships systems. Informal groups are important to the employee because in them he finds security through the acceptance, understanding, love, and sense of personal worth he gets from the other members, and participates in the decisions that affect the members.

The key things for the manager to understand about informal groups are:

1. Normally, managers can never be full members of informal groups above or below their present hierarchical level.

2. Special pains should be taken to see that informal leaders are kept well informed on organizational matters. Remember, they can smell a "snow job" a mile away.

3. Managers should pay attention to what they are told by members of informal groups, especially by informal leaders. These people have access to information and feelings managers can't possibly pick up through other communication systems.

The grapevine

Often, the grapevine is considered to be a separate communication system. Most observers report that the membership of grapevines tends to be the same as that of informal groups. Normally, we think of the grapevine as carrying inaccurate information very quickly. However, the grapevine also carries accurate information and very quickly, and it probably carries more accurate than inaccurate information. Contrary to popular belief, the grapevine seldom sets out to destroy an individual or unit, though it is capable of doing so.

When the grapevine is carrying inaccurate information, the manager should check the following things:

1. Does the information being transmitted make sense—not to the originator, but to the receiver? Usually, originators of messages or

information have dealt a long time with the subject and have sat in on many meetings and discussions and have much back-up data. The information they release makes sense to them in terms of their total orientation, but they forget that the recipient does not have this rich background. A good test here is to try out your proposed release on persons not familiar with the issue. If they understand the directive or communication, you probably have a good release.

2. When a rumor is prevalent, ask, "Is it prevalent everywhere, or only in certain parts of the organization?" If it is prevalent only in certain parts, then the odds are fairly strong that specific managers are inappropriately filtering the information flow, and they must be made to release the available information they are holding back.

3. The manager must understand that everyone tries to make incoming data make sense. If it does not, people will invent additional data in order to make the data they have make sense. Note the number of times you will look at something, then turn away because the information does not make sense. You will then turn back for another look to get additional data. For example, an organization in the Midwest operated a production floor. The machinery was quite good, but not the latest available or as versatile as the organization desired. They found a buyer of the old machinery in Maine and began to crate the machinery for shipment. Employees saw this happen and noted the address. This was a factual piece of information but they did not know why. Quickly, a rumor spread: "We're moving to Maine. Do you want to go to Maine? They're shutting down our operation. What a lousy way to treat us. Let's slow down and maybe strike." When this came to management's attention, management said, "How stupid. We're getting new machines. We may even increase the work force. Certainly the jobs will be better." When asked whether they had told this to the employees, management replied, "Of course not. We didn't think it was any of their business to know we were selling the old machines." This is an example of some available factual data and the invention of additional data by employes to make the limited data they possessed make sense—to the detriment of the organization.

Often, management has some unpleasant news to impart to employees and makes the following assumptions.

1. What is bad news for management and the organization will be bad news for the employees.

2. Employees have limited capacity to absorb bad news. If we release all the bad news at one time, we will upset them, thereby creating poor morale.

On the basis of these assumptions, management decides to release the bad news in phases—perhaps five of them. So, on Friday afternoon at four o'clock, the first phase of the bad news is released. (Management always releases bad news at four o'clock on Friday, apparently on the assumption of "Let the employees worry about it on their own time.") Additional parts of the bad news are released on the next four Fridays. Finally, on the fifth Friday, the last part of the unpleasant news is released, and management says, "You now have it all. That's the whole story." Do the employees believe it? No! The communication among employees is, "If you think this was bad, wait until next Friday." Another thing wrong with this approach is that it establishes a pattern. The next time management has a piece of unpleasant news that can be released all at once, the reaction among the employees is, "Remember the last time. It took five weeks for us to get the whole story." They won't believe you.

The points for the manager to remember about the grapevine are:

1. What is bad or unpleasant news for the manager of the organization is seldom that bad to employees. They listen to the manager's communication with boredom and respond, "So, what's new?"

2. Employees, as humans, have a much greater capacity for absorbing unpleasant news and adversity than we think. Human beings find strength to cope with great adversity.

3. It is better for employees to have the full dose of adverse information, digest it, get upset, react—and then get down to the business of coping with it. Phasing unpleasant news only prolongs the period of being upset.

One interesting comment about the grapevine was made by a company president of long tenure. He observed, "The president is always the last to know what is on the grapevine. Further discussion indicated that the informal group—the grapevine network the employee is in—seldom carries information about him. That information is usually in the grapevine network one echelon below him."

EXTERNAL COMMUNICATION SYSTEM

Not all communication having to do with organizational matters and information exists solely within the organization. Nor are organizational matters discussed only within the enterprise. Some studies have indicated that one of the major topics of discussion by employees after office hours is their job and job-related matters. Seldom does an organization attempt to control—at least in a formal way—this external system of communication.

By external system we mean the every-day contacts that employees have with nonorganizational people—feeding information about the organization to the outside world and the outside world feeding information about the organization to those inside it. Among these outside contacts are suppliers, unions, professional schools and societies, friends, neighbors, husbands, wives, children, consumer groups, groups served, politicians, news media of all kinds, task and study groups, columnists, consultants, etc.

If the organization does concern itself about this system, it is generally revealed in the following ways:

- An organization may tell a supplier, "If you reveal what you are delivering to us, in what quantity, and at what location, we will cut you off." With this information, a competitor or adversary would not have much difficulty figuring out a probable development and of what magnitude.

- The organization may attempt to keep certain sensitive or unpleasant information from employees or the public. Public agencies may badly abuse this policy, which resulted some time ago in "right to know" legislation.

- The organization may make half-hearted attempts to tell its employees that they are public relations ambassadors and to put their best foot forward when talking about the organization to outside contacts.

- The organization may hire public information or public relations persons.

Such techniques, however, are usually slanted at the general public and not at employees. And, as everyone knows, no one believes a PI or PR person. We know they are paid to tell only what is good about the organization—not what is bad. Any time you receive information from a PR or PI person, you always seek out someone in the organization and say, "Now, give me the other side of the story—or the rest of the story." Using PI or PR persons is understandable. We all practice good PR. Seldom do we tell even our closest friends about our most serious personal or family problems. We try to project our best image. Even in the yard, with neighbors observing, few of us will chastise children or wives or husbands. We smile at what irritates us and under our breath mutter to them, "Wait until I get you in the house." Observe how we prepare for guests, our behavior in front of guests, or watch the frantic efforts to prepare for a visit from the minister.

Much of the information we pick up about our organization—especially the secret, confidential, sensitive, or unpleasant type of information—is usually received from the external sources. For example, federal personnel in the greater Washington area avidly read the daily newspaper columnists who specialize in news and developments about the federal agencies. Information obtained from these sources is 24 hours ahead of that from the work relationships system and often as much as six weeks ahead of information derived from the formal system.

SUMMARY

The question often arises whether or not the last two systems discussed—the grapevine and external system—are appropriate systems for the manager to use. Most managers agree they can, at times, be legitimate. Certainly, the grapevine is used for many purposes—in emergencies, for example. If the organization is to let employees off work because of heavy snow, this information almost invariably is carried by the grapevine or informal system. If the organization depended in such a case on the formal system, employees would probably not receive the word of early release until hours after their regular release time.

Some organizations use the grapevine to send up trial balloons to test employee reaction. If the reaction is favorable, the item is put in the formal system. If the reaction is not favorable, the organization can always issue a release stating, "Some unauthorized person has spread the unfortunate false rumor that . . ."

Most managers also agree that the external system is a proper one to use on occasion. Certainly, employees use their unions and professional societies to bring pressure to bear on the organization. Some employees will demonstrate with outside groups against their own firm. Employees write letters to the newspaper editor. Managers will use outside study groups or task forces for this purpose, a particularly effective technique if he knows someone on that task force. Also, it is not unheard of for people to use cocktail parties for the same purpose.

What is the major importance for the manager's becoming aware that there are *several* systems of communication within the organization? The manager's effectiveness as both a communicator and a decision-maker and planner are reduced if he does not understand this fact. Each of the four communication systems has a separate membership, and the kind of information carried in each system is quite different. Most of the information carried by informal groups will never be found in the formal system and seldom in the work relationships system. Armed with this knowledge of the several systems, the manager is better able, when looking for information upon which to make a decision or plan, to determine which system or systems he needs to plug for information. Similarly, if he wants to disseminate information widely, quickly, or reinforce its dissemination, knowledge of the various systems tells him into which system or systems he needs to feed the information.

Communication continues to be a problem which plagues organizations. Too often, the organinization or manager looks for the one gimmick which can solve the problem. Or, the organization falls into the trap of thinking that the problem calls for a very extensive, sophisticated communication system. Actually, as we have seen, most communication misfires result from the violation of relatively simple, commonsense practices. Too often, managers comment, "I get so tired of communicating; it seems that half my days are spent in communication activities." The manager should understand that one of the major responsibilities for which he is paid is effective communication. Communication, for the manager, is not a bothersome impediment to be tolerated; it is the major substance of his job.

NOTES

1.
The initial report of these significant findings is in: Ralph Nichols, *Are You Listening?*, New York: McGraw-Hill, 1957; the findings are expanded in Ralph Nichols and Thomas R. Lewis, *Speaking and Listening,* Dubuque, Iowa: W. C. Brown, 1965.

Giving Effective Leadership to Employees

5

The price of leadership, in and out of work organizations, has become extremely demanding in the past decade. As society and shared values became more and more fragmented, the expectations from the manager and other organizational leaders became more and more difficult to accommodate. Some have referred to this as a "revolt against authority." When demands are not met, the individual or group will take their grievance or demand directly to the top. In many organizations, lower and middle echelons are almost routinely by-passed. Some months ago, the author met one morning with the County Superintendent of Schools for a major metropolitan county. The proposed 15-minute conversation took over an hour. By count, the Superintendent handled 14 phone calls. The content? Calls from mothers complaining, "My child missed her bus. What are you going to do about it?"; "The bus was three minutes early this morning, and I had to drive my child to school"; "Sally's bus driver was rude to her"; "Bus 115 is quite dirty. What can you do to see that it is cleaned?"; etc., etc. The Superintendent earns a salary of about $50,000 a year and is undoubtedly the highest-priced bus dispatcher in the country.

This is not an isolated example. More and more individuals and groups are by-passing lower and middle echelons and going directly to the "head man or woman." Leaders in lower and middle positions feel that their job and function are being steadily eroded. A closer look indicates that what seems to be happening is that authority and leadership, as traditionally defined, are undergoing radical change. No longer will individuals or groups blindly follow orders or directions. The organization is having to face this problem and select more capable people as leaders who can think and flexibly, but appropriately, apply policies and regulations. This means that the decision-making process is being conducted at lower levels of the organization, nearer to the scene of action. Concurrently, more power and authority are being delegated downward. Managers and other leaders are finding that often, people are not really rejecting authority and leadership; rather, the base of authority and leadership can no longer be rooted in position, grade, and tenure. More and more leaders are beginning to understand that leadership that is followed must stem from such bases as technical expertise, ability to get a job done, values that are respected, and ability to coach and develop others. In all candor, we should also add that personal charisma is also sometimes a basis for leadership.

How should the manager handle this leadership role? A number of attempts have been made to understand leadership, and each has added something to our knowledge. More and more, the manager is discovering that there is no single correct leadership style. We shall briefly sketch each of the major approaches and conclude our look at leadership with a summary of what staff people seem to be saying about what they want from their leader.

APPROACHES TO LEADERSHIP

"Leaders are Born"

Prior to 1900, and for two decades following, we were influenced by the notion that "leaders are born, not made." In many of the countries from which our parents emigrated, leadership was largely a function of birth and family position. Of course, some workers rose to high leadership positions, and this was the dream of every worker, but leadership positions tended to be filled from a very small part of the population. In most communities, the members of boards of community organizations and agencies came consistently from two percent of the population. This segment of the population was referred to as "Silk Stocking Row" or "Blue Bloods." Only within recent years have minority-group members, client or consumer groups, and labor union members been placed in leadership positions in these organizations.

"Leaders Can be Made"

A democracy finds it quite difficult to accept the concept that leaders are born. More and more, Americans came to believe that "leaders can be made or developed." If leaders can be developed, it is logical to ask, "What distinguishes a leader from a follower? In what ways is the leader different?" One must know these differences in order to understand what one must develop or look for in leaders.

The trait approach

The first approach, called the trait approach, was directed toward the traits (physical, mental, or psychological) that set leaders apart from followers. Initially, the search for differences between leaders and followers centered on physical traits. Researchers studied jaws, chins, noses, head shapes, palms of hands, eating habits, eyes and eye set, plant constellations at birth, etc. Today, we scoff at such naive approaches, but the impact of some of these observations is still with us. For example, for a while it was felt that leaders have prominent jaws. Even today, we speak of heroes and leaders as having "a square jaw" or "a determined jaw." (Observe how the cartoonist draws the jaw of Dick Tracy.) If one had a receding chin, one could only hope to be follower.

Researchers also studied eating habits. Peaceful people, e.g., Seventh Day Adventists and Indians (the country), tended to be nonmeat eaters. If one liked one's meat raw or rare, one was virile and aggressive. If one liked meat well done, one was characterized as a follower. To this day, many people look with suspicious eyes at someone who eats well-done meat.

Scores of studies followed these avenues. Gradually, it was found to be a relatively fruitless search. One study indicated that only five percent of the traits in over 100 such studies appeared in four or more studies. Occasionally, today, the search is renewed. One recent study group concluded that there are only four predictors of success: highest rank the person had held in military service, father's position, highest educational level attained, and wife's father's position. Another study group at about the same time reported that the only difference they could find between successful and nonsuccessful leaders was that the successful leaders tended to be older and heavier than the younger leaders.

Situational Leadership

About 1940 the search began to be directed toward the situations within which leadership was practiced. It became obvious that not all leaders would or could use the same style in all settings. For example, a railroad track foreman and a hair stylist in a fashionable women's hair salon are both supervisors, and both practice and follow good supervisory processes, but it would be quite difficult to envision these two persons exchanging positions.

Initially, it appeared that there was much to recommend this approach. For example, a company is having a picnic, and in the afternoon two baseball teams are formed. One youngster works in the mailroom, but has had some semipro baseball experience. On his team are both his boss and his boss's boss. However, for the duration of the game they will follow the leadership of this young man and take directions from him. Or, take the example of a boss and her secretary in an office. At the office there is no question that the boss has the ascendant position. But if both attend a social function in the evening, the secretary, because of her husband's position or her family's social position, far outranks her boss and is so treated at that event.

The situational approach to an understanding of leadership had much to warrant further research, but it fell out of popularity.

Functional Leadership

The situational approach was succeeded by the behavior approach, sometimes called the functional approach. According to this theory, the kind of leadership position a person holds will determine the different kinds of leadership functions he or she performs. Four major such leadership, or behavior, functions have been identified:

1. *Symbolic function.* Here, the personal characteristics of the individual leader are secondary to the symbolic meanings the posi-

tion and the incumbent leader have for the followers. Examples of this kind of leader are the Pope, royalty, e.g., the Queen of England, and gurus.

2. *Problem-solving function.* The major function demanded of these leaders is their ability to identify and solve problems. Leadership positions of this type are supervisors, managers, company presidents, and staff personnel.

3. *Advisory function.* The primary function of these leaders is giving advice, information, or counsel. Examples are teachers, ministers, psychiatrists, doctors, and lawyers.

4. *Initiating function.* These leaders are good at "thinking up" ideas, but usually are not good at implementing their ideas. Their major role is to think, plan, and conceptualize. Examples are "think-tank" members, "brain-trust" members, and long-range planners.

Leadership Styles

From the mid-1940s until about 1960, the thrust was on studying the styles of leadership, and a number of researchers were quite active in this area. Since many of the studies were done on leaders of children's groups, the application of the research to adult work organizations came under a good deal of attack. However, some major leadership styles were recognized and formed the basis of the content of many management and supervisory development programs. The three major styles that were identified are:

1. Democratic

2. "Laissez-faire"

3. Autocratic

The usual approach in management development training programs was to have managers listen to each of the styles and then form discussion groups to determine which was the most appropriate style for the manager to employ with his or her staff. Since no manager could admit to doing nothing, that eliminated the "laissez-faire" style. Nor could (or would) any manager admit to being an autocrat. That left the democratic style, and this would be dutifully reported out and certificates awarded. It was only toward the end of the period of this research focus that one researcher reported that he had found a style more prevalent than any of the three identified—the benevolent autocrat—and that this leadership style tended to be found most often in governmental organizations. This type of leader was often described as "Always what he asked you to do was 'for your own good.' " Others, less kind, described him as so adept that "You don't feel it going in."

Leadership Matrix

The 1960s did not see much original research in leadership. It became popular to take the different styles and to put them into matrix form. Managers then took tests—written, oral, and simulations—to identify their location in the matrix and what kind of leadership style they employed with staff people. Labels were assigned at major points on the matrix to identify the most common leadership styles. The manager was then encouraged to question whether or not this was the best style to employ and whether or not the manager was using a range of styles; the manager could then map out developmental steps to improve his or her leadership functioning.

Managerial grid

One of the most popular of these matrix-type approaches has been the Managerial Grid Program. The matrix has two dimensions—the manager's concern for people and the manager's concern for production. (Note that these two dimensions are very similar to the "task" and "maintenance" functions described in Chapter 3.) Each of these dimensions has a nine-point scale ranging from low to high. Tests reveal the manager's location on these two dimensions. The intersection of these two dimensions identifies the manager's leadership style (see Fig. 5–1).[1]

Other matrix approaches

A number of similar matrix approaches exist. Rensis Likert developed a matrix that looks at the styles of exploitive-authoritative, benevolent-authoritative, consultative, and participative-group.[2] In other approaches described by other researchers, leadership styles

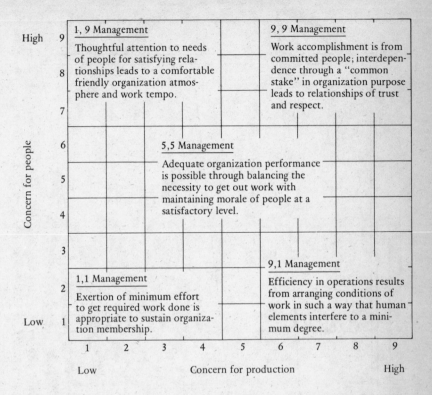

High 9 | **1, 9 Management** | | | | **9, 9 Management** | | | |

[Grid description:]

1, 9 Management
Thoughtful attention to needs of people for satisfying relationships leads to a comfortable friendly organization atmosphere and work tempo.

9, 9 Management
Work accomplishment is from committed people; interdependence through a "common stake" in organization purpose leads to relationships of trust and respect.

5,5 Management
Adequate organization performance is possible through balancing the necessity to get out work with maintaining morale of people at a satisfactory level.

1,1 Management
Exertion of minimum effort to get required work done is appropriate to sustain organization membership.

9,1 Management
Efficiency in operations results from arranging conditions of work in such a way that human elements interfere to a minimum degree.

Concern for people — High 9, 8, 7, 6, 5, 4, 3, 2, Low 1

Concern for production — 1 2 3 4 5 6 7 8 9 — Low ... High

FIG. 5–1 The managerial grid ® (R. R. Blake and J. S. Mouton, The Managerial Grid, *Houston: Gulf Publishing Co., 1964, p. 10. Reprinted by permission.)*

are given such names as diplomatic, participative, free-rein, informal, technocrat, rules-centered, group-centered, and individual-centered. One of the simplest models, but one that seems to be quite useful to managers, is the leadership model developed by Robert Tannenbaum and Warren H. Schmidt, called the "continuum of leadership behavior."[2] This model is shown in Fig. 5–2.

Managers have been asked, regarding the Tannenbaum-Schmidt model, "If you have a decision to make and the consequences of that decision are quite significant, do you tend to make that decision alone

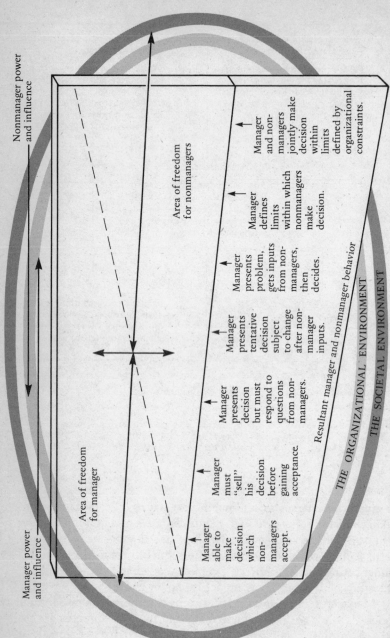

FIG. 5-2 Continuum of leadership behavior. (Robert Tannenbaum and Warren H. Schmidt, "How to Choose a Leadership Pattern," Harvard Business Review, **51**, 3, May–June 1973, p. 166. Reprinted by permission.)

Nonmanager power and influence

Manager power and influence

Area of freedom for manager

Area of freedom for nonmanagers

Manager able to make decision which nonmanagers accept.

Manager must "sell" his decision before gaining acceptance.

Manager presents decision but must respond to questions from nonmanagers.

Manager presents tentative decision subject to change after nonmanager inputs.

Manager presents problem, gets inputs from nonmanagers, then decides.

Manager defines limits within which nonmanagers make decision.

Manager and nonmanagers jointly make decision within limits defined by organizational constraints.

Resultant manager and nonmanager behavior

THE ORGANIZATIONAL ENVIRONMENT

THE SOCIETAL ENVIRONMENT

or involve a group?" Most managers report that they consult with others on their staff but, under this condition, will make the decision alone. Managers also observe that professionals will demand that the manager function heavily toward the right-hand side of the Tannenbaum-Schmidt model, whereas lower echelons will accept leadership that runs toward the left-hand side of the model.

LEADERSHIP IN TODAY'S ORGANIZATIONS

It will be observed that many of the attempts to understand leadership focus heavily on the problem-solving and decision-making functions in the manager's job. This is quite consistent with the school of management thought that views an organization as a collection of problems to be solved, and the process of organization as assigning problems to those persons most qualified to solve them.

Flexibility

The trend today is not to "push" any particular style of leadership as being "best." There probably is no one single most effective style. Rather, the emphasis today is on flexibility in the knowlege and use of leadership styles. The manager may use two or more styles with the same group on any given day. Of course, each manager will have a favorite style which, for that manager, is most authentic. However, the manager will make a serious attempt to match leadership style with the needs of the group or the individual employee.

As managers strive for a flexible leadership style, they often ask, "But how do I know when to use which style?" The answer is not simple, but the most appropriate leadership style for a given situation can be found by analyzing the following forces:

1. *Forces within the manager.* How does the manager define leadership? What is the manager's image of an effective leader? How much ambiguity can the manager tolerate? How much confidence does the manager have in subordinates? How much does the manager believe in participative management?

2. *Forces in the staff.* Do staff people regard the decision as important and affecting them? Do they want to be involved? Do they have the necessary knowledge and experience to solve the problem?

Are they overly dependent? Will decision-making responsibility frighten them?

3. *Forces in the situation.* Does the organization encourage participative decision-making, or does it expect the manager to make decisions alone? Is the decision of an emergency nature? Is time a factor? What is the nature of the problem?

Many managers state that the critical thing, when staff people are involved in problem-solving and decision-making, is not the specific style of leadership used, but whether the style of leadership to be used and the type of control that will be exercised are made very clear to the staff. Often, the staff will believe that they are to be involved in making a decision, only to find that the manager has already made the decision and has called the group together simply to "let them talk" so that they "come to see it my way, but they'll think it is their idea"; or, at the end of the meeting, the manager will pull out the decision already typed and ready for implementation. This is one of the fastest techniques known to stymie participative decision-making.

Promotions

A discussion about leadership cannot be separated from a manager's thoughts about promotion. Most managers want to progress in the organization. They are, of course, interested in displaying and manifesting the best possible leadership in their current work groups. But most managers also realize that leadership ability is one of the qualities weighted heavily by top management as it makes promotions. For example, in an effort to get some insight into how managers really feel about leadership qualities that account for individuals being promoted to higher leadership positions, the author divided participants in the study into small groups. One group was instructed: "Reflect on the training programs you have attended in management development sessions on leadership, books and articles you have read, and anything that appears in your organizations's printed materials. What seems to be the major critical qualities of an effective leader?" A second group was told: "Each of you individually identify one person in your organization whom everyone recognizes is progressing at a faster pace than other employees. What leadership or other personal qualities seem to account for this rapid progress?" A third group was not given instruction until the other groups were already at work. This group was told: "Forget the nonsense. As you view who is promoted in your own organization, how is it really done? What personal qualities are rewarded?"

As might be expected, the first group reported out such items as technical expertise, good communication skills, good delegator, likes people, good human relations, good decision-maker, loyal, and industrious. (You can almost hear the drum and bugle corps playing as all recite the Boy Scout oath.) About one-third of the items identified by the second group coincided with those noted by the first group, and normally, such a list will not have more than one or two negative items. Additional items listed might be: being in the right place at the right time, luck, rides in the right car pool, belonging to the same club in which the decision-makers have membership, aggressive, "yes-man," taking work home, won't question policy, drives subordinates quite hard, and makes sure his work is noticed. The items reported by the last group were entirely different; for the first time there appeared such items as: "brown-nosing," "back-stabbing," taking credit for the work of subordinates and others, "having the goods on somebody in a critical position," "massaging data to own advantage," use of cocktail party contacts and conversation, "operator," gets rid of those who might be a challenger, "word merchant," "buck passer," "apple polisher," has family pull, parties with the right people, follows the party line. Granted, the exercise engaged in by the third group can be a catharsis, but after all the fun has been wrung from "letting it all hang out," most participants are quite adamant that these are the kinds of behaviors their organizations really reward. It makes the futility of so many training programs stand out in bold relief as one reflects, as participants return to their real-life jobs, that people behave for the rewards.

As participants in this study became more reflective and objective, they were asked to focus on the following question: "Assume that two candidates in your organization are being considered for the same promotional opening. Both have the same tenure and experience. As best you can judge, both seem to be about equally qualified. Under this condition, what kinds of factors will eventually result in management's selecting one of the applicants for promotion?" The following factors, rank-ordered, were the ones most frequently identified:

1. A *male* will get priority over a female.

2. A *white,* in most organizations, still gets priority over a minority-group member. There are, of course, some organizations in which the reverse is true.

3. *Good looking.* This is noted in the attempts by political candidates to feature their best side to the cameras. A recent article looked at this subject and reported on the very difficult time an ugly person has in getting promoted.

4. *Young.* Everyone wants the youthful image in leadership positions. Several organizations have reported in recent months to the author that the average age of their supervisors and top management has dropped five to seven years in the past three years.

5. *Tall.* Many personnel departments comment that their organization promotes a short candidate only reluctantly.

6. *Healthy.* The slightest inkling that the candidate has a health problem is the "kiss of death" in terms of promotability. Mid-managers report that they go to extreme lengths to hide physical disabilities from their boss and organization.

7. *Stamina and energy.* The promotable must take work home, be available on weekends, not complain about field trips or long hours, and never admit to being tired.

8. *Mobile.* Employees who admit that family or other reasons prevent or hinder a move ensure that they will receive limited consideration for promotion. Most managers report that in their organization, one might get away with turning down one transfer, but to turn down two transfer requests is to ensure that the employee will never again be considered for promotion.

9. *Married.* The married candidate still has priority over the single candidate, though managers report that this factor is changing.

10. *Religion.* This factor, too, seems to be changing. However, many managers still report that the "right" religious affiliation can facilitate a promotion.

None of these ten characteristics will appear, of course, in a company's promotion policies, although managers insist that they are used fairly extensively in making selection of personnel to be promoted.

One other consideration is increasingly being identified—*visibility*. This is quite noticeable among government interns as they look around for their first permanent assignment after their internship. Almost invariably, they look for an opening that will put them in a position where they and their work can be directly observed by the promotion-makers. The philosophy is: "One ounce of visibility is worth five pounds of nonvisible performance." Managers will at first deny that this is true; in their more reflective moments, however, they will admit that there is a great deal of truth to this observation.

Many government interns report that they find the transition from school to the work place very difficult, and this is an area which should be researched more extensively. One of the more difficult transitions is in the area of leadership. Many interns have commented, "In the selection process, most organizations weight 'leadership' very heavily. Much attention and credit are given to the college candidate who has held an impressive number of leadership positions. However, we have never been in a work organization. Our leadership positions were in groups composed of children, and the emphasis was on personality, good looks, or athletic or social accomplishments. Personal charisma also played a large part in our getting these leadership positions. One had to be extroverted, aggressive— the 'rah-rah' type. Often, one sponsored radical causes and engaged in extreme forms of advocacy. Suddenly, when we join the work organization, we are told: 'Hey, calm down. This is not what we mean by leadership. Don't rock the boat.' We get confused. The very characteristics that were weighted so heavily and that got us our childhood, youth, and school leadership positions are suddenly not acceptable to the work organization. What the work organization means when it uses the term 'leadership' is quite a different animal."

Situational Leadership

Such discrepancies have led to an exploration of whether "leadership" is a generic term, with a generic set of useful and desirable behaviors, or whether it is one thing when practiced in the area of voluntary organizations and in nonpaid positions and an entirely different concept when practiced within the work organization. As managers have analyzed this possibllity, they have identified the ways in which nonpaid leadership positions and leadership in voluntary organizations differ from leadership as practiced in the work organizations. These differences in leadership are shown in the list that follows.

Work organizations	*Voluntary organizations*
Leader is paid	Leader normally is not paid
Followers are paid	Followers are not paid
Followers are interested in advancement	Followers are most interested in achieving organization's goals
Penalties are financial and more severe	Penalties are seldom enforced and are nonmonetary
Leader can "tell" and "sell"	Leader must "sell" and "persuade"
Leader's expertise is important	Leader's personal charisma is important
Authority is derived from above	Authority is derived from followers
Organization prescribes work to be done	Members prescribe work to be done
Leader can direct authoritatively	Leader must direct out of persuasion
Leader is a specialist	Leader is a generalist
Leader is task-oriented	Leader is people-oriented
Leader has work-life tenure	Leader has short tenure
Leader normally is profit-oriented	Leader is service-oriented
Fixed structure	More informal structure

Limits on creativity	Usually open to high creativity
Organization chooses leader	Followers choose leader
Greater risk to economic security	Little or no risk to economic security
Commitment of leader to followers is usually not great	Commitment of leader to followers is great

These differences, of course, are not constant, nor are they all present in every organization—work or voluntary. Nor, of course, are we suggesting that the shades of differentiation are always as firm, finite, and discrete as we have drawn. However, even with all these allowances it still remains fairly evident that leadership as practiced in the work organization is quite different from leadership as practiced in the voluntary organization. Perhaps we have too long tended to treat leadership as a constant, when we should be viewing it as a flexible concept that has significant differences, depending on the setting and milieu within which it is practiced. Therefore, perhaps we should go back and take another look at the situational approach to leadership.

Leadership in Work Organizations

Workers' expectations of the manager

Are there any keys as to how leadership should be practiced in the work organization and what work followers expect of their leader— the manager? Two clues may be helpful here. First, when workers are asked what they expect from their boss, their responses consistently reveal the following types of expectations of the boss:

- *Technical expertise.* The boss is expected to know his or her field. Workers can learn from them, because workers know the boss knows how a job should be done.

- *Planning.* The boss's planning shows; when a job is to be done, the boss has seen to it that personnel are ready, equipment and supplies are there, the facility is ready, and all materials are there and ready—and what is more, they are ready *on time*.

- *Decisiveness.* Workers may not like the answer, but they get an answer.

- *Fairness.* The boss is fair. This does not mean that the boss treats everyone alike. On the contrary, the boss does treat workers differently, but the treatment is fair in terms of the individual's ability, tenure, and the parameters of the job.

- *Loyalty.* The boss goes to bat for his or her staff. The boss may not agree with what the staff people want, but if they are insistent, the boss will make every effort to present their case fairly to higher management.

- *Consistency.* The boss is consistent. As one supervisor put it, "I have made a most helpful discovery. I have learned I can work with a boss who is an SOB—provided the boss is consistently an SOB. But I can't work with the boss who is a good guy or gal today and an SOB tomorrow. You can't figure such people out."

- *In good with higher management.* Part of the recognition, ego, and status employees enjoy stems in large part from the recognition and status their boss receives from management. If the boss is in trouble with management, employees working under that boss also feel that they are in trouble with management. The message is clear here. Any time a person in a supervisory or management position is in trouble with management, the organization had better take steps to ameliorate that condition or get rid of the supervisor or manager. To fail to do so is to create a morale problem within that unit and to incur many requests for transfer out of that unit, resignations, tardiness, absenteeism, and all the other problems associated with low morale.

If only the boss would . . .

Another clue as to the kinds of leadership behavior workers want from their superior came from the survey of 1000 supervisors and managers which was cited in Chapter 2. These supervisors and managers were asked, later in the program, "What would you say to your boss if there were one thing, if he would do it, that in your opinion would most contribute to the effectiveness of yourself and your work unit?" The following is a rank-ordered list of the responses.

1. *Share the company objectives with me.* This response was a surprise as the item in the first place. Apparently to a degree not suspected by most managers and organizations, staff people often do not really understand or comprehend the goals and objectives to which their individual efforts, energies, and capabilities are being directed.

2. *Provide better, more honest communications.* We noted in Chapter 4 that one of the major functions of a manager is to communicate. This survey confirmed this fact. The word that was of interest here, however, was the number of times the adjective *"honest"* was used. Supervisors and managers were queried as to why they used this word, and their consistent response was along the line of: "We receive many communications from management. However, these communications are heavily filtered. We are told we are part of management, but we are not treated as if we were a part of management. The information and communications we receive are always 'doctored' and are the same stuff issued in public information and public relations releases. We are big boys and girls now. We know how to take the bad news and data along with the good. Level with us. Let us know the honest-to-god facts and data. We can handle it. But don't treat us like children who have to be protected. We can make decisions that are effective and handle operational matters effectively only if we have the straight scoop."

3. *Know my problems.* When asked to expand on this item, supervisors and managers responded, "We have staff meetings or meetings to deal with problems. Almost invariably our boss sets the tone of the meeting and asks our help in 'how we can help solve a problem.' Once in a while it would be most refreshing and helpful if the boss said, 'What are your problems and how can I help you solve or reduce them?' "

4. *Set the objectives. Let me do the job my way.* This response is a recognition that there is seldom a single right way to accomplish a task. Each of us has a different methodology that is known and comfortable to us in accomplishing a job. What the supervisor and manager is saying is, "Tell me what is to be done, the results expected, the time frame within which it must be accomplished, and any other parameters I need to know, but don't spell out the detailed procedure for getting there. I will meet the objective within the

parameters set, but do allow me to use the means I know best and that work for me." Most employees fully understand that, on occasion, there is not room for individual choice of means. For example, in a governmental organization, frequently not only the objective, but also the means for reaching that objective are identified and defined in the enabling legislation. Most employees have no difficulty whatever in making this distinction and accepting it.

5. *Involve me in the decisions that affect me and my work unit.* This, of course, is quite consistent with the philosophy of participative management. Employees do have an excellent record of supporting and implementing what they help to create. In addition, employees have an excellent record of following their own suggestions.

6. *Eliminate duplication of effort.* This point was most frequently suggested by governmental employees. Apparently, in many organizations two or more units are charged with the same job or functional responsibility. Employees recognize, we learned, that sometimes duplication of effort is deliberately planned. For example, if the organization is trying to find a breakthrough in product, service, or product or service application, it may assign the same problem to two or more units to see what solutions each can devise.

7. *Back me up in personnel/grievance decisions.* This item was checked with a number of groups. What the supervisor/manager is saying is: "Management wants this personnel complaint or grievance handled at my level. Management knows what guidelines, laws, and criteria will obtain and what the final decision will be if the grievance hits the formal channel. However, they don't want to face this outcome. So they ask me to solve it at my level, but with an entirely differennt hoped-for outcome, guidelines, legal interpretation, and criteria. Most of the time these grievances hit the formal channel and I am overruled. I get tired of being placed in this position. I now no longer 'see' these violations. Who likes to have a record of being overruled 100 percent of the time? This is another instance in which I would like to be treated as an adult. Give me the same guidelines, laws, and criteria that management must apply in adjudicating these grievances."

8. *Treat managers as if they were human.* This item has a note of pathos in it. In effect, managers are saying: "I am asked to know human relations and to apply the concepts to my subordinates. I, too, am a human. Accord me the same human relations considerations you ask that I accord my staff."

9. *Get rid of the deadwood.* The deadwood referred to can be at a higher level, peer level, or subordinate level. It is astounding to realize the number of employees who do not contribute to the accomplishment of organizational goals. Most organizations are running a fair-sized pension or preretirement or make-work program. This is not to say that long, faithful service does not create its obligations. But surplus employees who only get in the way of efficient operations should be handled in an entirely different way than is currently done by most organizations.

10. *Tell me what is expected of me.* This, of course, is related to the first item, "Share company objectives with me." Most top managers are amazed at the frequency of this observation or request. It has two implications:

a) To some managers, this statement refers to the fact that they never, or seldom, receive a performance appraisal. They would like to know how they are doing, what the organization really thinks of them and their work performance, and where they stand.

b) To other managers, this statement means that they do not know the major goals of the organization, its objectives and purposes, and so do not really understand how their unit and the unit's work fit into these objectives and goals.

When we speak of organizational leadership, these guidelines from subordinates probably do a pretty good job of sketching the kinds of leadership behaviors that subordinates look for in a manager who is effective and whose leadership the subordinates want to follow.

Some other considerations

Several miscellaneous items should be mentioned before we finish our discussion of organizational leadership. First, one of the roles of an organizational leader is to mediate between the individual and the organization so that both can receive maximum satisfaction. For the organization, this turns out to be maximum productivity, at the lowest cost possible, with the greatest efficiency and highest quality possible. For the employee, this turns out to be maximum individual job satisfaction, motivation, and a feeling of moving toward self-actualization.

Second, the manager should realize that the group maintenance function is best left to someone else. Almost invariably, the staff will look to the manager to provide the task functions, but will look to an informal leader to provide the group maintenance functions. In almost every office there is a Myrtle who looks out for birthdays, wedding anniversaries, special recognitions, Christmas parties, and provides a "friendly shoulder to cry on." Observe that as the discussion in a conference relates to establishing a special hospitality room and plans are being made for an "end of conference dinner and bash," the group will turn almost invariably to a member and say, "You're our 'booze' chairman." This person is the informal leader, and the manager should not attempt, normally, to assume the function of an informal leader. These informal leaders assume the maintenance function and should be allowed to do so.

Third, the manager should avoid the trap of viewing informal leaders as likely prospects for new supervisors. Most organizations have found, as we have earlier observed, that these persons do not usually make good supervisors; rather, they function best when "outside" the formal system. Put them in the system, and they lose their effectiveness with staff. They do not work well, normally, within the parameters, obligations, and requirements of the formal system.

Rather than trying, through training programs, to change the basic managerial or leadership style of a subordinate supervisor or manager, the manager might consider matching the leadership style of the supervisor or manager to the psychological makeup of the subordinates. For example, some people are dependent and will probably remain so for the rest of their work career. Some supervisors and managers tend to operate most comfortably in an autocratic, telling, and close supervision style. Rather than try to change both, why not place dependent staff under an autocratic supervisor? Dependent employees like to be told what to do, do not like responsibility, and like to have their work checked. All of this dovetails nicely with the inclinations of the autocratic supervisor or manager. It should make for a happy marriage. Similarly, why not try to match the participative manager or supervisor with employees who enjoy being independent and who like to work in a team setting?

Lastly, supervisors and managers do not fully appreciate the fact that subordinates do emulate the behavior and work habits of their supervisor or manager. "As the Abbot sings, so does the Novice." The manager needs to understand this fact, as well as recognize that employees can also emulate bad habits and behavior. It does little good for the manager to plead, "Do as I say, not as I do." For unfortunately, "What you do and are speak so loudly, I cannot hear what you say."

NOTES

1.
For a thorough explanation of how the grid program works in organizations, see Robert R. Blake and Jane S. Mouton, *Building a Dynamic Corporation through Grid Organization Development,* Reading, Mass.: Addison-Wesley, 1969.

2.
Rensis Likert, *New Patterns of Management,* New York: McGraw-Hill, 1961. The ideas presented in this book are expanded in his book *The Human Organization: Its Management and Value,* New York: McGraw-Hill, 1967.

3.
Robert Tannenbaum and Warren H. Schmidt, "How to Choose a Leadership Pattern," *Harvard Business Review,* 51, 3 May–June 1973, pp. 162–171. This is a reprint of the original article, published in the March–April 1958 issue of HBR, and reprinted in 1973 as an HBR Classic.

Practical Guides to Help the Internal Consultant Influence the Organization

6

THE STAFF FUNCTION

About 20 years ago, organizations began employing unprecedented numbers of employees known as "staff." (The use of the word "staff" thus far in this book has referred simply to "employees." However, the word "staff" sometimes has a more limited definition, one which we will explore in this chapter.) Organizations had always had such persons, but in far fewer numbers as compared to the total number of employees. Before these "staff" persons were employed, the "staff" functions had most often been performed by what were called "line" personnel, who were those directly involved in fashioning or selling the product or service. Thus, production workers, sales workers, marketing workers, maintenance workers, and management fell in this category. Persons who fell into the "staff" category were not directly related to producing the product or service; rather, they served, or supported, the "line" personnel. Some employees were difficult to categorize. For example, were research personnel staff or line? Organizations varied in the classification of such workers. Generally, however, the differentiation between staff and line was fairly clear.

Initially, staff personnel seldom had authority over the line. On an organization chart, their relationship was noted with a dotted rather than a solid line. In the absence of authority and power, staff personnel had to "sell" their services by using their best persuasive talents on line personnel, who were free to accept or reject their services.

Many persons who elected to go the "staff" route were by nature self-effacing, nonaggressive, and preferred to avoid the bustle and hassling that was often associated with line operations. Accordingly, staff would prefer to sit in their offices, waiting to be consulted by line personnel. Frequently, no knocks were to be heard on the door. Being human, staff had to fill the available time, so they wrote papers on how important they were, prepared speeches and papers for their professional organization on "Are We a Profession?," spent time at professional meetings talking about "How Can We Get the Ear of Management and be Recognized," and were concerned with getting more pay and getting the dotted lines leading to their box on the organization chart changed to solid lines.

For about a decade the battle lay dormant. Line and staff began to accept, or tolerate, each other. Occasionally, one heard or read about "the line-staff conflict." Subtly but surely, this state of affairs changed. Staff people began to proliferate and began to wield a good deal of influence over line operations. From 1958 to 1970, American industry added about 12 million persons to the work force. However, the number engaged in turning out products remained fairly constant. Most of these 12 million workers went into service organizations and staff positions. Who are these people? They are management analysts, training personnel, computer programmers and others with computer-related functions, technicians, engineers, scientists, operations research personnel, systems personnel, attorneys, medical personnel, etc.

Some of these staffs became so large that the managers of these operations began to find that many of their managerial problems were almost identical to those of the line manager. More and more organizations and line managers became aware that staff personnel were not only offering consulting services but were, in many instances, "running" the line personnel. For example, supervisors and managers became aware that they were no longer able to hire or fire an employee on their own initiative. Before an employee could be fired, the line manager discovered that he had to confer with personnel who handled exit interviews, looked at union implications and possible public relations aspects, personnel who were responsible for grievances, those responsible for the payroll aspects, and those who were involved with terminal-benefits implications.

Staff people are "knowledge workers" and persons who possess knowledge and information are in a position to significantly influence an organization. The influx of the computer increased the impact and importance of knowledge. The computer began to take over many of the organization's decisions about inventory, resource management, costing, and marketing. Most staff persons are highly professional and tend not to like hierarchy and strict functional lines; they would prefer to work on a total problem in a matrix-type organization. This factor also contributed to the blurring of the distinction between line and staff.

Today, there is a tendency for line and staff to work together in a team effort. In some organizations the "staff" positions play the major role in organizational decision-making. Organizations also recognize that the line manager and line supervisor are internal consultants to the organization and that offering advice and counsel to management and attempting to influence the organization is no longer the sole province of the staff person. The term "organizational internal consultant" is now used to include any staff member who in any way attempts to influence other persons, groups, or management within the organization.

THE FUNCTIONING OF ORGANIZATIONS

Depending on background, education, and experience, every consultant—internal or external—will develop a way of looking at and understanding organizations which, for that consultant, will help answer the question "How can you really understand the functioning of an organization?" Few managers ever reflect on the principal way they view an organization, but most managers will find that they have such a view. What is important for the manager to realize is that this way of viewing an organization will significantly affect what the manager looks for and suggests as corrective action when things go wrong. Among the most common ways of looking at organizations are the following.

1. An organization is basically a set of methods or procedures. When something goes wrong, look for breakdowns in this area. A manager who holds this view will make sure that policies, regulations, rules, and manuals are current and are followed. Such a manager usually leans toward the approach of scientific management and devotes much time to up-dating organizational charts, functional statements, and job responsibilities and job descriptions.

2. An organization is mostly a matter of having clear goals and commitment to those goals. Managers with this view like the approach of achievement motivation. The personnel in the organization are quite capable and skilled and want to do a good job. To release this capability and energy, the manager only has to make clear the goals toward which efforts must be directed. This type of manager likes the grid-program approach in training and is a firm believer in management by objectives.

3. An organization can best be understood as a system of communications. When anything goes wrong within the organization, look for a breakdown in communications. Managers with this view will ask the training office to sponsor courses for staff members in interpersonal communication, listening, rapid reading, and intragroup communication. Such managers will write voluminous directives, route everything that crosses their desk, hold frequent staff meetings, and probably issue a monthly or weekly departmental bulletin.

4. An organization is a system of personal and interpersonal relationships. Managers who adopt this view have probably read that three-fourths employees who are fired are terminated because of their inability to get along with others. Human relations is high on this manager's list. If the manager has a secretary, she probably keeps a "tickler file" on all employees' birthdays so that the boss can send them a birthday card—exactly on their birth date. The manager is most likely to recommend laboratory and human relations training to solve problems within the unit.

5. An organization is to be understood in terms of representing a given amount of energy output and properly channeling that output. Managers with this view believe that people have views and generate fairly predictable amounts of energy. If channeled properly, this

energy should result in high production. If not handled properly, the energy will dissipate itself, or discharge, on whatever channel or item is handy. Such misdirected energy will be used in bickering, griping, office politics, grievances, empire-building, vested interests, and personal goal-directed activities. This type of manager will also like the concept of management by objectives and is probably a firm believer in team-building activities.

6. An organization is to be understood in terms of role theory (discussed in Chapter 1). Dysfunction in the organization results from some individual, individuals, or groups not "playing" their organizational roles properly. The remedy is to identify the roles needed in the organization and to assist people and groups to play the roles properly. This type of manager will depend heavily on coaching and counseling.Most often, the roles and approprite role behavior will be defined and taught according to the image the manager has for the various roles.

7. An organization is to be understood as the product of its own time and external environment, but it can never divorce itself from the tradition, history, and culture from which it has emerged. The manager who holds this view will insist that there is no right way to manage—no set of processes to be followed blindly—and that management is an art. This type of manager will encourage staff to be as broadly read as possible—likes the Great Books program, likes staff to read and study as cosmopolitanly as possible, and may even conduct courses in local community colleges on such subjects as "Alexander the Great's Insights into the process of Decision-Making."

8. An organization is to be understood as an extension of the personality and management philosophy of the manager or chief executive. Many managers deny that emulation of the leader is a significant dynamic in organizations and units. However, many managers hold that the opposite is true: managers, through their behavior and example, exert a tremendous influence on subordinates and employees. These managers say that if the consultant will observe the behavior, performance, values, and attitudes of subordinates, the consultant can do a fairly accurate job of predicting the personality, behavior, and values of the head of that unit or organization. It would therefore

follow that appointing a new manager or changing the behavior of the incumbent manager will have predictable, major changes in the workers who are subordinate to that manager.

This list does not exhaust the ways in which managers, and other consultants, view organizations. Which view of the organization is right? Probably none. Each has its insight and is therefore valuable in adding to our understanding of an organization. However, it is probably quite true that each of us has a particular model in mind, such as sketched above, that we believe basically explains the functioning of an organization. This model will influence us mightily in what we look for when something goes wrong within the organization, what the data add up to, and the remedial suggestions we offer to correct the malfunctioning.

Internal consultants, as well as external consultants, will have a model as to how an organization can best be understood. As one such consultant said, "I have about decided that what is important for the manager and the consultant is not what model he or she holds, but rather that the manager's behavior be consistent with that model. If this is done, all managers will do an effective job." Thus, for example, when employing an external consultant, it is probably quite important that the model held by the manager be consistent with that held by the consultant. To do otherwise is to run the significant risk of reducing effective communication and giving staff conflicting and confusing signals. This is not to say the manager should stay locked into a single model; it is to say that the manager's actions and behavior need to be consistent with some model of organizational understanding.

INTERNAL CONSULTING

Internal consulting varies in some very significant ways from external consulting.[1] Sometimes the manager asks an external consultant, "Tell me how you handle this kind of consulting problem." Although such counsel can be quite helpful, the manager who does not understand the differences his role as an internal consultant makes on the process can make some very grievous errors. Internal consultation differs from external consulting in the following ways.

1.   The internal consultant is always on hand and available, but the external consultant is available only at specified times. Since these times must be scheduled in advance, the external consultant cannot always be available or present at critical process points.

2.   The internal consultant is part of the system receiving consultation. Indeed, the internal consultant and/or that function may be part of the problem.

3.   The internal consultant is not free to leave at the end of the consulting relationship—or before.

4.   The internal consultant does not receive special pay for performing this function. It is understood that the internal consultant's pay does include the skills of consultation, but the pay is not as closely related to the results as is that of the external consultant. If the internal consultant does a poor job, it is not likely that his or her paycheck will be held up, but this can happen to an external consultant.

5.   The internal consultant can devote more time to the client, since the internal consultant's remuneration is not dependent on the number of days worked with that client.

6.   The internal consultant is not usually accepted as an expert to the degree accorded an external consultant. It is, unfortunately, still true that often "a prophet is not without honor save in his own country.

7.   The internal consultant often does not have the varied experience that the external consultant does. The external consultant is continually moving from organization to organization and has more data and experiences from which to draw and make generalizations. Generally, too, the external consultant's experience comes from a variety of organizational settings—not from just one industry, business, or discipline.

8.   The internal consultant tends to be in a more specialized field, e.g., computers, personnel, training, accounting, sales. Although the same may be true for the external consultant, more often he or she has a broader base of interest and knowledge.

9.   An internal consultant can get by with shoddy performance for a longer length of time than can an external consultant. Most external

consultants know that they are no better than their last two or three jobs. Many internal consultants will dispute this generalization, but usually an internal consultant can get by with up to three years of marginal or submarginal performance before the machinery can be set into operation to release the internal consultant.

10. The internal consultant often operates from a position of low influence in the organization, and this dynamic will be discussed later in this chapter. The mere fact that the organization pays a good fee to bring in an external consultant means that this "outsider" will be accorded a hearing disproportionate to that of the low-influence internal consultant.

11. The internal consulting system is usually not quite as demanding on the internal consultant as it is on the external consultant. The system, paying the external consultant, usually demands results and often wants those results more quickly than is true of the demands it makes on the internal consultant. Further, the internal-system consultant is "one of us," and the system and its members are much more tolerant of mistakes and low-quality work.

12. The internal consultant is the person in the middle. Often, the internal consultant's own job or unit is affected by the consulting problem. It is frequently, therefore, more difficult to be objective and to see the "big picture."

13. Being within the system, the internal consultant is often better able to sense and feel when things are starting to happen—or not happen. The external consultant has a much more limited life within the organization and is largely dependent on the diagnostic assessment and evaluation of others as to what is happening. This filtering can be very misleading.

14. The internal consultant, being part of the system, has access to sensitive information which can significantly affect the change project or change effort. Sometimes this information is so sensitive that it is not made available to the external consultant.

15. The external consultant is a system imposed on the client group; the internal consultant may be so imposed, but more frequently is requested to assist with the problem.

16. The ability, personality, and skills of the internal consultant are often quite well known within the organization. Normally, this is not true of the external consultant, with the result that much more time needs to be spent with the external consultant in the maintenance function early in the consulting relationship.

The Process

The manager should be aware that any internal-consulting relationship is a *process* rather than a single event or in-put. Eight distinct steps or phases in the relationship can be identified. The manager will note that the phases or steps are not too dissimilar from those usually outlined for the mechanistic model for problem-solving, decision-making, or planning. In these mechanistic processes, the steps generally taught in management development programs are:

1. Identify the problem

2. Collect data

3. Develop alternative courses of action

4. Select one course of action

5. Implement the course of action selected

6. Get feedback, evaluation of the feedback, and make any necessary modification of the decision or plan. This, of course, sometimes means that one needs to go back and redefine the problem.

The phases that can be identified in an internal (or external) consulting relationship are given different terminology, but the manager will recognize in them the steps identified for problem-solving.

1. Awareness that there is a problem. Sometimes, this awareness comes from the person who has the problem. The person will come to the manager and say things like:

- "I have a problem"
- "I have low morale in my unit. I'd like to talk to you about how it might be corrected."
- "I'm concerned about our turnover—or excessive scrap or quality control."

- "I'm catching the devil from management and they expect me to do something. So I have come to you . . ."

Sometimes, this awareness comes from the manager, who will take the initiative to approach the person with the problem—suspected or real. The manager will use all kinds of diagnostic tools and data: performance comparison with other, similar units; comments from persons in or out of the unit concerned; a gut feeling that all is not well, but not being able to pin-point the problem or not even knowing for sure that there is a problem. Most effective managers have learned that this uneasy feeling is quite often a valid indicator. It seems to become intuitive with experience.

2. Entry into the system. Bluntly stated, once the manager becomes aware that there is a problem, he or she often asks, "But how do I get in?" Of course, if the person with the problem has come to you, the entry problem is usually quite simple. Not always, however. Particularly if management has directed the potential client to seek your counsel, that person will sometimes have a discussion with you and then say to management, "Well, I talked with "Y" like you requested. Things still aren't any better." Managers, as internal consultants, develop with experience their own techniques to gain entry into the system with a problem. Sometimes, this is done by direct confrontation; sometimes, higher authority directs that the relationship be entered into; one's boss can open doors; a personal visit might do the job; a subordinate, either your own or that of the other person, might be the best entry; legislation sometimes opens the door; and, of course, an edict by top management can open the portal.

3. Development and definitions of the helping relationship. At this point both the person being helped (client) and the internal consultant need to be honest and open with each other about their mutual expectations from the relationship. How does the client view the internal consultant and the service to be provided? Does the client want a study, a diagnosis of what is wrong, and a prescription for correcting the problem? Does the client expect that the internal consultant will simply provide extra hands—be a "do-er"? Or, does the client see the internal consultant as a hatchet man to do the dirty work the client is reluctant to do?

The internal consultant needs to ask such questions as: "What is my motivation for offering help in this situation?"; "What do I really want to see happen?"; "Do I have the resources and knowledge to offer the help that seems to be needed? Would I be more helpful to the client if I were to suggest another resource?" By the same token, the internal consultant needs to understand and get answers to the following:

- What are the performance standards?

- How much time has been committed for the internal consultant's activities?

- What kind of involvement and commitment will the internal consultant have from other staff and resources?

- Where will the work be performed?

- With whom will the internal consultant work within the client system?

- What kind of budget will be needed? Whose budget?

- What will be the criteria for success or failure?

- Who will evaluate the results?

- When and/or under what conditions will the consulting relationship be terminated and the job or relationship considered to be completed?

These consideration must be faced. Too often, these items emerge later in the relationship, when it is extremely difficult to discuss and reach any agreement on them. After such a discussion, it may very well be that either or both of the parties may decide that no relationship should be entered into. It is far better to discover this fact at the beginning. Unless such specific matters are discussed and resolved, the relationship can drag on for months and years.

4. Clarify and diagnose the nature of the problem or difficulty. This step, problem identification, or "situational familiarity," includes the collection of pertinent data. This step is an attempt to avoid rushing into the situation like an eager young bull and, on the basis of very limited data, coming up with instant solutions. More and more internal consultants are finding that the definition of the problem is the most time-consuming aspect of problem-solving and consultation. Therefore, the internal consultant should always question the first definition of a problem. Most consultants have not kept percentages on this matter, but most agree that the first definition of a problem is often wrong. At least to some degree, in about 40 percent of their consulting relationships, the initial problem definition is wrong, too broad, or too oversimplified.

An example of this was related by an internal consultant from the management system unit of a manufacturing firm. The internal consultant was asked by a plant manager to assist him plan a reorganization of the plant manager's central office group. The request seemed logical, since the plant had been taken over in a merger about a year before, and it was quite understandable that there might be a better way to organize. However, as the internal consultant collected data, everything seemed to be running pretty well, employees concerned thought that the present system was efficient and productive, and all available records and reports seemed to bear out this state of affairs. It was not until a great deal of time had been spent on collecting data and considering optional organizational restructuring models that the internal consultant identified the real problem. The plant manager had an executive assistant whom he did not like and whom he did not want in his management group. He wanted this assistant reassigned to the national office. The plant manager did not have the guts to confront this issue with the assistant on a one-to-one basis. Rather, he chose to put his entire organization through the throes of a reorganization so that he could get rid of one position and one man. This type of fallacious problem definition will be encountered more frequently than the new manager realizes.

5. *Assess the change possibilities.* Is the client ready to change—really ready to change? The internal consultant should particularly watch for such comments as: "They say I must do something." Seldom will meaningful change result from such negative motivation. The manager must not only make a judgment about the system's readiness for change, but also satisfy himself that the system has the capacity for change. Does it have the staff, resources, knowledge, and facilities to implement the changes that are being thought about?

6. Structure the change possibilities. This is the process of determining possible courses of action or solutions that may solve the problem. It is in this phase that the internal consultant can often make the most valuable contributions. When a problem is all-absorbing, and especially when personal feelings or emotions are at a high level, it is extremely difficult for the person with that problem to see or think clearly and to see more than one possible solution. This will come out as, "What I've got to do is. . . ." At most, the person will see only two solutions, and these tend to be at the opposite ends of a continuum —"either/or" and "black/white" types of choices. The manager, whose view may be more objective, should attempt to find solutions that are more toward the middle of the continuum. Frequently, such solutions will be the best answer to the problem and will never have occurred to the client. For example, a man having trouble with his wife may see only one way out: "I must kill her." Actually, of course, there are all kinds of options—divorce, separation, taking a mistress, finding a hobby, joining a religious order, seeking marital counseling, etc.

7. Transform change intentions to change efforts. No study that the author can find indicated what percentage of organizational decisions and plans, of a significant nature, are ever implemented. In the field of government and urban studies, it has been estimated that only one in ten such plans is ever implemented. The percentage within work organizations is probably somewhat higher, but not much. Organizational persons expend a great deal of time and energy coming up with decisions and plans and then fail to put them into effect.

The critical requirement for the manager in this phase is to encourage the client to take the indicated corrective actions. It is important here that the first steps taken should have a high-odds factor of success. If the initial implementation efforts are successful, it significantly increases the chances for the totality of the change intention to be put into operation.

8. Termination of the consulting relationship. It has been stressed that this date and time should be initially resolved during the phase of "development and definition of the helping relationship." For the manager, this usually is not a clean break. The internal consultant is within the organization and is therefore always available. What is usually involved at this point is that the formal consulting relationship is terminated and the project considered to be at an end. The manager and the client revert back to the ongoing relationship within the organization.

The Internal Consultant's Role

It is not always easy for the manager, as an internal consultant, to decide what kind of specific consulting role to take with the client. One of the postures taken most frequently is that of a technical expert, giving expert advice and answers on the basis of one's technical expertise. Most managers today believe that this concept is too limiting. When managers are asked to describe the roles they most frequently take in a consulting relationship, the following are the ones most frequently identified:

1. *Technical expert.* "I am there to give my best advice and answers from my education, experience, and training. Whether or not my advice is accepted is not my concern."

2. *Decision-maker.* "I join the client in making a decision about what to do with the problem."

3. *Data-collector.* "I will collect pertinent data and facts for the client and may help to analyze the data. Beyond that, I don't get involved."

4. *Alternative-identifier.* "I not only help collect data, but I will also actively participate in identifying alternative courses of action for the client. I will not usually be a part of the final selection of the alternative chosen."

5. *Process-observer.* Until the past decade or so, this is a role that few managers attempted to assume. In recent years, however, many managers have come out of schools of business administration which taught about group process, and many more managers have attended laboratory training activities, so that they now feel qualified to take on this role. "I will not take part in the deliberations. I do observe the dynamics that are occurring within the group that are facilitating or blocking its working on the problem, and these observations are fed back to the group."

6. *Advocate.* "I have my own biases and prejudices, which I prefer to think of as valid and tested generalizations and values. I will take a position and advocate a given course of action and fight hard for its adoption." More and more managers seem to be accepting this role as valid. A decade ago this stance was regarded as "taking sides" and as beneath the professionalism of a manager or internal consultant. Needless to say, with this role goes high risk. If the ideas advocated are not accepted, the manager runs the risk of losing authority, power, status, prestige, and sometimes his or her job.

7. *Doer.* "What the unit or client needs is another pair of hands. The unit has enough 'thinkers.' I can best serve by helping out as an additional staff member."

8. *Hatchet man.* "My role is to do the dirty jobs the client does not want to do."

9. *Teacher-trainer.* "My job with the client is to help instruct or teach others, out of my expertise, so that increasingly they can provide the service or expertise they now look to me or my unit to provide."

As is usually true, there is no one right role for the internal consultant to take. It is true that each of us probably has one or two roles we normally assume with a client. For us, these roles are comfortable and fit our leadership style and inclinations. The key is to be found in flexibility. What role does the client need at this moment in time? What role will most advance the client and his or her group toward the solution of the problem? The manager will probably take on several roles during the course of a consulting relationship. Indeed, it is not unusual for the manager to take two or three roles within a given meeting with the client. Early in the consulting relationship, the manager may assume the role of an expert, move to that of a data-collector, later provide the skill of a trainer-teacher, and end up being a strong advocate for the alternative chosen.

Many managers and supervisors have commented that the process of arriving at a decision, making a plan, or solving a problem, although difficult, is fairly readily attainable. A much harder task, they report, is the process of "selling" the decision, plan, or solution to their boss, management, or the organization. It is often difficult to get change initiated and implemented.

This task is particularly difficult when one operates from a position of low influence in the organization. Too often, the middle-level manager will propose a decision, plan, or solution and, if it is not immediately accepted, proceed to sulk: "Well, if that's the way this organization feels about my good ideas, I won't propose another thing." Such managers then settle firmly into a stodgy rut. Seldom are new ideas immediately bought in any organization. The managers who make an impact on their organizations are the ones who understand this phenomenon and have the ability to keep coming back again and again. Such managers have an excellent percentage of ideas ultimately accepted by the organization.

Influencing Top Management

Initially, in working with managers to help them think through the ways available to them to influence top management and the organization, most plead that there are limited means open to them. It is difficult to get them to reflect on the many techniques they, or other managers, use to influence the organization. They often state such generalizations as:

- "Almost every boss wants to appear as a 'good fellow' in the eyes of his subordinates. Few bosses enjoy or want to be disliked— or don't mind if they are not wanted or liked. Such an attitude works to the subordinate's advantage, because it influences the boss's decision-making and behavior in a direction that is favorable to the subordinate.

- "It is easier for a boss to say 'yes' to a subordinate than it is to say 'no.' Most of us intensely dislike saying 'no.'"

Once managers get to *thinking* about how to assert their influence, however, they are usually amazed at the number of means and techniques they discover are open to them. It is not unusual for a group of six managers to identify 80 such means and techniques within an hour's discussion. Among the frequently identified are:

- Talk the idea over fully and frankly with your boss.

- Wait for an emergency or reorganization and then move in with your idea.

- Maneuver so that the boss or organization will think that the ideas are theirs.

- Use the chronological reading file to get your idea on record. The boss looks at it, and often his boss does, too.

- Engage in a slow-down, sick-in, walk-out, or join a union to bring about the change that is desirable.

- Use outside social contacts. Talk to someone in an influence position, preferably in an informal setting such as a cocktail party.

- Point out vividly the advantages that will accrue to the organization, clients, program, or staff if your idea is accepted.

- Instill in your boss or organization fear of competition or other unpleasant consequences if the change is not bought.

- Work through staff specialists and let them sell the idea.

- Take action while the boss is on vacation or at lunch, so that when he comes back, he is committed to a decision you have made.

- Let your professional society bring pressure to support your point.

- Show how your idea will help the manager or organization solve a current operational problem.

- Use the work-improvement suggestions systems, i.e., suggestion boxes.

- Try to persuade a member of an outside organizational committee, board, or task force and let them promote your change idea.

- Refuse to carry out an assignment; this is particularly effective if several join in the refusal.

- Use outside help, e.g., newspaper "letters to the editor," to air your views.

- Manipulate information. Give only information that is favorable to the action you want.

- Use internal politics.

- Show or demonstrate how your idea will increase efficiency, cut costs, or provide better service.

- Use outside consultants to reinforce your position.

- Enlist the support of informal leaders.

- Convince someone to whom you have access at your level or, preferably, just about your level. Keep enlarging this circle of informed people, and soon you will have a cadre of persons at all levels who accept your idea.

These are only a few of the kinds of ideas that are suggested. Some of them will be considered unfair and unethical by most managers. The idea in listing them here is not to recommend them, but to indicate that managers have many means of influence open to them. Another reason for listing a variety of influence methods is to emphasize that each manager will often discover that he or she has a limited number of means that are *effective.* Managers seem to use six basic influence patterns:

1. Some managers will use only traditional and highly ethical means to influence their boss and organization, e.g., doing good staff work, presenting the best solution, working through staff meetings, and depending largely on the logic of their conclusions to make the "sale."

2. Some managers focus on influencing their boss and letting him, in turn, influence the organization.

3. Still other managers will attempt to manipulate the organizational system and structure in order to bring about change.

4. Still others depend on aggressive, even militant, techniques to bring about change.

5. Some managers depend heavily on outside groups and individuals to effect change in the desired direction.

6. Lastly, some managers will attempt to influence the organization by traditional means, but if this is not successful, they wait for

the organizational milieu to change—a change in management, an emergency, legislation, etc.

Managers should realize that they have a large number of means and techniques available to them to influence the organization and that these means are limited only by their own ethics and values. Managers may find that they are using too narrow a range of methods and techniques and need to increase their knowledge and skill in order to increase their arsenal of influence techniques.

In this discussion, there is a possibility of being misunderstood. No one is saying that a manager should not first attempt to sell ideas by logic, reason, and the intrinsic worth of the idea. This should almost always be the first attempt and be part of the ongoing way in which the manager attempts to bring about change. One of the major concepts implied here is that of "finished staff work." Too many managers do not understand this concept and, unfortunately, depend on gimmicky and flamboyant means to influence their boss or organization.

EFFECTIVE STAFF WORK

Too often, managers believe that they have engaged in effective staff work, when in fact they have only collected a mass of data to be "dumped" on the boss's desk. This approach says, "See how bright I am. I have collected the data. Now, you sift through it, find the right answer, and let me know what the answer is, so I can use it to guide me in operational decisions." This is not completed staff work. Part of what any manager is paid to do is not only to collect data, but to sift through the data, analyze it, and come up with one or two possible solutions. It is this solution, or solutions, that should be given to the boss, together with pertinent back-up data, so that the boss can make an intelligent decision choice. The following guidelines are identified by managers as among those by which the effectiveness of staff work completed by subordinates.

1. Does the solution solve or contribute to the solution of a current operational problem? This, of course, often relates to timing. A submanager will come up with a carefully thought-out plan or

decision, but in the context of the boss's or management's current preoccupation with existing emergencies or significant problems and issues, the idea has not a ghost of a chance of being either heard or bought.

2. Differentiate between fact and inference.

3. Practice situational familiarity. Make an intensive effort to understand the problem.

4. Know the existing parameters within which a solution to a problem must conform.

5. Know your organization—its traditional way of meeting similar problems, its policies and regulations, and its way of doing business. Of course, the organization may be wrong, and these items may need to be examined, challenged, and changed. But more often than not, the solution must fit within this organizational context.

6. Present your solution fairly. If there are significant adverse data that would indicate a different solution, don't bluff, hide the data in footnotes, or bury the data on p. 289 of a 357-page report. The manager who must make a decision is a big boy, too, and has a right to know the full data out of which the solution was fashioned.

7. Combat the idea that "bosses only want to hear good news." Most of them would like to have *all* the news. Managers can make effective decisions only to the degree that they have total and accurate data.

8. Understand the implications of your solution. What other departments, personnel, or units are affected? How? Have you consulted with them? Thought out how they will be affected? How does your solution propose to meet these realities?

9. Test your ideas as you go along—with co-workers, the boss, subordinates, and significant others who will be affected by the decision or who will be involved in its implementation. Don't withdraw into a sylvan hideaway and think you can come up with a pristine decision, pure and sparkling, untainted with the dirty realities of operational life.

10. If the problem definition given to you to solve passed through more than one person, check back with the originator to verify the problem definition, parameters, and expectations. Three out of five times, you will be glad you did.

11. Lastly, try this test: "If I were the boss, would I be willing to accept the solution I am proposing and stake my organizational reputation on its being right?"

Upon the completion of a consulting relationship with an individual or group, the manager is often troubled by the question, "But, did I do any good?" If the manager did not toss off a "pat" answer, the odds are fairly strong that he did do good. One of the things that differentiates an effective internal consultant from an ineffective one is that the effective internal consultant has learned that problems are rarely identical. People, the internal consultant learns, can feel two entirely different ways about what appears to be an identical situation. Two women give birth. The events appear identical. But one woman hates her child; the other loves hers. Motherhood is not a state in which everyone has similar feelings and emotions. Every person or group situation has similarities and dissimilarities from every other person's situation. Understanding the *difference* is what separates the ineffective manager from the effective manager. This is why managers who have impact within their organization take violent exception to the statement frequently heard in management circles: "All you need to be a successful manager is a lot of experinece and a good memory."

The manager also needs to understand one other factor. Some research has indicated that when a person receives counsel about a desirable course of action (whether or not that person sought counsel), the advise is rarely acted upon immediately. "Let me sleep on it" or "Let me think about it." The research indicated that after receiving counsel, the person would consult a third party about whether or not to accept the counsel. Interestingly, the third party contacted tended to be at a peer level and not a professional in the field in which the counsel was given. The client who wanted to reject the counsel would most often look up a person who was most likely to say, "That's bad advice. Forget it." The client who wanted to accept the counsel would look up a third person who was most likely to say, "That's good advice. You should take it." This study also found that the client was more likely to break a commitment made to the counselor than to this third person. The implication here is clear for the manager. Do not expect the client to immediately accept your counsel. Give the client a reasonable time to check out your advice with a third party. Of course, if the internal consultant wants to be Machiavellian, the consultation will be given in a setting where, for 24–72 hours, the only persons available for checking are those favorable to the internal consultant's point of view. This is one of the major techniques underlying brainwashing.

Probably some of the best indicators as to whether or not the internal consultant has been effective in the consultation relationship are the following guides:

1. The organization, unit, or individual has learned to cope more adequately with the problem or problems which initiated the consulting relationship.

2. The organization, unit, or individual has learned how to function more adequately in clarifying future problems as they emerge and to make appropriate decisions about seeking consultative help when needed.

3. The organization, unit, or individual has learned how to learn. That is, the client is better able to solve similar problems that might arise in the future.

4. The organization has learned new procedures and new types of organizational patterns to help it maintain a healthy state of flexibility in adapting to new conditions and in utilizing potentialities for creative improvement in its functioning and productivity.

5. The organization sees the need for data-collection, feedback, and diagnosis on an ongoing basis.

6. The organization has recognized the benefits that are derived from periodic evaluation of its own effectiveness.

7. The internal consultant is invited back.

8. The internal consultant is recommended to other potential client individuals or groups.

9. On a follow-up evaluation 6–12 months from the termination of the consulting relationship, the client or client group can point to specific action steps that resulted from the consulting relationship.

10. The manager has a gut feeling of having done a good job and that the consulting relationship "worked."

NOTES

1.

A good, but limited, discussion of this subject is included in the following article: John K. Baker and Robert H. Schaffer, "Making Staff Consulting More Effective," *Harvard Business Review*, Jan-Feb. 1969, pp. 62–71. For a more in-depth discussion of the internal consultant's job, see: Anton K. Dekom, "The Internal Consultant," AMA Research Study 101, New York: American Management Association, 1969.

The Manager's Role in Organization Development

7

THE CONCEPT OF ORGANIZATION DEVELOPMENT

One of the most difficult concepts for the manager to comprehend emerged full-force during the 1960s. Actually, it had emerged a few years previously, but became quite popular in organizations only during the period 1960–1970. This concept of "organization development" (O.D.) is basically difficult to understand and is so global in nature as to almost defy a short definition.[1] The specific activities that go into an organization-development program are legion. There is a tendency for organizations and managers to seize upon one of these activities and to make the mistake of identifying that single activity as organization development.

Basically, organization development is concerned with increasing organizational effectiveness. Obviously, what contributes to organizational effectiveness can run the entire gamut of organizational activities. Some O.D. practitioners behave as if this were the first time in organizational life that organizations and managers have been concerned with this matter. Most experienced managers know that this is not true. As one explores the various approaches to O.D., five major ones can be identified.[2]

1. *Literal organization development.* Some O.D. practitioners view the organization as developing from a simple structure to a very complex one, or from a very small organization to a very large organization.

According to this view, organizations pass through three distinct stages: early development, adolescence, and maturity.

2. *Training and educating people to function more efficiently.* This approach can be further subdivided into four orientations:

a) Those who believe that personnel should be trained and educated quite generically, on the assumption that anything one learns will help one become a better manager and better employee. The liberal-arts focus is used.

b) Those who believe that the organization should concentrate on training its managers—through either outside resources or in-house management development programs.

c) Those who believe that a management development approach is not effective because it trains managers individually; thus, when they return to the work organization, they are limited in their ability to change the work standards and the unit's behavior, and they will usually not utilize their training insights, but will "behave where the rewards are." This school of thought focuses on team training. Those who work together and have to relate intensively together are trained together. Hopefully, this will contribute toward changing the group's values, work standards, and patterns of work behavior.

d) Those who believe that the organization should train all employees. These organizations will focus their training not only on supervisors, managers, or professional staff personnel, but will also offer extensive programs to clerical and blue-collar workers and will frequently also engage extensively in technical and on-the-job training.

3. *Training for personal insight.* This focus really belongs under the training approach, but the large number of organizations and O.D. practitioners who utilize the approach warrant identifying it as a separate one. According to this view, most organizational problems are directly traceable to poor interpersonal skills and self-insight and erupt into frequent interpersonal conflicts. These O.D. practitioners emphasize that training will contribute to personal insight and awareness—of how one's behavior affects others and vice-versa—and that this will be particularly true if opportunity is provided for

practicing new and more productive behavioral skills. This approach relies heavily on laboratory training and sensitivity training or personal-growth laboratories.

4. *Systems development.* Some people equate organization development with systems development and therefore center their attention on the development of subsystems within the organization, although viewing the total organization as a major system made up of a host of interdependent subsystems. These persons are likely to be less people-oriented in their approach to organizational problems.

5. *Personal and systems development.* An increasingly popular approach is to view O.D. as concerned with both the human and non-human elements within the organization. Anything that is done to improve the functioning of either of these elements can be called organization development.

It should be remembered that the approaches we have identified are only the major ones. Further, within each of these major approaches a number of techniques are employed to effect the training, and these specific techniques are often confused with O.D. For example, it is not unusual to observe that a manager or O.D. practitioner utilizes role-playing or simulations in O.D. training and refers to these as O.D. Because of the confusion about the term, some O.D. practitioners and authors have coined new terms to avoid the biases and tunnel-vision that surround the term O.D. Gordon L. Lippitt, for instance, uses the term "organization renewal."[3] In England the term "organizational effectiveness" is often used to describe the O.D. process.

Although there is a risk in attempting to identify the heart of the O.D. concept, the manager can basically understand the concept by viewing it in the following, albeit oversimplified, context. Any organization, to function effectively once it reaches the size of about 100 employees, will find that there are certain elements that must exist within the organization. Among these critical elements are:

1. *Predictability.* It is impossible for a large organization to exist if the individuals and units in that organization are unable to predict what others are doing, what they will continue to do, with what quality control, in what numbers, and in what time frame they will

do their work. If a manager sends a request to the personnel department for an employee replacement, the manager must be able to predict that Personnel will find the best-qualified applicant available and that that employee will probably be made available for work within two weeks.

2. *Standardization.* Most employees often chafe at this element, but without it organization life is chaotic. Every manager cannot be permitted to determine: the qualifications for personnel employed, how much money each employee shall receive, standards for promotion, what equipment and supplies shall be bought (among other things, volume price and interchangeability of supplies and materials must be considered). This is the purpose of inventory control systems, procurement systems, wage-salary systems, promotion systems, etc.

3. *Regularity and stabilization.* The organization must function on a fairly regular basis so that there is not a frenzy of work in one month and nothing whatever scheduled during the following month.

How does an organization get these basic elements of predictability, standardization, and regularity and stabilization? It gets them through the development of such items as: policies, regulations, rules, manuals, various types of systems, and functional and program statements. As any manager who has been around organizations longer than six months knows, once an organization develops these items, there is a tendency to "lock into them" and to strenuously resist changing them. They are now in print and give a feeling of security. "Don't rock the boat" is the by-word. The organization may not be functioning effectively, but at least it is functioning. And to change one item may call for changing other items. For example, to change policy "A" may mean that policies "D" and "H" will need revision, and to change these policies will call for other revisions to regulations and manuals. It is these items, in the aggregate, that young people and minority groups initially began to refer to as "the establishment." The term "establishment" has now been widely accepted in all our vocabularies.

The Organization's External Environment

Let us leave this discussion of the organization and look now at the external environment of the organization. This external environment also affects the humans within the organization and creates internal dynamics with which the organization must cope. Any organization exists within the context of its external environment, though too many organizations and managers behave as if this were not so. There are a number of social and economic factors in this external environment to which the organization must appropriately respond. More and more, the popular press has been terming these social and economic forces and dynamics "revolutions." What are the major ones? As managers reflect on the ones that affect their organization, they most frequently identify the following areas (it is recognized that not all these social and economic revolutions will affect all organizations):

- Minority groups
- Women's liberation movement
- Concerns about ecology and the environment
- Raw resources
- Sex
- Morals
- Religious
- Personal dress and hair styles
- Changing meaning of work and motivation
- Politics
- Technology
- Education
- Revolt against traditional authority
- Governmental regulations and controls
- Vandalism and theft
- Drug use and abuse

This list is not an exhaustive; rather, it is indicative of the kinds of social and economic dynamics in the external milieu of organizations. Some of the persons and groups identified with these "revolutions" are peaceful and attempt to bring about change in quiet and traditional ways. Others are aggressive, militant, and even destructive, for they believe that it is impossible for the establishment to change voluntarily, peacefully, and in traditional ways and that the only alternative is to burn, blow up, and destroy the establishments and to build anew.

These social and economic forces often dramatically affect the organization. For example, the current energy shortage and ecological considerations are having a major impact on the decisions and planning of public utility companies and in the automotive industry. Governmental organizations have had to change a host of personnel policies, including recruitment policies, in response to the demands of minority groups and women liberationists.

O.D. asks the question, "Is it not possible for people internal to the organization to work toward the goal of making the organization appropriately responsive to these social and economic forces and dynamics?" The answer is "yes," and this is what O.D. is basically all about. Of course, O.D. is also concerned that this responsiveness will help ensure the organization's survival and will help meet the needs of the people within the organization.

How, then, shall O.D. practitioners make the organization more appropriately responsive to its external environment? They will do this primarily by affecting the problem-solving, decision-making, and planning processes within organizations. The manager and organization shall be encouraged to take a proactive stance toward these dynamics—not a reactive stance. Decision-making and problem-solving skills of individuals and work groups shall be improved. Problem-solving and decision-making shall be located downward to the level closest to the existence of the problem and where the skills and resources for solving that problem exist. This is why most O.D. programs focus heavily on problem-solving, decision-making, and planning. Because many of these processes within organizations are no longer an individual function or responsibility, they require that the decision, plan, or solution to a problem be arrived at within a group; therefore, any O.D. program will normally also engage intensively in team-building and team-effectiveness training.

Today, O.D. is not seen as the prerogative of specially employed O.D. experts. Every manager, supervisor, and person in the organization who has a "sphere of influence" is considered to be an O.D. practitioner—a change agent. The O.D. staff at one time was assigned to a central office. The general trend today is to locate them out with the line manager.

Defining O.D.

We can now look at definitions of O.D. Perhaps the one that best reflects the previous discussion is that by Dr. Gordon Lippitt: "The application of the planning, development, and problem-solving process to the overall functioning of the organization in such a way that it strengthens the physical, financial, and human resources; improves the process of interface; helps the organization mature; and is responsive to the environment of which the organization is a part."[4] Most of the definitions are along this line, though they are slanted toward the approaches we discussed earlier.

One of the concerns increasingly being raised is whether or not O.D. practitioners hold a set of assumptions about effective organizations and use these value judgments to evaluate both the effectiveness of their work and their organization. As would be expected, it is extremely difficult to gain concensus about such value judgments. As a result, many O.D. practitioners are leaning toward the following definition of O.D.: "The conscious movement of an organization, or major subunit, toward desirable organizational goals (however the organization defines these goals), through the use of planned interventions." This means that if an organization desires to become the most autocratic organization in the nation, the O.D. practitioner would help it plan interventions to reach this goal, and this would be O.D.[5]

Figure 7–1 shows the context of specific training, educational, or operational activities as they relate to the concept of O.D. As is indicated in the upper left-hand box of the figure, interest in organization development usually begins when one or more concerned members of management wonder whether or not their organization is as appropriately responsive as possible to the organization's external environment. This manager, or managers, will then involve other persons to help arrive at an answer. These "other persons" may be internal to the organization or they may be external persons, such as consultants. Involving these other people will usually result in the collection of data to determine "the state of affairs in the organization." Assuming that the "state of affairs" is not all that management

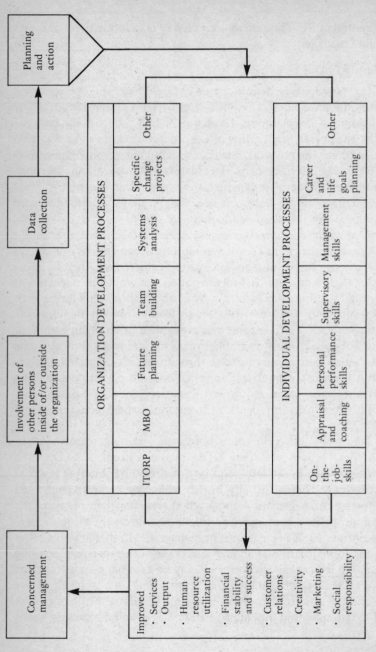

FIG. 7-1 Organization renewal processes at work. (Reproduced by permission of Organization Renewal, Inc., 5605 Lamar Rd., Washington, D.C.)

desires, the data collected will be used for planning corrective steps. Often, these planning steps are of a training nature. At this point, the organization may elect to go one of two ways: (1) it may focus on improving the organization development process, or (2) it may focus on improving the individual's development processes. Of course, the organization may opt to go in both directions simultaneously. Figure 7–1 also shows the typical activities that often occur in both of these processes.

It is these specific activities that managers and organizations often confuse with the total O.D. process. Some of the hoped-for outcomes of these specific activities are listed, e.g., improved services, output, human resource utilization, financial stability and success, customer relations. As management assesses these activities and their contribution to the desired outcomes, management often will make further plans for other parts of the organization to be looked at, and the process will basically repeat itself.

THE DEVELOPMENT OF ORGANIZATIONS

As an organization begins the process of organization development, a commonly encountered question is, "But what should an effectively functioning organization look like? Do organizations develop? If so, through what stages do they grow? If they do go through stages, are there predictable problems and concerns at each growth stage?"

Almost all managers have some guides or concepts that assist them in understanding organizations. Some managers hold that an organization has "arrived" and is mature when it:

- Receives "X" amount of return on its investments
- Has "X" percent of growth per year
- Has cornered "X" percent of the potential market.

Other managers use different guidelines to identify effective organizations. Among those frequently mentioned are:

- Clarity of the organization's purposes and goals
- Optimal use of human and physical resources
- Synergistic functioning

- Responsible relationship to environment
- Flexible guidelines for operations
- Functional feedback system, i.e., leveling
- Environment of trust among individuals and groups
- Efficient problem-solving and decision-making process.

Growth Stages

One of the most helpful concepts in assisting the manager to understand the development of organizations through growth phases is the "organizational growth stage" model developed by Drs. Gordon L. Lippitt and Warren H. Schmidt.[6] For convenience and easy reference, we will sketch the six growth stages, the key issue that faces the organization at that phase, and will indicate the kinds of problems normally encountered by organizations at that growth stage.

1. To be born

Every organization can normally identify the point at which it was born, i.e., when some entrepreneur decided to go into business in order to sell a marketable service or product. Similarly, governmental organizations usually can identify some specific piece of legislation that brought them into existence, and every subunit within an organization can identify when it was created by management edict.

The key issue faced at this growth stage is "How much and what am I willing to risk?" Among the problems encountered by the organization and/or owner(s) at this growth stage are:

1. The organization's creators and staff are excited and have high hopes. But few of these people have good organizational skills; rather, they tend to have high creative skills in their field.

2. The organization attracts high-risk personnel, who are not always easy to control or standardize.

3. Usually, one person or a small group (normally, the owners) controls and dominates the organization.

4. It is not unusual for the personnel to wear many hats, since there are insufficient funds for specialization, and most employees "double in brass."

5. Most often, there are good communications. Everyone is dedicated to the major goals, they like one another, the staff is small, and the problems encountered and operational developments and status are freely shared. Frequently, the key persons interact socially, and there are few secrets.

6. The organization puts a high premium on creativity and innovativeness. Anything that will save costs, make a sale, improve the product or service, or open new markets is eagerly accepted.

7. The emphasis is on the "selling" function. The organization usually has limited funds, and the product or service must be put on a paying basis within six to twelve months.

2. To survive

At this stage of growth, "making it" is a touch-and-go situation for the organization. Initial capital is disappearing at an alarming rate. Cash flow is a critical problem. Some clients are slow to pay. Those who encouraged the owners to get into the service and product field are not buyers of that service or product, although they are long on advice and good wishes. The fight for survival is for real. Some estimates indicate that of all the small businesses created within a given year, about 40 percent are bankrupt at the end of the first year. Of those surviving, 40 percent are bankrupt at the end of the second year.

The key issue at this stage is "what to sacrifice" to keep going. Shall the owner(s) mortgage and risk losing their homes, properties, and life insurance? Do they dare continue to ask their family to make personal and individual sacrifices? The problems encountered at this stage are:

1. Hard selling takes priority over creativity and innovation.

2. Many innovative ideas do not get off the drawing board. To move ideas from the ideation stage to a service or product with a market takes time, funds, and staff energy—none of which is in great supply.

3. The key person is very active, spending much time on the road in an effort to make critical contacts and to sell the product or service. It now becomes evident that this person came out of a

specific functional area and tends to view all problems too simplistically through the eyes of that specialty.

4. The organization is very cost conscious. Some employees begin to feel the organization is penny-wise and pound-foolish.

5. Any employees who are "tenure-conscious" become quite anxious and begin to look around for another job.

6. If there is more than one owner, they begin to increasingly clash over the "right direction to take." Staff begin to choose up sides. However, there is still the feeling we are "one happy family," and these issues are not generally dominant.

7. Some employees begin to see the need for systems and standardization. Management replies, "Don't bother me with talk about a promotion system, a wage-salary system, a training system—we may not even be around next year. If we make it, talk to me then."

8. There is a tendency to "lock into" packages and operating procedures that seem to work, even if these are wasteful.

9. If the organization is becoming successful, there is rapid expansion, and the various key persons wearing "many hats" find that they cannot keep on top of their jobs. Many things go undone. Communication begins to slip.

10. The control of the organization is still in the hands of the key person or persons. If the venture is not successful, they engage in penny-pinching activities such as turning off lights, personally checking the books and expense vouchers, and doing minor equipment repairs.

3. To become stable

The organization has made it through survival, and the emphasis now goes into consolidating gains and getting on top of the many things that previously had to be neglected. The organization now usually becomes systems conscious and attempts to get away from crisis management. The key issue at this growth stage is "how to organize." Among the more critical problems are the following.

1. Since most of the key persons are either sales-oriented or oriented toward their own specialty, few of them know how to organize the enterprise effectively.

2. The usual procedure is to hire assistants for those who are overburdened. No one looks at the big organizational picture or the better way to align functions. Even though overburdened, most key persons see any limiting of their functions as a threat to their ego, status, and importance.

3. Lines of authority are unclear. The organization may begin to uncover a large amount of overlap and duplication.

4. The personal differences of the key persons begin to become sharper, and various camps of position begin to form. Coupled with functional unclarity, this situation increases communication difficulties.

5. Some of the more innovative and capable personnel begin to leave as they become bored with standardized operations. "The excitement has gone out of this outfit." Increasingly, the organization is left with a cadre of nice, willing, loyal employees who place seniority, tenure, and security above all other matters.

6. Employees become more concerned with creature comforts .

7. There is increasing disenchantment with the boss or bosses, who are regarded as paying inadequate attention to internal matters and organization.

8. The organization does begin to institute systems, but these are often poorly thought out and are not integrated with other systems being developed.

9. Office politics begin to play an important part.

10. Employees begin to spend an undue amount of time griping about the way the organization is being run.

4. To gain a reputation

Few organizations are content simply with being stabilized. Something within management and the employees wants the organization's product or service to be recognized as good. One driving force is, of course, repeat business. In addition, the organization would like to have a good community reputation and a good reputation with customers, clients, and suppliers.

The key issue at this stage of growth is "how to review and evaluate." This review and evaluation initially focuses on the product or services and is then extended to concerns related to the local community and to the employees. The organization wants to be known as a "good outfit" by the community and as "a good place to work" by employees.

Some of the problems encountered at this growth stage are:

1. The organization becomes very conscious of quality control and attempts to negotiate with employees over the issue of high production and high quality.

2. The organization may begin to limit the number and kinds of customers called upon.

3. The organization looks for ways, methods, and techniques to improve existing products, services, and markets.

4. The founders of the organization consider getting out at this phase and turning the organization over to professional managers. Often, a founder will become chairman of the board or take on special assignments.

5. The organization learns how to organize around needed functions and to be less dependent on strong personalities. Persons affected may not understand this dynamic and may either seek to get out or begin to form a conservative clique within the organization.

6. Some employees begin to feel that the organization "cannot be all things to all people."

5. To achieve uniqueness

At this stage, the organization is not satisfied simply with having a good reputation within its field. A number of other organizations also have a good reputation. What the organization now strives for is to become unique, so that when unusual problems are encountered, this is the organization that is turned to and so that its products and services will be recognized as the leaders in their field. In addition, the organization is felt to be unique in the way it deals with its staff. The community feels that the organization is "one of a kind" and is very pleased to boast of its presence in the community.

The key issue here is "what and how to change." Almost inevitably, when an organization becomes unique, it decides to drop some of its services or products and to specialize in a narrowed field of endeavor. Much activity at this stage goes into defining the organization's objective and determining the business the organization really wants to be in.

Among the problems encountered at this stage are:

1. Disagreements occur among employees, units, and key personnel about the business the organization is in, what services or products should be dropped, and what services or products should be expanded.

2. The organization may turn down certain contracts, resulting in strained relationships with its sales force.

3. The organization may consider the merits of "zero growth" or declining size. The repercussions of these discussions are to be found at all levels: "Do you want to stay an assistant sales manager the rest of your life?"

4. The organization senses the deterioration of team relationships and begins to focus on team-building activities and group problem-solving and decision-making.

5. There is a trend toward participative management, and the comment is often heard, "We're turning the organization's operations over to committees."

6. The organization often decentralizes at this point, with all the attendant problems of decentralization.

7. As it specializes, the organization may feel that it does not have within its own ranks innovative and creative people who can make the organization unique. The organization may sponsor courses and programs in value analysis, innovation, and creativity. It may look outside the organization and bring in creative persons. This, of course, has an adverse impact on the employees.

8. A fair number of employees are concerned about maintaining the status quo and forgetting those "grandiose ideas of innovativeness, specialization, and uniqueness."

6. To contribute

This is felt to be the most mature stage for an organization. The organization fully realizes its interrelatedness with the community, its industry, and the larger society. It now has funds and staff time to explore those interests. The organization becomes concerned with such questions as: "What are we doing to our people? How can we help them to develop and grow? What is our debt and obligation to our local community? What does it need that we can supply? What is our obligation to our society and our national way of life? How can we help government solve some of the nation's social problems?"

The key issue at this stage of growth is how to share and contribute. How many strings shall be attached to the sharing of the organization and its resources? What is the best way to make needed contributions?

Problems faced by the organization at this stage are:

1. Shall the organization consider retaining certain products or services that are relatively nonprofitable, but which seem to be doing some good to society or to the community? For example, a division may consistently be at a break-even point, but to disband that division would throw 300 people out of a job in an already economically depressed community.

2. The organization's key members are active on committees and in organizations, at both the local and national levels, which are concerned with the social consciousness of organizations.

3. The organization defines what is meant by social consciousness and begins to comprehend that the implications are—well beyond participating in the United Givers Fund and employing a token minority-group member.

4. The organization tends to splinter into "special interest" units, which on the surface may look like a matrix organization. Often, however, the units or special groups do not have a central, orga-

nization-related purpose or goal, but rather represent various vested interests.

5. Communications often tend to be professionally oriented and are neither functionally related nor leveling, though on the surface they may appear to be so.

6. It may be subtle and not obvious, but there is functional professional distrust and very sophisticated, "civilized" organizational in-fighting.

7. Often, there is great concern with self-actualization opportunities for employees, efforts to restructure jobs for job enrichment purposes, and experimentation with concepts of matrix organization.

8. The organization may begin to experiment with employee sabbaticals for community service; encourage employees to become involved with community, civic, and national affairs; and experiment with the concept of meeting job requirements without the trappings of traditional standardization. For example, employees may be required to get "X" amount of work performed, with the hours and days within which it is performed quite flexible.

Leadership in Developing Organizations

One last implication of the growth-stage model should be discussed, and although the observations that follow are not yet well researched, the generalizations are admittedly pragmatic in nature and seem to have validity. The need for organizational leadership seems to be closely related to both the organization's *present* growth stage and the next *higher* growth stage. Three distinct types of organization leadership seem to be involved. During the growth stages of birth and survival, the leadership that the organization needs, and which seems to attract these qualities in managers and entrepreneurs at these stages, is based on the following qualities:

- A deep, abiding belief in the service or product being sold or promoted
- A love of "selling," persuasion, and winning
- An ability to be knocked down and to keep coming back again and again

- A desire to be innovative and creative
- A desire to "best" the greatest of odds
- An extroverted, outgoing personality
- A goodly amount of personal charisma
- Tremendous amounts of stamina and the willingness to work long hours.

However, when the organization moves into the stabilization and reputation growth stages, the organization no longer needs these qualities; rather, it now needs reflection, systems stabilization, and the ability to "settle down" the organization. At this point the organization needs a leader who likes desk work, who is comfortable and happy drawing up organization charts, preparing functional statements, writing job descriptions, designing systems and understanding the relationships of each system to the others, conceptualizing, and operating as an administrator. As we have mentioned, the skills are those of an administrator, and the tasks are those related primarily to a "desk job." The manager who is successful at these functions tends to be introverted and self-effacing.

In the growth stages of uniqueness and sharing or contributing, the organization needs a manager who is highly reflective; has high ethical and moral standards; is concerned about what the organization is doing to the people who work for it; is concerned with the organization's responsibility to the local community, the region, the nation, and the nation's way of life; tends to write or speak well; has a national reputation; and has distinct abilities as a senior statesman and a spokesman for the goals, values, and aspirations of others.

In part, these qualities seem to be a function of age. It is amazing how, as managers reach the zenith of their career, they become more moral, more ethical, more contemplative, and more concerned about how their organization is contributing to the welfare and self-actualization of employees, the local community, and the nation. Observers have always noted how people get more religious, mellow, and become more moralistic and ethical as they age.

One of the implications is that organizations probably should pay a good deal more attention to matching the innate leadership style of managers to the present growth stage of the organization and the growth stage into which it is emerging. The manager who is good at shepherding an organization through the growth stages of birth and survival usually is inept at giving the organization the needed leadership when it emerges into the stabilization growth stage. Desk work bores this manager. If placed in such a job, the odds are fairly strong that much of his or her time will be spent on the road and making field visits while the work needed to be done to stabilize the organization goes unattended.

Unfortunately, when new units or projects are created which call for the skills of seeing the organization through birth and survival, the persons eligible for leadership consideration usually occupy desk and administrative positions. Because of tenure and grade, the person tapped to head the new unit or project generally does not have the leadership inclinations appropriate to the demands of the task and feels more at home and comfortable with organization charts and conceptual tasks. Such a person who is suddenly thrust into a leadership position that calls for a "hard sell" generally does a miserable job.

A vivid example of this was encountered in a State Department of Agriculture. The department felt it had had enough of planning; what was needed was implementation of plans already made and a position of consumer and community advocacy. To attain this objective, the department decided to encourage and create regional and county advocacy groups of rural citizens. The person selected to head this departmental activity was the Bureau Chief of Operations, who was doing an exceptionally fine job in his current position and was well respected and liked by the employees. The new leadership position called for skills in the creation of new suborganization. Mass meetings were scheduled for interested citizens. Anywhere from 75 to 200 citizens attended these county and regional meetings. The new Assistant Deputy of Agriculture, the former bureau chief, was supposed to attend these meetings and give dynamic leadership to the creation of county and regional advocacy groups.

Usually, he could be found, cookies and coffee in hand, in a corner with his back to those attending. When reminded that his role was that of selling the program and that he should be in the thick of things, promoting the concept, he would mutter between bites of a cookie, "But I hate people. I hate selling." It was obvious that this person was much happier and better suited to the routines of administration and helping his organization to become stabilized. His lacks became so painfully obvious that within three months he had to be released.

Unfortunately, seldom can a manager receiving such a promotion go back to his former job. It did not happen in this instance, and this capable administrative leader had to find employment in another organization. This is a classical and typical example of a manager who can give effective leadership to the organization in the stabilization phase, but is completely unable to provide leadership in the creation of a new unit.

Most organizations do not believe it is possible to train and develop leaders to provide all three leadership functions equally well—birth and survival; stabilization; and reputation, uniqueness and contribution. Probably, through training, the organization gains at best mediocre leadership performance. It is therefore probably far better not to tamper with the innate needs, qualifications, capabilities, and interests of managers. The organization should capitalize on the manager's strengths rather than attempt, through training, to make the manager equally skilled in providing leadership to the organization in all its six growth stages. Rather, the organization should concentrate on matching the manager's and leader's innate skills, capabilities, and strengths to the current growth stage of the organization and subunits within the organization.

"MATURE" ORGANIZATIONS

Managers sometimes ask, "But, if an organization goes through growth stages, is it not true that ultimately they must die?" Most students of organization development dodge this question. The assumption is that organizations, through O.D., have truly found the perpetual fountain of youth; if they will conscientiously self-renew themselves, apparently they can forever stay mature and virile. There are instances of this phenomenon. The National Polio Foundation, for example, knew some years in advance of the discovery of the polio vaccine that such a discovery was inevitable. The only uncertainty was who would make the breakthrough and on what date. The organization had decided that when the vaccine was discovered, the organization could further emphasize polio for a limited length of time by continuing to focus on polio vaccinations and public education, undertaking the care of polio victims for their lifetime, and performing similar services in the polio field. Instead, however, the organization made plans that, when the vaccine was discovered, it would broaden its base of interest and move into the field of other diseases. This is a good example of an organization being proactive and taking self-renewing steps to protect against its demise.

However, it is true that organizations do die. Only a small number of organizations which appeared on the major stock market exchanges 50 years ago are there today. It is also probably true that a large number of organizations should die and not attempt to perpetuate themselves. But it is probably also undoubtedly true that many organizations could prolong their mature life in a contributing and positive fashion through a self-renewal process by changing product and service lines, or applications of these lines, in such a way as to stay viable, profitable, and dynamic.

No definitive study exists, but it is generally felt by those who subscribe to the growth-stage model of organizations that probably 70 percent of American organizations are content with reaching the stage of stability. For these organizations, the benchmark for success is to continue to keep a given percentage of the market, grow a certain percentage annually, and have an acceptable return on investment. If these criteria are met, the organization considers itself effective and successful. These criteria were fairly acceptable in the past, but it is quite doubtful that the public today will accept these benchmarks as valid criteria for an organization's continued existence. More and more evidence is accumulating that new criteria will emerge by which the public, and also stockholders, will evaluate the organization. Social responsibility is one such guideline that seems to be emerging. Another guideline appears to be that "an organization exists not only for profits, but also for the development of people through their work."

Managers of governmental organizations will frequently contend that it is improper for a governmental organization to aspire beyond the stabilization phase. These managers argue that a governmental organization has certain tasks and objectives laid down by legislation and that the organization's function is to discharge these objectives as efficiently and economically as possible; to go beyond this is improper, although not for organizations in the private sector. These managers insist that for a governmental organization to aspire for reputation or uniqueness is to be self-serving and to lose sight of the purpose of their existence, which they view as being the efficient carrying out of the legislative programs for which they are responsible.

Other governmental managers take sharp exception to this position, arguing that the public interest is not well served and that legislative objectives are met in a mediocre manner if the governmental organization does not strive for growth stages higher than stabilization. The FBI, NSA, CIA, National Park Service, and IRS appear to be governmental organizations which do not subscribe to their organizations' "knocking it off" once they have reached the stability stage of growth.

NOTES

1.

In the past five years the literature on organization development has mushroomed. The following books from the Addison-Wesley Series in Organization Development are highly recommended for those who would like to improve their comprehension and expertise in organization development: Richard Beckhard, *Organization Development: Strategies and Models*, 1969; Warren G. Bennis, *Organization Development: Its Nature, Origins, and Prospects*, 1969; Robert R. Blake and Jane S. Mouton, *Building a Dynamic Corporation Through Grid Organization Development*, 1969; Jay Galbraith, *Designing Complex Organizations*, 1973; Paul R. Lawrence and Jay W. Lorsch, *Developing Organizations: Diagnosis and Action*, 1969; Richard J. C. Roeber, *The Organization in a Changing Environment*, 1973; Edgar H. Schein, *Process Consultation: Its Role in Organization Development*, 1969; Fred I. Steele, *Physical Settings and Organization Development*, 1973; and Richard E. Walton, *Interpersonal Peacemaking: Confrontations and Third-Party Consultation*, 1969.

A compilation of papers on organization development, setting out case examples of O.D. efforts in 12 organizations in government, schools, business, and industry, is found in J. Jennings Partin, ed., *Current Perspectives in Organization Development*, Reading, Mass.: Addison-Wesley, 1973.

A useful book for the manager who is curious about O.D. and wants to learn more about it and the manager who is already involved in an O.D. program or who needs a practical handbook of methodology and examples is Jack K. Fordyce and Raymond Weil, *Managing with People,* Reading, Mass.: Addison-Wesley, 1971.

2.
Leslie E. This, "Organizational Development: Fantasy or Reality?" Pamphlet No. 7, Washington, D.C.: Project Associates, 1969. This study examines the various major interpretations often erroneously labeled "O.D." It also identifies the directions toward which O.D. activities seem to be trending and the set of conditions which must exist for O.D. to be effective.

3.
Gordon L. Lippitt, *Organization Renewal,* New York: Appleton-Century-Crofts, 1969. This book not only examines the concept of organization development, but also contains helpful suggestions to the manager as the dynamics in the O.D. process are analyzed. Dr. Lippitt was influenced by the concept of self-renewal in Dr. John Gardner's book, *Self Renewal: The Individual and the Innovative Society,* New York: Harper & Row, 1963. Dr. Lippitt applied the concept of renewal in this context in its application to organizations.

4.
Gordon L. Lippitt, *op. cit.*

5.
Wendell L. French and Cevil H. Bell, Jr., *Organization Development: Behavioral Science Interventions for Organization Improvement,* Englewood Cliffs, N.J.: Prentice-Hall, 1973. This book does an excellent job of describing the various approaches to O.D. and clarifying some of the major issues. The bibliographical references to the behavioral science literature is one of the best in any book.

6.
This model was initially explained in Gordon L. Lippitt and Warren H. Schmidt, "Crises in a Developing Organization," *Harvard Business Review,* Nov.–Dec. 1967, pp. 102–112. The concept is further expanded by Dr. Lippitt in his book *Organization Renewal, op. cit.*

How to Improve your Planning Accuracy

8

The process of planning has long been the butt of much management humor. One can find such observations as:

- "Any fool can lay out a five-year plan, but it takes a manager of rare ability to hop from crisis to crisis."

- "Long-range planning is where you lose sight of both the forest and the trees."

- "Don't plan vast projects with half-vast ideas."

Planning, of course, is a form if decision-making. It is the proposed course of action an organization elects to take in response to the dynamics in its environment—internal and external. Planning is a proposed solution to existing and anticipated problems.

Dr. Walter R. Mahler points out that a manager deals primarily with four kinds of problems when planning or making decisions:[1]

1. *The puzzle-type problem.* In this type of problem, all the data are available. The solution to the problem lies in finding the best relationships among the data. For example, in designing the wing of an aircraft the designer has all the pertinent data: possible materials, stress information, behavioral characteristics of materials, temperature resistances and characteristics, expansion and contraction data,

weight, cost, etc. The wing can be designed within the parameters of predictable and known information.

2. *The risk-type problem.* Here, much of the data is known, but one can never know all the data. Those who bet on horse races can find all kinds of information about the horses entered in the race: performances on last several races, assigned jockeys, track conditions, etc. However, the bettor can never know exactly how each horse and jockey will perform in a given race.

3. *The strategy-type problem.* These are problems dealing primarily with humans—their feelings, moods, personalities, and all their other unpredictable elements. No matter how much data one has, it is usually impossible to predict the precise response of another person. For example, a manager who says to a secretary, "My, that's a lovely dress you are wearing this morning" can never be sure if the response will be, "Thank you, that's good for my morale" or "What's been wrong with the other dresses I have been wearing this week?"

4. *Ethical-type problems.* These involve the value systems of the manager, organization, and those affected by the decision or plan. The higher one goes in the organization, the more decisions of this nature are required. A simple example occurs when a manager must release one of two employees during a reduction in force. One is a male, single, has no responsibilities except for himself, and is in his late twenties. The other employee is male, married, has three children, and has just bought a house. Both have the same tenure; both get along well with others; and both have the same technical expertise. Who shall the manager release?

Managers vary considerably in their innate ability to plan. Some seem to have excellent memory recall, can identify all the data that bear on the problem, can formulate possible courses of action, and can select a course of action or plan that is valid. This manager's planning seldom has to be modified. Another manager, in what appears to be an identical situation, does not have this capability. Seldom can this manager's plans and decisions be made fully operational before two or three modifications have been made to work out the "bugs."

STEPS IN PLANNING

To assist managers who do not have a facile planning ability, and to serve as a checklist for more capable planners, students in the planning field have designed a series of steps to guide the planner. Frequently, this is called the "scientific" or "mechanistic" model for planning, and it is very similar to the model used in problem-solving and decision-making. Most managers are quite familiar with this model, which usually includes the following steps.

1. Define the Problem Precisely

More and more managers report that a major part of their planning time is spent in this phase. The complexities of modern organizations and of society have made problem definition very difficult. The manager may be particularly suspicious of the first definition of the problem; indeed, most managers report that the initial problem definition is wrong, in full or in part, about 40–60 percent of the time.

The manager needs to be very sure of the context within which the problem exists. Some call this "situational familiarity." It is not a bad rule to employ one of Murphy's laws: "Everything is more complicated than it looks."[2] Alexander Pope, in his "Essay on Man," commented on this when he said, "Some people will never learn anything, for this reason—because they understand everything too soon." Albert Einstein commented, "Too many people find the right answer. Too few know how to find, or ask, the right question." The Edsel, Nixon-Kennedy debates, and the ill-fated Cuban invasion are all examples of probably good decisions that went awry because they were not addressed to the proper question or problem.

The problem-definition stage should also include defining the parameters within which the solution must be found. Many managers are quite adamant that this is one of the most frequently overlooked aspects of problem definition. Says the manager, "I and/or my work group are asked to make a plan or a decision. Much time goes into formulating the decision or plan. When it is submitted to higher management, they say, 'We can't accept the plan or decision. We can't invest the required employee labor, the time framework is wrong, and we can't commit the facilities, equipment, personnel, funds, or raw resources to the implementation.'" When a problem is given to another person or group, it should include the boundaries within which a solution or plan must be made.

2. Collect the Data

One can err in two directions. First, one can insist on having all the data possible before making a plan. For most significant organizational problems, one will probably never be able to collect all possible data. To try to do so is to encounter paralysis by analysis. This is often one of the major areas of friction between line managers and professionals. The professional insists on delaying the decision or plan, pleading, "I don't have all the data." The line manager replies, "But I don't have time to wait for all the data. I need the decision or the plan now." Additionally, one of the ways managers can avoid ever making a plan or decision is to continue to collect data until the decision or plan is no longer needed.

Effective planners advise the manager to concentrate on securing data that are not already known. Often, much effort goes into compiling information, or subtle aspects of that information, which is already available. It is not unusual to observe a planning group spend an entire morning arguing about a piece of data which could be made available within 15 minutes through the requisition of existing reports or computer print-outs.

The second danger the manager should avoid is securing information and data only from friendly sources. This is a real temptation, but the manager should realize that these sources will offer only what they think the manager wants to hear. Thus, the manager's best source of data and information is "enemies," because they will provide the needed data that the manager could never get from other, friendlier sources. To the degree that the plan does not incorporate these adverse facts, it will be a faulty plan. Better to find this information out now and incorporate it into the plan than not to incorporate it and in the implementation phase have the data emerge and destroy, or at best modify, the plan. As Carl Rogers once observed, "The facts are always friendly." We may not like them, but they are data and must be considered.

One police official in Los Angeles commented on this point after the Watts disturbance, saying: "After the Watts riot we did some soul-searching. How could we have been so wrong and made the mistakes we did? We had tried to check on our effectiveness and acceptance in the community. Everyone told us we had an excellent department—so good that other police departments came to observe our operation. After Watts, we discovered that we had been asking the right questions—but of the wrong persons. We had asked our own officials, our city administration, our peers, social and fraternal clubs—generally those who were our friends. And they told us what we wanted to hear. Of course, some data they did not have because of who they were. We should have been asking these same questions of the indigenous black leaders, the black ministers, the man in the street, the people who were being stopped and frisked, and the black militants. They would have given us data that would have significantly affected our planning."

Of course, one can also secure too little data. On balance, this is probably the most frequent error. The manager depends on memory, does not separate fact from inference, and is heavily dependent on his or her past experiences. (Some refer to this as going extinct through instinct.)

Managers will find that their planning can be greatly expedited, and the accuracy of their planning improved, if they will take time to locate good sources of information within and outside the organization. These sources can be people, but they can also be books, periodicals, and other printed information sources. Such resources, especially the people, can be invaluable to the manager. The manager will find no dearth of people who will supply information, but the manager must look for reputable sources who will provide accurate information. If these persons can also correctly assess the importance and implications of the information, they are even more valuable. The kinds of people resources whose input the manager must learn to avoid or minimize are those who repeat every rumor they hear without ever checking its frequency or accuracy; those who have personal objectives and goals and who skew the information so that it favors those personal objectives; those who routinely distort and embellish information; those who are angry and vicious by nature and whose every input is designed to tear something down; and those who are recognized as acting as messengers for others who are attempting to feed the manager highly filtered information.

3. Develop Alternative Courses of Action

Earlier, we observed that a person or unit with a critical problem is often quite limited in the solutions structured to solve that problem. This limited structuring of choices is heightened when the individual or group has a great deal at stake personally, or when high values, feelings, and emotions are involved. One of the most significant contributions the manager can make in the planning process is to attempt to maintain objectivity and to consider every possible course of action.

A number of techniques have been developed over the years to help the manager develop alternative courses of action. Some of the ones most frequently employed are the following.

Checklists

These force the manager to consider new possibilities for solutions. Checklists may take the form of questions, such as "What happens if you make this part smaller?" "Larger?" "Turn it inside out" "Turn it upside down?" "Leave this part out?"

Attribute listing

This technique requires the manager to identify all the attributes of the problem and then look at each of these to see how it could be improved or used to find a solution to the problem.

Forced relationships

Here, one takes the various parts and forces two or more of them together and asks, "Have I found something useful or workable?" For example, the clock-radio probably was discovered by using this technique.

Brainstorming

Most managers are familiar with this methodology, the goal of which is the rapid generation of as many solutions as possible. Usually, a brainstorming group consists of 5–25 people, one or two of whom act as recorders and jot down the ideas mentioned. The major ground rules are: no one makes evaluative comments, e.g., "That is crazy";

one may not ask for amplification of an idea or how it would work; and members are encouraged to "piggy-back" on the contributions of others. Once the group is drained of ideas, the group or the leader goes through the ideas to see if one of them is a possible, innovative solution. It is at this point that judgment is employed and evaluation of the ideas is exercised.

Value analysis or value engineering

In value analysis/value engineering, the group is trying to get at the basic function of whatever is being studied. For example, "What is the basic function of a pencil or pen?" At first, the group members may confuse usage with basic function, e.g., "The basic function of a pen or pencil is to write with." Actually, this is the *end-usage* of the pencil or pen; the basic *function* is to make a mark. Next, the group is encouraged to ask, "What else will make a mark?" In this way an innovative idea for a writing instrument may be discovered.

Many who use this technique insist that about one-third of the group will not know anything about the problem under consideration and that these are the people who will ask the "stupid" and "crazy" questions that elicit the response "Everybody knows that. . . ." However, many of the breakthroughs come from such "stupid" questions. This is a good example of the fact that fixation is not always to be found in ignorance and lack of knowledge; often, the worst kind of fixation exists in the possession of too much knowledge—knowledge of things that "everyone" in the profession knows will or will not work.

Synectics

Basically, synectics is quite similar to brainstorming. In brainstorming the problem is disclosed to the group and innovative answers are sought; in synectics, however, only the leader knows the problem. The leader uses the broadest possible terms in defining the problem to the group. After the group runs out of ideas, the leader adds a few more specifics to the definition; this pattern is continued until the problem is revealed. For example, the leader may wish to involve the group in finding innovative ways of lawn care. The leader's initial, generic statement of the problem might be: "How can you separate something?" The assumption behind this technique is that if the group does not know the specific problem initially, they will be less inhibited in the suggestions they offer.

4. Select One Alternative for Implementation

In selecting the alternative course of action to be implemented, the manager should consider the following kinds of guides:

1. Which of the alternatives is most likely to be implemented by those who will have to carry out the plan or who will be affected by it? Seldom is there any single "right" plan. Often, managers are well advised to select a course of action acceptable to those who will be affected by it or who will have to implement it; otherwise, they may have trouble "selling" their plan, even if it is of higher quality.

2. It should be obvious that no risky course of action should be chosen unless there is also a great deal to be gained. Similarly, of course, the manager should be willing to select a high-risk course of action if the possibility of gain is correspondingly high.

3. In a rapidly changing world, it is true that often experience can be a liability rather than an asset. Nonetheless, past track records are often fairly good predictors of future performance. Thus, an employee or unit that has performed well in the past will probably continue to do so; a profitable item will continue to be profitable; and a productive territory will continue to be productive. Obviously, the manager should not follow such generalizations inflexibly; he should be continually on the lookout for data indicating that these things are changing. However, past performance should not be summarily dismissed. For example, many organizations find that training has its best pay-off for the already capable employee. Normally, the best that can be hoped for from training a submarginal or mediocre employee is continued mediocre or marginal performance.

In this connection, it may be well to remember an observation that is stated as "Pareto's principle": 80 percent of any phenomenon is accounted for by 20 percent of the factors involved. Similarly, many managers comment that 80 percent of their sales come from 20 percent of their salesmen; many social welfare organizations note that 80 percent of their national income and services performed come from 20 percent of the local units; and many managers have observed that 80 percent of work complaints and grievances come from 20 percent of the employees. Recently, a behavioral scientist commented that 80 percent of employees could be managed in a participative way and that 20 percent could not. No one maintains that such generalizations are scientific or that they are infallible. But often, such guides can serve the manager well in planning. For example, the manager is fairly safe in assuming that when two groups begin to work together for the first time, there will normally be a "honeymoon" period. The manager is also pretty safe in assuming that sooner or later this honeymoon period will end and that the two groups will then begin to bicker and fight.

4. Sometimes, the date by which results must be shown will indicate which alternative solution must be chosen.

5. Another excellent guide is to ask which one of the possible action courses will make the best use of already existing resources. When a new piece of legislation is passed and is to be implemented, the government is often accused of immediately proceeding to establish a new organization with separate staff, budget, facilities, equipment, supplies, etc. Few people ever ask whether this new legislation could be implemented through already existing resources. Sometimes, of course, impactful planning may legitimately call for an entirely new approach with an entirely new structure, staff, and budget. However, planners should always consider how an effective solution can be found through the use of present resources, structure, staff, budget, materials, supplies, and facilities.

5. Implement the Course of Action Selected

It is at this point that most plans come to a sudden death. No one has the courage to risk implementing the proposed solution; or, the planners have difficulty selling the proposed solution to those who are affected by it or who must carry it out. One of the major ways the problem of acceptance can be overcome is, of course, to involve in the planning those who will be affected by the planning or who must implement it. Often, however, managers object that to involve these persons in the planning process takes a large amount of time. This is true, but it is not wasted time. Everyone is heard, objections are raised, and feelings are vented. When the plan has been completed, the manager can usually proceed directly to its implementation. When the planning is done by one person or a small group, less time is needed. However, when the plan is announced, it can usually not be implemented immediately; instead, the manager encounters resistance to the plan—"I had data you didn't even request or know about"; "I could have told you that if you had asked me"; "This is why the plan won't work." In a large percentage of cases, the overall time is less (considering planning, overcoming resistance to the plan, and implementing the plan) when the planning involves others than when the planning is done by the manager alone or by a small planning group.

Obviously, geographic distance or the numbers of people affected sometimes make it impossible to involve everyone in the planning process. In these instances the manager should consider using representatives of the groups concerned in the planning process or taking special pains to keep concerned and affected persons informed through verbal and written progress reports and giving them the opportunity to make observations, comments, and other appropriate in-puts.

The manager should realize that seldom will there be only one workable plan. Most managers have had the experinece of bleeding and fighting strenuously for the adoption of a specific course of action, only to see another course chosen and discover that that course of action worked as well, and possibly better, than the one the manager was championing. Often, what seems to be most critical is not which course of action is chosen, but rather adopting reasonable courses of action and getting action started. Usually, *any* attempt to solve a problem will be better than taking no action at all. Unfortunately, few managers understand that the refusal or failure to make a plan or a decision is in itself a plan or a decision. The results of such failure to plan or to decide are usually much more adverse to the organization than an inferior decision or plan directed toward problem solution.

6. Get Feedback, Evaluate the Feedback, and Modify the Plan Accordingly

Plans for feedback should be incorporated into the planning. How is the plan going to be evaluated? What are the benchmarks by which the plan's effectiveness will be judged? Who in the organization will make this evaluation and must be satisfied? What kind of feedback data will be needed and when? Who will secure the feedback data? These are the kinds of concerns about feedback with which the planning process must deal. At times, the planners will find that they have developed an excellent plan, but that it does not address itself to the proper problem or question; then, the planning process must begin all over again, beginning with what is now a better understanding and definition of the true problem.

A consulting firm related an experience of this nature. When the National Alliance of Businessmen began to encourage the private sector to employ hard-core minority group members, many employers felt that their supervisors and key personnel office staffs needed training to help them to effectively allay fears of the regular work force and to insure the success of the program. A consulting firm, engaged by some employers to do some of this training, began to accumulate some good experience and training materials. The firm then decided that to capitalize on this new development, it needed to design the best possible five-day training program for industry and business. It committed several thousands of dollars for this purpose and put several of its best training persons to work on the project. In two months an excellent training program was developed and materials were printed. But there were no takers. For a number of reasons, the endeavor to employ the hard-core faded fast. The consulting firm had come up with an excellent decision and plan—the product was the very best—but the firm had asked the wrong question. The question was not "How can we develop the best possible training program in this content area?"; rather, it was "Is there a market for this training program which will warrant our developing it?"

Why the plan is modified

This mechanistic model of planning and decision-making is taught by many schools of business administration and is the model most often taught in supervisory and management development programs. The manager looks at the model and comments, "Gee, if everyone in my organization would just follow this model. I wish my management did. Why, following these steps would almost always result in the best quality plan possible."

This is probably true. However, as most students of planning will honestly observe, "This is not the way planning and decision-making is accomplished in most organizations. Perhaps many hardware decisions are made in this way, but not most plans and decisions which involve people in implementation." This is a valid observation. For major plans and decisions made by organizations, it is probably most often true that the quality decision or plan developed by using the scientific or mechanistic model is seldom the one that is selected or implemented. The "perfect" solution is almost always modified. It is entirely possible that the modifications will result in a plan or decision that is 180 degrees out of phase with the quality plan or decision arrived at by using the model.

What are the factors that will result, almost inevitably, in the modification of the "quality" plan or decision? There are three major sets of factors. The first set consists of factors in the external environment: outside politics and political considerations, e.g., a change in political administration; community/public reactions with resulting good or bad public relations and organizational acceptance; an act of God, e.g., snowstorms, floods, tornadoes, plane crashes with key company personnel aboard; a change in the public's buying habits or preferences; an unpredicted technological breakthrough; a recession; a change in the availability of resources; a change in the international situation, e.g., a shift in the "cold war," international crises, including monetary; changes in related organizations, businesses, and industries, e.g., a strike at a related industry or business; a shift in public attitude; public-media exposés, investigations, or editorial views; and activities by special-interest groups, e.g., environmentalists or consumer groups.

A second set of factors that may result in modification of a "quality" plan derives from within the organization. Such factors include: "internal politics," e.g., the organization may listen to the individual or group that screams the loudest, or it may hold that the major criterion of the "best" plan or decision is profitability or the plan that will most help the company to survive, or the organization may contend that "company policy" must be served at all costs and that it must follow company tradition and history in making similar plans; higher-level decisions or plans may dictate lower-level decisions or plans, i.e., the lower-level plans must be consistent with the ones from the higher level; fear of both union and employee reactions; organizational panic; the influence of certain groups in the organization which may be sponsoring an alternative plan and will probably get their way unless the quality plan is modified; the biases and prejudices of top management; a sudden shift in company direction; and the death, illness, or transfer of a key influence person.

Finally, modification of a quality plan may occur as the result of factors within the planner. These factors may take the form of statements such as:

- "I follow the 'party line'—the way the organization makes similar decisions."

- "I slant the plan so it will please or protect the interests of my boss (or peers or my professional society or my subordinates)."

- "I always consider 'what's in it for me.' "

- "I examine the decision to see if it will conflict with any of my other interests, pet theories or preferences, and biases; if so, I may 'juggle' the plan."

- "I will normally take the path of least resistance. Why rock the boat?"

- "I generally slant the plan, if necessary, to please an important client, customer, or consumer."

- "I dislike conflict. I will modify the plan to please a vociferous complainer, agitator, or advocate of another plan."

- "I consider the personal consequences if I don't go along with another plan approach, already made, that relates to the plan I am making."

- "I always hold out for the quality plan. I will not compromise."

These are only some of the major factors identified by managers when they reflect on how and why they modify "quality plans." New supervisors or managers often find this difficult to accept. To them, the quality plan should always be sought and defended. The experienced manager, by contrast, fully realizes that most significant plans are modified to some degree by these factors. Of course, one can argue that these factors are realities and data and that the modified plan, a response to these factors as valid data, is really the quality plan, although younger employees may contend that this is a "cop-out."

A division director in the United States Department of Agriculture who was responsible for research stations throughout the country was aware of these factors. Some of these research stations were manned by no more than five persons. Some stations were researching pests and diseases that had long since ceased to be a threat to agriculture. Some of the stations were staffed by incompetent, aged personnel. Some of the younger staff talked to the research director before he went to the "Hill" to make his request for funds before the Agricultural Appropriations Committee. They pointed out how his plans could be more quality-oriented. Patiently, the research director listened and then commented, "I know you folks think I am an old fogey. Our research planning has bothered me for years, but I have learned to accept reality. I know how to plan a quality research program. I know we don't need all these stations and that many of our operations are ineffective and not needed. I know we would be better off and more efficient if we consolidated the research stations, researched vital areas of concern, and located these research stations near a university which offered top research laboratories, staff, and equipment. All this I know. But the moment I suggest closing a local research station, the "flak" I receive jeopardizes our entire budget. The local community is up in arms: 'This is one of our major showplaces. Old Dr. Jones has been here for 21 years, is Deacon of the Baptist Church, and is chairman of our local fund drive. And his secretary, Mrs. Wilson, is a widow with five small children to support. If the station closed, I don't know where she would find a job.' You can multiply this phenomenon by 40 communities. And anyone who thinks I don't have to respond to these factors in my planning is hopelessly naive."

It is also true that the higher one progresses in the organization, the more there are of these factors to which the manager must respond. Often, these factors are so sensitive and confidential that the manager cannot reveal them to subordinates. It is a safe bet that if any subordinate manager were aware of the factors which affected a seemingly nonquality plan received from "on high," that manager would, in the same situation and facing the same factors, probably come up with a similar plan. It is true that "no boss ever looks so smart as the day you inherit the boss's job." Suddenly, the newly promoted manager becomes aware of the multitude of forces and factors that modify quality decisions and plans.

Obviously, these are difficult modifications for the manager to make, and often the manager is disturbed by demands for modification to what seems to be a higher-quality plan. When managers are asked what guidelines they follow in determining how far they will be pushed in modifying what to them is the better plan, they identify such internal guides as:

- "How I will look, afterwards, to myself, my boss, and to my family and significant others if they discover the forces to which I responded and how I modified the quality plan."

- "Which plan will adversely affect the least number of people."

- "My present mood; I try not to be in too high or low a mood when I make the final choice."

- "I consider the impact of the plan on other organizations and the precedent I may be setting."

- "I ask whether there might be a 'creeping decision' in the plan. If I make this decision, what next one(s) does it call for me to make?"

- "I will not violate my profession's code of ethics."

- "I am an organization man. I always go with company precedents or desires."

- "My career comes first; I'll recommend any plan that will further it or that will put me in good with my boss and the organization."

- "I will go with any plan that will get the required return on investment."

- "I will not jeopardize quality of service, quality of product, or safety."

BLOCKS TO EFFECTIVE PLANNING

Planning and decision-making are admittedly difficult processes. However, it has been noted several times that these processes are two of the most critical ones for the manager and are the stuff out of which his or her career is in large part fashioned. Often, one of the critical dilemmas for the manager is the relationship between two positions. The general manager of one of the nation's largest aircraft divisions summed it up succinctly when he noted, during an in-plant seminar on planning and decision-making, that managers are constantly plagued, in their decision-making and planning, with the problem of coming up with what is the proper and best balance between:

- Too little or too much information
- Making the decision or plan too early or too late
- Pressure of subunits phasing out and phasing in
- Relying on technology that is either too advanced or obsolete
- Adopting the posture of one's competitors or striking out in a new direction
- Holding lengthy discussions and deciding to take action
- The advantages of having the manager make the decision or plan alone versus the benefits of participative decision-making or planning
- Milking a current product or service to the bitter end versus abandoning it while it is still marginally profitable
- Making the highest-quality product possible versus simply meeting the needs of the job order specifications (the "perfect" plan or decision versus employee/customer acceptance)
- Performing economically on current orders and business, but at the same time retaining the capability of expanding quickly.

When managers are asked to identify the blocks they encounter to effective planning, the lists of factors identified become legion. In descending rank-order, the following were listed by 100 managers in one organization.

1. Inadequate communication
2. Insufficient data
3. Faulty or inadequate problem identification or definition
4. Insufficient time to plan
5. Unclear parameters for the plan (staff, budget, time, facilities, equipment, material, etc.) in the planning request
6. No emphasis on planning; the organization prefers to work on a crisis basis
7. I don't like to plan
8. Nobody will cooperate in the planning process
9. We don't have a range of alternatives to choose from in our planning
10. The timing is bad for submitting plans
11. The knowledge or views of the planners are too limited
12. My organization resists change
13. We don't know the organization's major goals; objectives are not clear
14. We don't involve the people who have to implement the plan or who are affected by it
15. It is never clear who is to do what or when
16. The planning approver is not knowledgeable or is disinterested
17. We plan only after a problem has become acute
18. The plan is never followed up
19. Nobody respects the abilities of the planners
20. Past plans were too optimistic
21. Goals are too ambitious
22. People resist any plan
23. Premature implementation
24. If the plan doesn't show an immediate dollar return, it hasn't a chance

25. Planning is not coordinated; others are doing similar planning

26. There's no point to planning; too many unforeseen things are beyond my control or vision

27. If I commit myself, I will be held accountable

28. The boss and organization shoot from the hip; so should I

29. I don't have the authority to implement my planning

These blocks to planning have been tested with 500 managers in 12 other organizations. No new blocks were identified, but as would be expected, the rank-ordering of the blocks varies with each specific organization.

MODELS FOR EFFECTIVE PLANNING

Dr. Gordon L. Lippitt, in his book *Organization Renewal,* [3] holds that an effective plan will:

- Optimize the effective utilization and development of the human resources in the organization
- Improve the interfacing process in the organization
- Contribute to the next growth stage of the organization
- Be responsive to the environment in which the organization exists.

Cyclical Planning

Because of the rapid changes in the organization's internal and external world, including technological changes, the overall model for planning has undergone some significant changes. Twenty years ago, the model was that people did their own planning, which might involve a three-month to five-year period. Once the planning was done, and a course of action decided upon, the planning steps and phases were implemented sequentially. At the end of whatever time period had been set for the planning, the planners took stock and reviewed the process to determine whether or not their planning had been effective and had met its goals.

The approach today is quite different. The present model employed is shown in Fig. 8–1. In this model, the planners have an

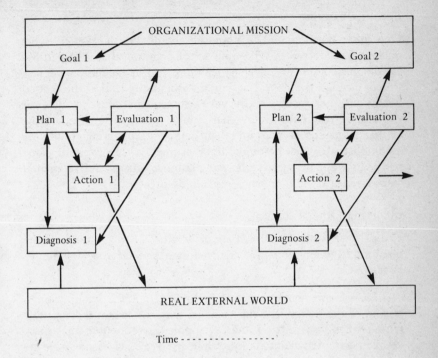

FIG. 8-1 Cyclical planning model.

overall plan in mind for a five-year period. However, since the planners realize that the world is moving much too fast for them to be able to plan confidently for this span of time, the planning is broken down into phases. Phase 1 of the plan is implemented and action is begun. Feedback is secured to determine if the planning effects are those that were predicted. If so, Phase 2 of the plan is initiated. If not, based on the feedback and its analysis, modifications are applied to Phase 2 and action is again initiated. This process is continued throughout the planning implementation and is called the cyclical method of planning. The planners are not irrevocably committed to a specific course of action; rather, the planning implementation is continually modified as warranted by the feedback.

Reverse Planning

One other development in planning should be mentioned. Some managers are intrigued with a model of planning that is sometimes called "perfection" or "reverse" planning. In this model, the planner thinks through the steps that would sequentially lead to the desired results and then focuses on the very last steps that must be taken for the desired results to occur. That is, one works in reverse, asking, "What last steps need to be taken before the planning results are accomplished? What before that?" Presumably, this gives the planner a different perspective on the planning phases and sequential steps needed to accomplish the planning objectives.

Involving Other People

The planner is often troubled about whether or not to perform the planning function alone. Experienced managers offer several guidelines.

1. For a major plan or decision involving the total organization, a region, or the nation, the top manager may think that the top staff whose functions—research and development, production, sales, marketing, personnel, maintenance, administrative services, etc.—are involved should be included in the planning process. These persons, reasons the manager, know more about their functional area than I know. Therefore, it makes sense to involve them in the planning process and to include them as part of the planning group. However, very frequently this is not the best approach. Each of these persons will view the plan from a narrow perspective, e.g., "What do I have to gain or lose?"; "What will this do to my employees and my unit?" Usually, report the managers, under this condition the manager should make the decision alone. Certainly, the manager should consult with pertinent others. But normally, these pertinent others are overly concerned with their own gain—and that of their staff and units—and are therefore unable to be objective and arrive at the best quality solution as it must be applied totally within the organization.

2. If there are two major considerations—acceptance of the plan and the *quality* of the plan—and if quality is of overriding importance, the manager alone can usually make the best plan. However,

if the overriding consideration is the acceptance of the plan by those who will be affected by it or who must implement it, then the groups or individuals concerned should be part of the planning deliberations.

3. If the planning involves the recall of much data and information, a group can outperform the individual manager. In this instance, the manager is advised to use the group-planning approach.

NOTES

1.
Walter R. Mahler, Mahler Associates, Inc., Midland Park, N.J.

2.
Murphy's laws are explained in Chapter 13.

3.
Gordon L. Lippitt, *Organization Renewal*, New York: Appleton-Century-Crofts, 1969.

Overcoming Resistance to Change

9

People often comment that there are only three inevitable things in life: taxes, death, and change. Few persons are more conscious of the reality of change than the manager, for no manager is employed to maintain the status quo within an organization. A major portion of the manager's work life is spent assisting the organization and employees adapt to their ever-changing internal and external environments.

The manager has to cope with two kinds of change: planned and unplanned. Unplanned change falls into two categories:

1. *"Acts of God,"* e.g., hurricanes, tornadoes, floods, earthquakes, droughts, and untimely deaths of key personnel in accidents. Although the manager knows that statistics exist on the frequency of each of these events and the total number of persons annually who will be affected by each category, it is impossible to pinpoint when and where they will occur and who will be affected. The manager and organization can take some steps to protect themselves, e.g., take out insurance, but in the main one can only perform limited planning to cope with such events before they occur.

2. *Changes are ignored.* The other instance of unplanned change occurs when the dynamics and forces in the organization's internal and external environments are identifiable, their impact on the orga-

nization is fairly predictable, but the organization elects, consciously or unconsciously, to ignore them. In this instance, the dynamic or force ultimately looms so menacingly that the organization can no longer ignore it and must react to it.

Planned change occurs when the internal and external forces and dynamics are identifiable and the organization takes a proactive stance toward them. That is, the organization identifies the force, factor, or dynamic and may use its individual and organizational resources to change the direction and intensity of the phenomenon. At the same time, through its problem-solving, decision-making, and planning processes, the organization assesses the probable impact the force will have on the organization, the organizational response that seems most appropriate, and the specific courses of action the organization will take.

Planned change is based on two assumptions:

1. Man can change his environment. The concerns of ecology are ample testimony that this assumption is valid.

2. People can change their attitudes, values, and behavior. Although the manager personally may not be able to change people, they have the capacity to change themselves.

PLANNING CHANGE

When one plans change, one "lays out an array of possible futures" and then consciously elects one of those futures. A colleague experienced the full impact of this concept recently and commented, "For years I have known this concept intellectually, but it had never gotten to me at the gut level. My son was just back from military service, and I met him for lunch during a visit to the West Coast. The evening was quite memorable for me; it was the first time I had had a hard drink with my son, and what was more memorable, he paid for it. During the evening my son discussed his career plans. He had three choices: to remain in the military, to follow his college program in business administration, or to make a break and go into a field that had recently "turned him on"—theatre arts. At the same time, he was dating three girls and was sure he would marry one of them. One was the domestic type, one was quite athletic, and the third was artistic. As we sat there talking, the term 'array of futures' suddenly came to my mind; never before had I seen that concept so clearly. My son had a multiple combination of choices, and each combination would mean a significantly different life for the next 40–50 years. I then began to see my planning function in the organization more vividly than I ever had before. One of my roles is to help the organization figure out the best future in which it can live for the next 5–15 years."

Planned change is a proactive stance. Occasionally, the difference in organizational orientations toward change is vividly seen. A recent conference was conducted for managers of utilities to assist them in determining the position their utility should take in response to the pressures of the ecologists and environmentalists. The program consisted of speakers outlining the activities of these groups, factual data on the seriousness of pollution, the tenor of legislative feeling, and the pulse of public sentiment about the issue. These managers were divided into two camps: one did not plan to take any action until forced to do so by legislation; the other group was already taking action—installing antipollutant devices in smoke stacks and taking corrective action regarding water contamination. Seldom does one see a more vivid contrast between a reactive and a proactive posture toward change.

The Influence of the Past

Few of the specific change problems a manager deals with in the organization will have emerged solely with the manager's work career. Most of these problems will have had a long history and will have preceded the manager. The manager will deal with these problems during his work career, but most of them will be with the organization long after the manager leaves. This is probably one of the most overlooked phenomena by young people who are attempting to solve organizational and societal problems. Too often, their approach reflects their naive belief that the problem has emerged only recently and can be corrected fairly readily. Often, this is not true, and one needs the perspective of the past, present, and future to fully comprehend the problem and understand how to undertake its solution. President Lyndon Johnson recognized this very well; his 1969 State of the Union message to Congress stated, in part: "Every

President lives, not only with what is, but with what has been and what could be. Most of the great events in his presidency are part of a larger sequence extending back through several years and extending back through several other administrations. Urban unrest, poverty, pressures on welfare, education of our people, law enforcement and law and order, the continuing crisis in the Middle East, the conflict in Vietnam, the dangers of nuclear war and great difficulties of dealing with the Communist powers, all have this much in common: they and their causes—the causes that gave rise to them—all of these have existed with us for many years. Several Presidents have already sought to try to deal with them. One or more Presidents will try to resolve them or try to contain them in the years that are ahead of us."

Is Change Resisted or Sought?

One of the yet unresolved questions about change is whether or not people resist change—or seek change. Different managers and students of change take both positions. There is much evidence that people do resist change. At a very simple level, if one's mate moves furniture about, one tends not to like the changes—especially if one's favorite chair or the television set has been moved. Farmers generally strenuously resisted the introduction of new farming methods. People of many countries still strongly resist the concept of population control and limitation of the size of families. Most managers are painfully aware that employees generally resist organizational changes. Many find confirmation of Newton's first law that "a body at rest tends to remain at rest."

On the other hand, there is a good deal of evidence that people not only enjoy, but actually actively seek, change. We observed in Chapter 3 that there is a good deal of research indicating that no species can tolerate boredom. As one listens to the comments of people in and out of the work place, one hears support for this research conclusion in such comments as: "I'm bored"; "I've got to get out of this rut"; "same old hum-drum"; "I've got to get out of this house or I'll scream"; "I need a change of pace"; "I need a vacation"; "I've got to get out of this monotony." Vacations, travel, rearrangement of the house furniture, seeking new restaurants, reading "escape" literature, hobbies and crafts—all seem to indicate that people actively seek change.

The truth seems to be that probably both things are true. People do want to escape boredom and actively seek change, but only on the condition that they can always return to a known, comfortable, and safe base. Even the apes, after staging mock battles to defend their territory, retire to their own territory to do whatever apes do to relax. Observe how often one comments, upon returning from a vacation trip, "It was wonderful to get away, but it sure is good to be home." A married person may flirt provocatively with another person at a cocktail party, let the other person pick up the cues for real and begin to take proactive steps, whereupon the flirting person retreats to the safety of his or her mate. We like change, but we also want predictability, stability, familiarity, and safety. Thus, if one can return to the safe, familiar, and stable, one will actively seek change.

Will a person ever seek change when this "out"—a return to the status quo and the familiar—is not possible? The answer appears to be affirmative, *provided* the person deeply and convincingly believes the change will be *significantly* beneficial. It is under this condition that people get married and drastically change their familiar life style; change jobs or change job locations to an entirely different part of the country, with the attendant disruptions to family and friendship ties; stop smoking or lose weight; or change job behavior.

Initiating Change

In initiating change, the manager needs to know something about the process that is involved. The current position of the item being changed is called the status quo—the present state of affairs. The manager would like to change this status quo, move the item being changed to a new level, and then "refreeze" the item at the new level so it will not slip back to where it was before the change effort began. This phenomenon can be seen in religious revivals and conversions. The revivalist minister views the status quo of potential converts as a state of sinfulness. The idea is to move the sinner, through the process of conversion, to a state of less sinfulness, or the state of being a "Christian," and to then avoid the phenomenon of "backsliding" to the original status quo.

It should be emphasized that if people are content with the status quo, they have no desire to change or to move in another direction. In this respect, much of the manager's change efforts will be directed toward "helping people become aware they have a need they don't know they have." Until this awareness of need is present, change simply will not occur unless it is forced upon the person.

The operation of this dynamic became apparent when the author was doing some work with one of the departments of a state government. One of the objectives was the establishment of local advocacy groups which would attempt to bring about needed change in rural communities, villages, and towns. During the organization phase, and in the process of determining what strategies might work best, 500 community leaders were asked to identify the last three successful community change projects on which they had worked; they were also asked to identify the last three unsuccessful community projects on which they had worked. These leaders were then asked to analyze these experiences to see if they could identify any dynamics or items that seemed to explain the success or failure of the change efforts. They consistently identified two factors that seemed to make the difference between success and failure. In the successful change efforts, the community leaders noted that people were intensely dissatisfied with the present state of affairs and fervently wanted a change. Second, the community persons identified a leader whom they thought reflected their values and desires and whom they saw as having the skills to help them secure what they wanted. In the unsuccessful change efforts, it was often noted that what appeared to be an effective leader was available, but since there was no dissatisfaction with the status quo, nothing happened.

Much of the manager's change efforts will need to be devoted to helping people become dissatisfied with the status quo—of unfreezing the status quo. This is true in all arenas of life. The salesman attempts to unfreeze the status quo in his relationship with a client or customer by buying drinks and meals, belonging to the same social clubs, taking gifts, remembering birthdays, writing notes of congratulation when the client or customer receives some award, etc. The male, in the courting process, attempts to unfreeze his relationship with the female through gifts of flowers and candy, meals, drinks, dressing well, opening doors, and listening and talking intelligently and interestingly. The training director attempts to unfreeze the manager's status quo through such techniques as conducting the training activity on a cultural island, using outside resources, books, articles, films, role plays, case studies, small group discussions, and bringing in a "status" manager to impart blessings on the training effort.

Force-field activity

One of the more useful techniques and concepts for assisting the manager unfreeze the status quo is the force-field concept, which was developed by Kurt Lewin[1] and is depicted in Fig. 9–1. According to this concept, any item the manager is attempting to change can be located somewhere on a continuum between "more" and "less"— however these terms are interpreted by the manager. The item's specific location on this continuum is that point at which a set of driving forces meets a set of restraining forces, i.e., the point at which

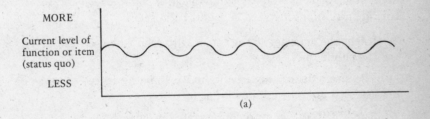

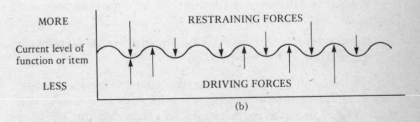

Fig. 9–1 Force-field analysis: (a) present level of employee morale; (b) action of restraining and driving forces. (Reproduced by permission of Organization Renewal, Inc., 5606 Lamar Rd., Washington, D.C.)

these two sets of forces are counterbalanced. For example, in Fig. 9–1, the change effort is directed toward improving employee morale. Driving forces, which "push" the change effort toward the "more" end of the continuum, in Fig. 9–1 are supporting employee morale where it now is and are keeping it from slipping lower; such items might include good pay, good interpersonal work relationships, company-provided benefits, recognition of the problem by the personnel department, which has undertaken a survey, etc. Restraining forces, by contrast, "push" the change effort toward the "less" end of the continuum. In Fig. 9–1, these restraining forces are operating to keep morale where it is and tending to not let it go higher; these items might include an impending strike, unsanitary conditions in the cafeteria, supervisors who tend to be autocratic, employees are not involved in decision-making, bad public relations concerning the organization's product, etc.

The key is in identifying all possible restraining and driving forces. Usually, this is best done at several meetings and by involving all pertinent persons who have knowledge of possible relevant forces. This identification of forces is useful because:

- It tells the manager all the forces with which he is dealing, even the subtle ones

- The strengths of the driving and restraining forces cannot be assessed unless we know what or who they are

- It may tell us where to concentrate our change efforts

- We might discover a hidden ally

- We may find that only one person or group is the main resistance force

- It is conceivable that we may discover that we are seen by the organization as the key problem.

Having identified the driving and restraining forces, the manager may think of two major strategies for dealing with these forces. First, the manager can add to the driving forces and attempt to "bull" the change effort past the restraining forces. Generally, however, this is not effective, since such adding of driving forces is obvious and will only cause the opposition to "roll in" counterbalancing forces. Second, the manager can endeavor to hold the driving forces constant and work to eliminate or reduce the strength of the restraining forces. Normally, this technique is not so obvious and is the better strategy, though in practice most managers will concentrate on the restraining forces but also add a few relatively nonvisible driving forces.

Managers are advised to never forget their friends in a change effort. There is a tendency to concentrate on the restraining forces and to assume that one's supporters are firm. It is good strategy to spend some of your entertainment funds on friends as well as opponents.

The manager will find that often only a thin line exists between a force being on the driving or on the restraining side. It is also possible for a force to be on both sides. For example, some supervisors may be for the change; others, against it. It is usually helpful to list key persons and groups, on both sides of the status quo line, by name.

Once the driving and restraining forces have been identified, the next step is to somehow weight the strength of each of the forces—particularly the restraining forces. It is obvious that all the forces do not have equal strength. If the restraining forces number 20 or less, the manager can work with 100 points and allocate these 100 points among the restraining forces. The points allocated should add up to 100 (or whatever number he manager decides to use). It is recognized that this weighting of the restraining forces is highly subjective, but it at least gives the manager some idea of the relative strength of each of the resisting forces. It is entirely possible that one restraining force may receive 90 of the 100 points. In this case, unless there is good evidence that the restraining force can be "converted," the manager should abandon the project. For example, if the plant manager is dead set against the change, that manager may well receive 90 of the 100 weighting points.

After weighting the restraining forces, the manager is then concerned with which of the restraining forces shall receive attention in order to attempt to change them. Several guides are used.

1. Ask, "Who, among the resisting forces, has a significant weighting and at the same time is ready or likely to change?" Some restraining forces should receive no attention at all—those whose adverse

position is so firm that any change is extremely unlikely. Some are so sensitive, full of potential dynamite, or unable to act or think rationally that the best strategy is to leave them alone.

2. Ask, "Who, on our side, has the best access to this person, group, or force?" In fund raising, a banker calls on another banker; friends call on friends; those who have performed past favors call on those who owe a favor, obligation, etc. The manager will need to be very careful here. If the group or individual has prestige, the manager might be tempted, because of ego needs, to gain access to this person or group, whereas in reality, it may very well be that the manager's subordinate has the best accessibility.

3. Last, spend a large percentage of influence-attempt time on group leaders who are resistive. Usually, it takes no more energy to convert a leader than it does a follower. The pay-off, however, is considerably greater. Some of the followers will follow the lead of the leader—or at least the followers will be somewhat inclined toward the manager's change effort if their leader is committed to it.

Taking unilateral action

Thus far, most of our discussion and techniques have focused on the skills and approach of consultation, persuasion, and facts. It should be noted that there is also a place for unilateral action. For example, some of the social changes introduced within the past ten years would not have been brought about solely by public information, facts, persuasion, and consultation. Laws and legislation can bring about change and may sometimes need to be employed. A decree of a company president can bring about organizational change even if the majority of employees in that company do not agree with the change, because presidential edicts tend to be followed in the organization. Changing the structure of the organization can bring about change in employee work habits and work relationships. And, it is not unheard of to replace a key resisting person in order to bring about change.

In considering whether or not to undertake a unilateral change effort within the organization, the manager will find these guidelines, suggested by managers with a successful record of introducing change, helpful.

1. It must be true that the product, service, or goals of the change

effort are valid, ethical, and sound and that the manager wholeheartedly believes that the change-effort goals are fully desirable. No change effort to increase consumer buying of an inferior product or service can be successful. If the organization's working conditions, pay, employee treatment, facilities, and management practices are below industry standards, no change effort to attain high employee morale can be effective.

2. The manager should review and study, and preferably write out, the current conditions which led to the conclusion that a change is needed. What is happening that is not satisfactory? Why is a change felt desirable? What contributed to these conditions? The manager should then write out what the conditions will be if the change effort is successful. In what desirable or positive ways will it be different from what now exists? Why was this change proposed? Often, the manager or organization will find that if the change effort is successful, the new conditions will not be that different from the ones currently existing. In such cases, the differences simply are not worth putting the organization or employees through the throes of the change effort.

3. The manager needs to ask openly and honestly, "What do I personally have to gain if the change effort is successful?" What are the motives, values, and personal gain that underlie the manager's promotion of the change effort? Often, these factors are subconscious, unrecognized, and never surfaced by the manager. But, an analysis will reveal that if the change effort is successful, the manager is the major one, or only one, who will receive benefit. The manager will receive a promotion, a large salary increase, an outstanding-service award, more staff, more budget, a better office, more exotic field trips—but the change does little or nothing for the organization or the staff involved in making the change.

WHY CHANGE IS RESISTED

Why do people often resist organizational change even when it appears that the change is desirable and will result in pronounced benefit to the employees? There are a few generalizations that can be made about change within and outside of organizations.

1. The manager can generally assume that any change will encounter some resistance. The manager should not be surprised at resistance; rather, the manager should be more surprised and ask questions when change encounters no resistance.

2. Resistance to change is usually related to the individuals' being protective of some security which they feel might be threatened by the change. This security may be either real or imagined. For example, one of the resistances displayed by participants in a managerial development program is expressed as "But, if I change some of my behavior, will I like me? I really like me as I am, and I don't want you to tamper with me." In other words, people seem to resist being changed personally more than they resist change itself.

3. Resistance can occur at a subconscious level. The rationale for the resistance may sound logical and mature, but the root cause of the resistance is subconscious or even unconscious. A mother may defend her overprotectiveness of a 30-year-old "child" on the basis of "I understand the organization and how it is trying to take advantage of my child. Life is cruel and my child is too trusting. Everyone takes advantage of nice people. I am trying to help my child get what is his, but at the same time, the organization is getting a good, solid citizen." Actually, the mother still views the child as an infant and cannot bring herself to let go of the child's dependency on her. Similarly, a manager may intensely relate his or her unit to another unit and justify the close relationship on the basis of organizational need, when the real cause of the relationship is a sexual or psychic need for the other unit head.

A large paper company was planning to introduce a change that appeared extremely beneficial to the employees, the union, and the organization. However, management became aware of strong resistance to the change but could not identify the root cause. Both the union and the employees gave what on the surface appeared to be fairly plausible reasons for the resistance, but which simply did not "ring true" on further examination. Management brought in a consultant to study the situation. Gradually, the basic cause for resistance was uncovered. Management, in the past three years, had introduced two other change efforts, both of which the union had supported, since the changes did benefit both the union and the employees, as well as the organization. Now, however, the employees and union felt that management could not be permitted to "win" the third change. This, they felt, would set a pattern that management's views always prevailed. The union had to "win" this engagement, even though all concerned agreed the change was good. Had management known of this subconscious motivation, it might have set up a "straw" issue or change so that the union could win and break management's string of successful change introductions.

Why do people resist organizational change? The more common reasons identified by managers are the following.

1. The influence of the person or group proposing the change may be unacceptable. If the employees do not accept or like the sponsor of change, they will find it extremely difficult to accept the change effort, even though it may be beneficial to them. Of course, the converse of this is often true.

2. An alternative proposal may be more attractive. Management may be sponsoring one change; the union or professional society another. Both are attractive and both, for a while, will be resisted.

3. Employees' allegiance may be with a group with a different proposal. Normally, employees will resolve the matter by accepting the proposal of the group to which they feel the closest ties and allegiance, regardless of the merit of the proposal.

4. The new goal simply is not important to the employee.

5. The change effort has not been adequately communicated to those affected by the change.

6. People have different ways of seeing reality. Capitalism does not mean the same thing to a Communist as it does to a citizen of the United States. A "boss" means one thing to a manager, and an entirely different thing to a subordinate.

7. The change will break up membership in meaningful informal groups. Some interesting discoveries have been made in this area. Informal groups usually have high meaning to most employees. Employees may view the change as desirable, but if the change will break up their membership in informal groups they hold valuable, they will resist the change: "You're breaking up my coffee-break

group (or lunch group or car pool or bowling team)." If the change can retain informal group membership, this is normally desirable. If the change must interrupt such membership, the manager should attempt to assure employees that they will find meaningful informal group membership in the new setup. Of course, some informal groups can work to the detriment of the organization; in this instance, a change may be consciously created in order to disband undesirable cliques.

8. "I'll lose prestige."

9. Change may be resisted simply because it is change.

10. "I'll no longer have access to secret, confidential, or sensitive information which gave me status in the organization and in the eyes of my peers and subordinates." Seldom will this resistance be expressed openly. When such loss of communication will result from the proposed change, the manager must be alert to this probable reaction and take such steps as are possible to allay this fear or to substitute other status rewards.

11. "I like the status quo. I don't see the need to operate differently."

12. The timing of the change may be wrong.

13. "The change will make my job more difficult."

14. "I don't know how others feel about the change; until I'm sure, I will resist commiting myself."

15. The purposes and goals of the change are not clear.

16. "I wasn't involved in planning the change."

17. The appeal for change is made for purely personal reasons, e.g., "I've been pretty good to you folks. Now I need your help and support. Do this for good old Charlie." The employees respond, "Sure, Charlie comes out smelling like a rose. But what's in it for me?"

18. Fear of failure may result in resistance to change.

19. The work habit patterns of the work group are ignored.

20. Excessive work pressure is applied.

Dealing with Resistance to Change

When managers are asked how they deal with resistance to change, they cite many techniques and approaches to allay, reduce, or eliminate the specific resistance. However, they also identify certain guidelines that they have found are helpful in heading off, reducing, or eliminating much of the resistance to change. Among the guidelines most frequently mentioned are the following.

1. Wherever possible, involve employees in planning and decisions that affect them directly or which they will have to implement.

2. Provide feedback opportunities so employees can air their opposition and feelings about the proposed change.

3. Be considerate of group standards, norms, and habits.

4. Be very certain that employees fully understand the objectives and goals of the change.

5. Be fully honest with the employees. Communicate openly and thoroughly. Don't tone down the negative aspects of the change. Don't try to maneuver employees or trick them in any way. Play it straight.

6. Much of the fear of change is honestly based; employees know that once the die is cast for the change, there is no return to the past, even if the change is not as effective as were past operations. In most significant changes, this can often be alleviated through the use of two techniques increasingly used by organizations:

   a) Try the change effort out in a small part of the organization. If it works, it can be expanded to other organizational parts. If it does not work, it can be modified before expansion of the change. Or, the organization can revert to the past operational methods.

   b) Introduce the change in phases rather than all at once. Try out phase 1; if it works, move to phase 2. If phase 1 does not work, either it can be modified or the organization can revert to its past operational methods.

TECHNIQUES FOR SUCCESSFUL CHANGE EFFORTS

For the past few years, the author has been interested in the techniques that are employed by successful change agents. There was reason to believe that some of these techniques might border on the unethical side, might not be made public by the managers, or ever appear in printed materials describing how to introduce change with the best odds for success. A number of techniques have been identified, and the author was impressed that most of them were quite ethical and that most successful change agents and managers use basically the same approaches. Among the techniques most frequently mentioned are the following.

1. In a reorganization or new organization, move in quickly with ideas and policies. Others are confused and haven't thought out the change, how to implement it, or its implications. It is much harder to get ideas into the organization or subsystem later; furthermore, it is much harder to get something out of the system once it has been adopted.

2. If you can't "convert" the opposition—and particularly if there is more than one opposition camp—get them to fighting among themselves, and they will leave you alone.

3. Any time a verbal communication passes through one person, assume that it is distorted.

4. The initial organization, patterns of working, projects selected to work on, relationships established, and initial directions will set the pattern for continuing operations and thrusts that may persist for years. These patterns are established within the first 72 hours of an ongoing group's life (such as a work group) and within the first two meetings of a group, such as a task force. The change agent should spend a good deal of time, in advance, thinking through the patterns that should be followed and should take special pains to see that these patterns are initiated early in the change or life of a group.

5. When working with committees, task forces, etc., *do your homework.* Most of the other members will not. Have notes, prepared charts, proposed organizational structure, functional statements, and similar items prepared in advance. The manager who has done his or

her homework and paperwork is in a position to exert leadership and influence. These items are not prepared slyly or secretively. Copies are prepared for other members. When ideas are asked for, they are distributed to indicate a possible way to proceed.

One of the change agents proposing this technique was observed in action. The governor of the state had decided to invite the 49 other governors to a meeting to discuss a national issue. The governor had appointed a task force of 25 persons to act as the planning group. This change agent, who was in one of the state departments, spent two days with key departmental personnel who were interested and drew up a series of proposed subcommittees with suggestions for chairpersons, a statement of duties for each subcommittee, a proposed organization for the group of 25, a tentative schedule of meetings, proposed dates, etc. At the first meeting of the planning group, no one knew how to proceed on such a large undertaking. The chairman asked for suggestions. In an unobtrusive way this change agent said frankly that he had had the opportunity to give the matter some thought and had some ideas that might give the planning group some directions and at least a start in the right direction. He then distributed his materials. At least 95 percent of his recommendations were adopted. Instead of showing hostility, the group seemed genuinely appreciative of the work that had been accomplished. Needless to say, this change agent basically got what he thought was desirable and got his departmental task-force members in strategic roles.

6. At the first meeting of a group, speak up early and get in your ideas. In its first meeting a group often is at a loss as to how to proceed. The group will spend an excessive amount of time on the first ideas proposed. It has also been observed that the first ideas given out to a group have a significantly better chance of being adopted.

7. When you know your change effort will alienate a group, approach them first before making a public announcement. You may win a few over, and usually adverse reaction is blunted. No one likes to be caught unawares.

8. See people face to face. Eye-ball them. Polarizations are crystallized by relying on memos, news releases, and other printed media.

9. If you are a consultant, stay in the background at public meetings. Being an outsider or nonresident is still suspect in most organizations and groups.

10. On any change effort you undertake, ask yourself: "What can the opposition make of this?" Then, assume that *they will.*

11. In the flush and optimism of a first relationship or activity, all will be love and light. However, assume that the honeymoon will end and that someone will make something of all that you now do—like buying a meal—or bending/waiving a rule or regulation in the interest of time.

12. When you say or write anything to anyone, assume that it is now in the public domain. There is no such thing as a confidence or secret. By the same token, when anything is reduced to a written charge or accusation, it looks and reads much worse than the reality actually is.

13. If someone is not performing or is blocking the change effort, fire that person or transfer him to an area where he can't hurt you. When you fire such a person, do it clean and quick. Don't let the person hang around to "poison talk" others.

14. Keep control of information; the possession of information is power.

15. Put a "blocker" or resisting key person on one of your committees. The person will not be so vocal or resistive, and group norms and affiliative needs will assert themselves. But don't put several such persons on a committee; they will then form a resistive clique.

16. Involve people who must implement or are affected by the change effort.

17. Sell strategic people before you begin to spread the change-effort discussion. Low-level persons are great supporters and good for the change agent's ego and morale, but they normally lack the clout to get things going or to "sell" the change effort.

18. Unless the need for change is clear, you will first have to create a "need for change" awareness. This is extremely time-consuming. Pick, where possible, change efforts which people want to "get going."

19. In disagreements, focus on points of agreement. The areas of nonagreement are then in sharper focus and are often easier to resolve. It is amazing how many groups can work effectively when they focus on their areas of agreement.

NOTES

1.
For more information about the force-field concept and its applications to organizational and societal problems, see: Kurt Lewin, *Field Theory in Social Science,* New York: Harper & Brothers, 1951. For a review of all of Lewin's major concepts and other contributions to the field of social science, see: Alfred J. Marrow, *The Practical Theorist: The Life and Work of Kurt Lewin,* New York: Basic Books, 1969.

Often, Organizational Media are the Messages

10

The field of human communication is indebted to Marshall McLuhan for clarification of the concept that often "the medium is the message."[1] Mr. McLuhan did not, of course, discover the concept. Many other observers of human nature and communication had observed the same phenomenon—"What you are speaks so loudly, I cannot hear what you are saying." What Mr. McLuhan did was to analyze the concept in depth, call our attention to many of its applications, and popularize the concept.

"THE MEDIUM IS THE MESSAGE"—CONTEXTS FOR USE

The concept has several applications and contexts within which it can be used. One of the first applications was to look at the various news media: television, radio, newspapers, magazines, etc. Most people had assumed, and most of the media seemed to accept the idea, that these media did not create news, but were simply reporters of the news others created. When asked to modify or "tone down" a news story, often the reporter or editor would reply, "Look, friend, I don't make the news. My job is simply to report it accurately."

Increasingly, however, this narrow view of the news media came under attack. There was mounting evidence that the media did in fact create news. For example, a militant radical may be unknown outside his or her own city and may even be relatively unknown within that city except within a very restricted area. The militant makes some dire threat, destroys a building, or creates some other violent disturbance which gets the attention of the media. Overnight, the militant and his or her views are to be read, heard, and seen throughout the country—and even the world. The media have created an instant public figure, given the radical's views wide exposure, and directly assisted in creating other aggressive incidents.

It will be recalled that this issue was widely discussed during the political conventions of 1968 and 1972. In another variation, as the funeral train of Senator Kennedy made its way from New York to Washington, it was constantly monitored by the media, which helped significantly to create a somber mood throughout the United States. This extensive coverage not only reported the progress of the train; it helped to create a national feeling.

A second context within which the concept is used is that often, the *use* of an organization's product(s) or service(s) is the true indication of what business that organization is really in. This is close to the approach followed in management by objectives, in which one of the early questions posed for the organization is a definition of its broad goals and objectives and a tight definition and understanding of its business. Many managers chafe under this kind of analysis. To them, the question is very simple: "My organization is in the business of making maximum profit, or manufacturing marmalades, or making 15 percent return on investment." The question cannot be answered that naively, however. Further, as the total organization answers this perceptive question, each subunit in the organization is required to answer the question for its subfunction.

The complexity of this question can be illustrated by the case of a manufacturer of interior paints, enamels, and varnishes which began to realize that it was losing its market position. The manufacturer viewed its business as making quality surface preparations that would protect those surfaces for the maximum time possible. The products were of high quality, provided long-lived wear, and were competitively priced. Nonetheless, sales continued to fall. Management got its key people together for a three-day conference to examine this problem. Part of the discussion centered on the question:

"What business are we really in?" This manufacturer discovered that most users of inside surface coverings were not interested, usually, in the product's long life. Wall and ceiling coverings were replaced simply because the wife or husband was "tired of this color." Gradually, the manufacturer came to the realization that they were really in the interior decorating business. This discovery called for all kinds of changes in the product: ease of application ("Paint it this afternoon and throw a party in it tonight"); use of aerosol cans; availability of a wide range of colors ("We can match any color you bring in"); and the provision of color charts and printed guides for users of these home interior decoration products.

The United States Department of Agriculture is apparently now going through a similar painful examination. Twenty years ago, if asked what business it was in, the department undoubtedly would have answered: "That's an easy question. The USDA is in the business of serving the American farmer." Many people, however, had observed that the number of American farms had declined from about 6.5 million to under 2 million in a period of about 40 years. At the same time, the number of USDA employees had grown to nearly 90,000. Either farmers were getting a lot more service, or some other usage was being made of the employees' time. For a while it appeared that the USDA might see itself as being in the welfare business, when one considered things like the Food Stamp Plan and its provision of foods to other needy nations.

However, it is becoming increasingly clear that the department sees itself as servicing primarily the consumer, though, of course, it still services the food producers. As the department began to adopt this new view, the agencies within the department had to look at their function and ask the same question. The Forest Service, for example, until fairly recently saw itself as primarily responsible for the management of the nation's forests. Today, it still has this function, but apparently sees itself primarily in the business of public recreation—the major use to which our national forests are put.

One other interesting example from a farm-related organization illustrates the pertinency of this question. One branch of this organization viewed itself as in the business of providing pamphlets and other printed materials and studies, which it presumed were ordered and used by farmers, suburbanites, and home owners. The branch decided to make a study to determine exactly who ordered the materials—to identify its clientele. The branch personnel were amazed when they found that more than 50 percent of their materials were ordered by junior and senior high school students who used the data as the basis of term papers. Said the branch, "Like it or not, currently we are primarily in the business of writing junior and senior high school term papers!" This discovery has significantly changed the operations of this unit.

One public utility also examined this question. Some of the utility's managers thought it was an exercise in futility: "Everyone knows we are in the business of generating and distributing electrical energy." The group exploring the question got nowhere until one of the managers asked, "Who primarily uses our output? What usage is made of our electrical energy?" No one was really sure. The data were secured, and it was found that well over half of the utility's energy output went into air-conditioning. Said one manager, "Like it or not, we are in the air-conditioning business." This discovery significantly affected the utility and its decisions relating to publicity, use of underground or overhead lines, location of substations, location of proposed new generating plants, areas of likely expansion of needed service, etc. This utility has recently even considered the purchase of an air-conditioning manufacturing plant.

It would be interesting to know whether earlier in this century the mail-order houses which provided catalogs to farmers and rural dwellers were fully aware of the uses to which their catalogs were put. The current issue was used by many rural people as a sex manual, and the out-dated catalog became the toilet tissue in outhouses.

The third context within which the concept is used is that any communication, written or verbal, involves both a message to be transmitted and the selection of a medium to carry that message. According to the concept, the medium selected to carry the message may itself carry a message that is more clamorous and itself communicate a message that overrides and overshadows the message it is transmitting. For example, people refer to second- and third-class mail as "junk mail." One never expects to find a significant message carried by these classes of mail. As soon as one sees the envelope and realizes the class of postage involved, one's reaction is "trash!" The message is junk and unimportant. This "message" is illustrated in the following example. Three friends always exchanged Christmas greetings. One Christmas one of the friends, for some unknown reason, sent his Christmas cards by second-class mail. One of the friends receiving the card was highly offended: "That's what he really thinks of us—second-class friends."

If the medium selected to transmit a message is complementary to the message being transmitted, the communication normally is quite effective. If the medium is not complementary, the receiver will tend to believe the medium selected as the more accurate communication and respond accordingly. This phenomenon has its counterpart in verbal communications coupled with the nonverbal signals given off as the verbal communication is transmitted. If a girl says to a boy, "I love you," but at the same time shudders, makes a grimacing face, and turns her head away, the boy should not have too much difficulty in knowing whether to believe the message or the medium. Similarly, if at a cocktail party someone says, "Tell me about your family. How are they?" and, as you begin to respond, the questioner looks around the room to see who else is there, waves and nods to other persons, and begins to move away from you, you should not have too much trouble assessing the warmth and genuine interest of the questioner.

The owner of a nursing home observed, "This home is filled with persons who are old or who are facing long convalescences. Theirs is a lonely life, and time hangs heavily on their hands. Each afternoon the mail carrier delivers the mail. The patients receive beautiful cards filled with tender verses of love and concern and letters that are brimming with kindness and thoughtfulness. They are sent by husbands, wives, children, relatives, and friends. However, five minutes after the mail carrier leaves, a constant refrain is heard throughout all the halls and rooms: 'but if only they would visit.' " The same sentiment, even though carried by an expensive greeting card or a personal letter, is not the same as when those exact words and sentiments are expressed in person through the medium of a visit to the patient. The medium of the personal visit is the critical message. It says, "I really care. I gave up several hours of my time, inconvenienced and troubled myself, drove through traffic, found a place to park, and gave up some other activity in order to be with you."

USING THE CONCEPT

You can test this concept through a simple exercise. Below are listed 12 items. Make two assumptions about the 12 items: (1) these are the only items in your in-basket; (2) there is no return address, so you do not know who the communication is from. Read over the 12 items and then, as best you know yourself and how you normally react to materials in your in-basket, select the five which you would pick up first to find out what the communication is about. Here are the 12 items in your in-basket:

1. A white bond envelope, individually typed
2. A white bond envelope, machine-addressed
3. A white bond envelope, addressed to your title only
4. A white bond envelope, hand-written address
5. A small package
6. A long-distance telephone memo
7. A telegram
8. A white bond envelope, handwritten and perfumed (for women, it has the scent of a man's cologne)
9. A local telephone call memo
10. A white bond envelope, addressed "boxholder"
11. An envelope that contains what appears to be a greeting card
12. A pencilled note, on yellow tablet paper with one staple through it, and your nickname on the outside.

After you have made your selection of five items, look at them and ask, "What does this tell me about what media I seem to respond to?"

Implications

This simple exercise demonstrates that readers respond to a number of things.

1. Different media (readers attach varying degrees of importance to those media)
2. Different kinds of paper

3. Different kinds of addressing. Normally, people rank-order addressing in this order: (1) handwritten, (2) individually typed, (3) robotyped, (4) machine-addressed on a label, (5) far down the list is the anonymous "boxholder," "occupant," or "resident."

4. The pattern each of us has developed over the years as to other factors to which we respond when we handle our mail. Managers most frequently identify the following factors as forming these patterns:

a) The sender of the communication. In the example we have used, this factor could not operate, since you were asked to assume that there was no return address immediately observable. Those who are influenced by this factor usually have two basic orientations:

1) Some managers always give priority to the communication from the highest-status person. If a dittoed sheet from the company president asks that paper cups used in the cafeteria be recycled for use by the Hidalgi Tribe in Borneo, this request will receive priority attention.

2) Some managers give priority to the communication from the "least-status" persons. These managers are oriented toward the underdog. A communication from a subordinate, a customer, or the night cleaning crew gets first action.

b) The trouble to which the originator went in preparing the communication. This possibly explains why a handwritten communication (obviously, there are also other reasons) receives a high priority.

c) Curiosity, i.e., in the example used here, the perfumed or cologned letter, small package, greeting card, and pencilled note will normally rank high.

d) "What's in it for me?" This is frequently related to curiosity, but the emphasis here is on looking out for one's self first; those communications which apparently will affect the receiver personally or his work unit will get first attention.

e) The frequency with which the medium is used. The receipt of long-distance phone calls or telegrams is, for some managers, an everyday occurrence; they may receive 20–30 of them each day. In this instance, such media will tend to be downgraded in importance. On the other hand, some managers seldom receive a long-distance phone call or a telegram, and the receipt of either is a red-letter day and a cause for celebration. Such managers respond like General Halftrack in the Beetle Bailey comic strip: "I've heard from the Pentagon." They are likely to call their wife and have her cook a roast and invite the neighbors so they can read them the wire they received.

It is interesting, in this connection, to observe the media that are "dreamed up" in organizations in order to communicate the elements of urgency, routine, secretness, etc. Sometimes, special memoranda or directives series are developed that are supposed to contain certain kinds of information or indicate the degree of urgency. Managers associate the sight of that piece of correspondence with a message without knowing what's in it—"Oh, oh, trouble"; "It's from the head office, now I'm going to catch it"; or, "I recognize the form. It's from Personnel. I've got the promotion." Initially, the use of such media has the desired effect. After a few days or weeks, however, people become aware that messages in these media are read by the intended receivers and go through the mail and distribution systems faster than the other media do. Within three months, the initial intent has been lost, and the medium is now relegated to the role of transmitting junk and routine messages. Therefore, the organization must continually invent new media to transmit priority and meaningful messages.

One Medium/Different Messages

It is interesting to observe that the same medium may, at different times of the day, or sometimes specific times of the year, carry a significantly different message. For example, the manager's initial reaction to a phone call at the office is usually "Business as usual. Routine. Somebody wants something that is work-related." However, visualize the manager at home in bed, sound asleep at 3:00 a.m. What is the "message" if the telephone rings now? Usually, "My God, some crisis, emergency, death, illness, real trouble, disaster." Some managers have noted, humorously, but perhaps with a grain of truth, that if under the latter circumstance, the manager's response is "wrong number," that manager is probably pretty ineffective and uninfluential at the office.

One cannot accept these generalizations blindly. One member of a rural electric cooperative noted, "It is true that most of us do not like to receive junk mail and get very annoyed at it. In our business, we get a lot or resistance to including 'fillers' with our billing statements. However, we do have some customers, and there are a lot of other similar people, who live such isolated and insulated lives that the receipt of *any mail* is welcomed. I have seen them save the kinds of things you and I routinely throw away. They read it. It seems to be assurance to them that someone is interested about and cares for them."

APPLYING THE CONCEPT

The implications of this concept for managers and organizations are legion, and they should not only be aware of the concept, but also consciously and actively explore how the media of their work behavior and organizational practices may be communicating to their employees and customers much more significantly than policies, regulations, and verbal messages. Managers have shared with the author ways in which they have found the concept applicable. A number of these are related below to indicate to the manager the extremely broad arenas of organizational life within which the concept operates.

1. The boss believes that good human relations pays off and initiates ways to communicate this interest in the employees as individuals. For example, the secretary is instructed to secure from the personnel department all the birthdates of the manager's subordinates and to set up a "tickler" file so a birthday card can be mailed to them three days before their birthday. The secretary is also given money to buy three dozen cards. Within a year, the "message" of this action to the employees is: "The manager couldn't care less. The manager's secretary has a file system; it's been systematized. I am a card or a number." This attitude is particularly heightened when a third employee thanks the boss for the card remembrance and the

boss hasn't the foggiest idea what the employee is talking about. These incidents are well publicized in the work group.

2. A manager's department is faced with a big job but only a short time to complete it. The employees all voluntarily work overtime and on weekends. Many of them are low-paid employees in low-grade Civil Service positions. At the completion of the job the boss buys a cake and soft drinks and gets the staff together for an informal celebration; thanks them, making a glowing speech about how vital, critical, smart, and innovative they are. Later that afternoon the boss talks to another manager and leaves the door to his office open. The voices became louder. Through the open door comes the boss's booming voice: "That's a damn silly misuse of those people. Why, any damn fool stupid GS3 could do that job." Which communication medium did the low-grade employees who overheard the comment believe?

3. You are a customer in a department store and need help in making a purchase selection. You wait 12 minutes for a clerk. (You drove 15 miles through heavy traffic to get to the store, and you will spend three hours on this trip.) Finally, a clerk comes over to you. But when you are three minutes into an explanation of your problem, a phone rings on a counter 20 feet away, and the clerk leaves you to answer the phone. The clerk listens for a while, then goes behind a counter and drags out three large volumes and begins to look up data. What is the message to you, the customer who is left waiting?

4. Two of your submanagers relate well together. They communicate face to face. Suddenly, one stops face-to-face communication and begins to send memos to the other submanager, who then stops face-to-face visits and also resorts to writing memos. You, the manager, can be badly misled if you think that what is important is what is contained in the memos. The medium is the message! Why did these two submanagers stop communicating face to face and begin to use the medium of memos?

5. Often, you will hear an employee comment, "I didn't mind so much what was said (or done); it was the way I found out about it." The employee learned about a piece of information that affected him or his work through the secretary, someone in the mailroom, at a

coffee break in the cafeteria, in a directive, in the company newsletter. The medium through which the employee gets such information and messages often tells him much about his real relationship, standing, and value to the person who should have given the message.

6. A manager puts an arm around a subordinate and says, "Let's go get a cup of coffee." What is important to the employee is not what is discussed over coffee, but the medium of the arm around the shoulder and the invitation to have coffee. That communicates something to the employee.

7. You are making an address before a group. At the end of your presentation there is a mad scramble for the exits. The only one who comes up to you is the meeting host, who says, "We really appreciate your coming. That was a great speech." Do you believe this message or the one communicated by the medium of the mad scramble for the door and the fact that no one in the audience came up voluntarily to ask a question or to express thanks?

8. An organization decided to inaugurate a training office and to engage in employee training. A member of the staff was made training director. A memorandum was issued from the President's office announcing the action and lavishly supporting the importance of the training program. The first group of supervisors was selected for a supervisory development program. At the initial session, they found that the program was being conducted in a former storeroom located in the basement. The room was still one-third filled with dilapitated crates and barrels. Two drop-lights hung from the ceiling. Old desks, battered and full of splinters, served as tables. Since the participants could not all sit at the table and there was no room for two rows of chairs, those in the outer row had to partially circle their legs around the chair in front of them. Which medium did the participants believe most adequately reflected what management really thought about training: the President's memo or the training facilities provided?

As the manager becomes familiar with the concept, all kinds of implications will become apparent.

- Does the way the manager and others, e.g., salesmen, dress, communicate something to customers and employees?

- Does the way you talk communicate something?
- Does the fact that you interact socially with certain people communicate something?
- Does the kind of car you drive communicate something?
- Does the location and appearance of your office communicate something?

Salesmen need to understand the concept too. When should they send a form letter, write, phone, or visit a customer? Does each of these media carry a different communication? On whose territory should they meet?

Those who handle customer complaints should look at the application of the concept. For example, if a customer has a complaint about the service, a department store can make three responses:

1. Send a form letter (known as the "bed-bug" letter). It lists the complaint (when this complaint is commonly encountered) and provides a list of six to eight of the most common explanations or replies to the complaint. One of these is checked.

2. Have someone call the customer, acknowledge the complaint, and attempt to resolve the problem by phone.

3. Send a representative to the customer to talk personally about the problem.

All three approaches may communicate the indentical message, but does the medium selected to carry the message change the message? Yes, sometimes. An interesting example occurred in a steel mill that was cooperating with the National Alliance of Businessmen's hard-core employment program. The steel mill was genuinely concerned about the problem and made a sincere effort to make the program work. One of the objectives was to let the hard-core know they were trusted and would be treated as any other employee or adult. Early in the training phase of the program, it became evident that some of the participants had no money for bus fare or for lunch. The company made arrangements to pay for these items and printed up tickets that would be accepted for a bus ride and for lunch. The reaction by the participants was immediate, disruptive, distrusting, and hostile. The organizational personnel were dumbfounded. Was this how their concern and interest would be repaid? Fortunately, the company was willing to learn why the participants were angry, engaging in absenteeism, and generally displaying hostility and disinterest in the program. The company learned a hard, but valuable, lesson. Many of these persons had come from "welfare families." In that setting they often were not trusted to handle cash, and chits and tickets of all kinds were used by social workers to insure that the family members got the item that was to be provided and were not given money that might be used for drink, gambling, drugs, etc. The participants saw that system being carried over to the work place. They were being told that they were adults and would be so treated —and would be trusted as capable men and women. But to the participants, the "message" in the chits and tickets for bus transportation and meals was that they could not be trusted to handle money. The medium of chits and tickets carried an entirely different message from that of concern and interest the company meant to impart and was communicating.

Of all the implications of the concept "often, the medium is the message" within organizations, one is most frequently mentioned by subordinates with a great deal of strong and negative feeling. The subordinate has a problem—either personal or work-related—and seeks out the boss to discuss it. The discussion begins, but during the course of the conversation the boss interrupts the discussion repeatedly to handle other matters or engages in other simultaneous activities, such as signing mail or reviewing correspondence. The subordinate says, "Usually the meaning is clear. These other activities have a higher rating than my tale of woe or my problem." When asked how they handle the situation, most subordinates reply, "I shut up quick and get the hell out of there." When asked how they feel about this situation, they reply, "I get the feeling I don't rate. My problems are considered small stuff. The manager couldn't care less about me and my problems. I thought the manager was there to help me, but I discovered that this is not so. I'm seen as an interruption to what the manager thinks is more important. So, I just muddle through and do the best I can; or, I simply ignore the problem I wanted to discuss until it gets so big it does rate getting on the manager's agenda."

Managers can get some insight into their own practice by honestly indicating how they would normally respond in the following situation. You are a manager with ten subordinate managers reporting to you. Your workload is about normal for any manager. During this week you are having appraisal discussions with each of your ten subordinates. You have completed the "adjective rating" sheet provided by your organization on each employee and have shared a copy of this with them before the appraisal discussion. You have also shared with each employee a copy of your written remarks, which includes a listing of weaknesses, strengths, and areas of improvement you consider should be actively worked on by each of the employees during the next year. You are now conducting one of these discussions with an employee, and you have been in the discussion about seven minutes. Usually, these discussions take about one hour. Following is a listing of incidents that could occur during this one-hour evaluation discussion. For which of them would you interrupt the discussion and handle the matter? Be quite open. What is your normal reaction or response when these things happen?

- You receive a local phone call. Your secretary says she does not know who it is from.

- Your secretary reminds you that you had said you wanted to dictate at this hour.

- Your secretary hands you a folded note. Do you read it?

- Your secretary signs for a telegram. Do you inquire what it is about or read it?

- Your secretary says you have a long-distance call but that she does not know who is calling. Do you take the call?

- A friend who is not in the organization drops by to visit you. Do you see and talk to the friend?

- A sales person drops by to see you. Do you see the sales person?

- A manager, superior to you but not your boss, drops by and asks to speak to you. Do you talk to this manager?

- One of your peer managers drops by and asks to speak to you. Do you talk to this manager?

- It is coffee-break time. The cafeteria will close in 15 minutes. Will you suggest that the two of you break the discussion and get some coffee, or that you continue the discussion over coffee?

- Your secretary says your spouse is calling. Do you take the call?

- Your secretary says that you have a long-distance call from the home office. Do you take it?

- Your secretary brings in correspondence you dictated earlier this morning. Do you read and sign it and signify to the employee "Go ahead, I'm listening"?

- You have a lot of correspondence in your in-box. Would you go through the in-box and read/review its contents?

- You are a government worker and your secretary says you have a phone call from a congressman. Do you take it?

- A subordinate comes into the office and says there is something important he needs to talk to you about. Do you talk to the subordinate?

- You are told by your secretary that a critical machine has broken down. Do you take time to check on the matter?

- You smell smoke and it is not tobacco. Do you investigate?

Obviously, there are no right and wrong answers, and much will depend on the interpretation managers put on such items, the assumptions they make about the item's prior history, and the probable implications of handling it or not handling it. Going through such an exercise will give the managers some idea about the extent to which they may be guilty of the most common implication—"Often, what managers allow themselves to be interrupted for communicates something to their subordinates which may be extremely detrimental to their relationship."

NOTES

1.
For an in-depth treatment of this concept and other media-related concepts that have many implications for the manager, see: Marshal McLuhan, *Understanding Media: The Extensions of Man,* New York: Signet Books, 1964.

Selecting an Organizational Structure for Maximum Results

11

It has been observed several times that a manager has two major concerns: (1) to maximize the individual employee's job satisfaction, and (2) to maximize production, efficiency, and quality at minimum cost. In Chapter 2 we focused attention on helping the employee to receive maximum job satisfaction. One of the major processes that assists the organization and manager secure maximum organizational results, and at the same time secure maximum employee job satisfaction, is the structuring of the organization, a process sometimes called "organizing." This process also directly relates to individual job enrichment and job restructuring, the implications of which were also discussed in Chapter 2.

Organizations and managers make extensive use of the organizing process in attempting to solve difficult organizational problems. Sometimes, the process is overused, and many employees complain bitterly about the number of reorganizations their companies go through. Newly promoted managers sometimes are snared by the belief that a major way to demonstrate their capability is to inaugurate a new organizational structure. An experienced government worker, whose agency was undergoing its fourth reorganization within three years, wryly commented, "I have observed that a reorganization rarely solves a problem; it merely changes its location." This seems to be the motivation behind many reorganizations: "I've had the problem for a year and I couldn't solve it; how about you taking it for a while?"

One of the earliest recorded examples of organizing is to be found in the biblical narration of the visit Jethro (Moses' father-in-law) made to Moses in the wilderness (Exodus 18:1–27). Jethro observed that his son-in-law sat to judge the people from "the morning into the evening." Jethro counselled Moses that to continue such a demanding leadership role was not good for either Moses or the people and that to continue to do so would jeopardize Moses' health.

Jethro gave Moses some excellent advice on how to organize such a large task—how to structure into an efficient organization. His counsel: "Provide out of all the people able men—and place them to be rulers of tens, rulers of fifties, rulers of hundreds and rulers of thousands. Let them judge the people. Every great matter they shall bring unto thee, but every small matter they shall judge; so shall it be easier for thyself and thy [rulers] shall bear the burden with thee." It has been noted that Moses took this advice; within one year, the children of Israel entered the Promised Land—after 39 years of previous wandering. Some, more cynical, also note that in the reorganization that followed, Jethro received a responsible position. This is not the first time a consultant has been employed by the consulting organization.

SCIENTIFIC MANAGEMENT

This pattern (rulers of tens, fifties, hundreds, and thousands) formed one of the most prevalent patterns of organizations and exists to this day within organizations. Many military organizations adopted the pattern: squads, platoons, companies, etc. With some modifications, this pattern was adopted by large industrial organizations. The version adopted in the United States and Western Europe was called "scientific management."[1]

Scientific management is based on the concepts of "specialization" and "division of labor." Specialization can be seen on an organization chart when the organization lists such major functions as sales, marketing, production, research and development, administrative services, etc. Scores of subspecialties exist under and within these broad categories. The concept of division of labor is related to breaking a job down into its simplest components. The assembly-line operation approach emerged from this concept. There was little thought about individual employee job satisfaction. The major concerns were with quantity, efficiency, and standardization. In part, this approach made sense at the turn of this century, when many persons in the work force had a very limited education and were immigrants who had formidable language and communication problems.

According to the principles of scientific management, management dealt basically with three inputs: men, money, and material. It ran these inputs through the process of scientific management, and the outputs were either a product or service; if management had followed the process correctly, these products and services would be profitable.

Elements of Scientific Management

The basic elements of scientific management were not complex. Organizations needed:

- A well-defined chain of command
- Specifically delegated power and authority from above
- Rules, procedures, regulations, policies, manuals, and written directives to cover all recurring variables in the work situation
- Impersonality in employee relations, i.e., treat everyone alike (Civil Service rules are excellent examples)
- Carefully delineated and defined job descriptions for each job
- Time and motion studies to help discover the most effective way to do a job
- A monetary reward system (employees wanted money above all else)
- Systems to provide unity, coordination, and interrelatedness of operations
- A policing system based on supervision. The job of the supervisor was known as POSDCORB:

> P: Planning
>
> O: Organizing

S: Scheduling

D: Directing

CO: Coordination

R: Reporting

B: Budgeting

You will note that there is nothing in the supervisor's job functions that relates to human relations, motivation, public relations, job enrichment, meaning of work, self-actualization, etc.—all the content areas that now make up the bulk of supervisory and management development programs. Indeed, as one searches the literature and magazines of the 1920s and 1930s, it is rare to find any reference to supervisory and management development courses and programs—inside or outside the organization. For the most part, this emphasis developed during and after World War II.

Scientific management is the system that has come to be known as the mechanistic model, or the formal organization. It gave an appearance of neatness and that all was in order, it assumed that people and units were doing exactly what their job descriptions and program statements said they were doing, and it eliminated all possible overlap and duplication. If the organization was not profitable, the basic assumption was that the organization was not properly following the method.

The scientific management system has come under heavy attack during the past 20 years, and especially during the last five years. Some of this criticism is understandable and warranted. However, the United States made tremendous progress under this system, and our affluence and standard of living were, in large part, made possible by it. When placed within the dynamics of its time, technology, environment, and prevailing national values, the system and method "fit." In part, the manager's problems today stem from the necessity to design other organizational methods and systems to respond appropriately to the forces and factors confronting today's organizations. Undoubtedly, with the perspective of two generations from now, the current efforts of even the most "liberal" organizational students will seem confining and ill-suited to today's milieu.

THE INFORMAL ORGANIZATION

Despite the effectiveness of scientific management, organizations did go bankrupt or faced serious problems of all kinds. It gradually became apparent that not that many companies could be applying the techniques of scientific management that poorly. What else, then, might account for less than ideal organizational functioning? One of the first insights came from the now famous "Hawthorne studies" at Western Electric.[2] These studies have been treated extensively in the literature and in almost all management development programs and will not be explained in depth here. Basically, the studies revealed that an organization is affected by not only the formal organization, but also the informal organization—the "people" organization. This informal organization comprises people's emotions and feelings, membership in informal groups, cliques, need for affiliation, irrational as well as rational behavior, and a recognition that employees have needs and that much of their energy is directed toward satisfying those needs, even if this works to the detriment of organizational objectives.

These and other studies brought the behavioral scientist into full bloom. The behavioral scientist began to study this informal organization almost to the exclusion of the formal organization. The formal organization was treated as something undesirable and was usually derided. It has only been within the past five years that behavioral scientists have begun to study, and seek to understand, the formal organization and its relationship to the informal organization. One current issue occupying the attention of behavioral scientists is the reality of power in organizations. Until recently, the existence and use of power was something to be deplored and avoided by behavioral scientists. Now, there is a flurry of studies devoted to understanding it and discovering how it can be used by behavioralists for "good" purposes and objectives.

Interrelationship with the Formal Organization

Some of the areas studied by the behavioral scientists indicate their interest in the informal organization, e.g., how the informal organization could modify the formal organization. For example, the formal organization may say: "No employee shall leave the building until

4:30 P.M." Employees will meticulously obey this formal edict, but the informal organization will institute the implicit work norm: "No leaving the building before 4:30. However, all employees will begin to clean their work places at 3:45, and no work will be accomplished after 4:00 P.M."

One manager had ten employees reporting directly to her. The organization permitted two ten-minute breaks. The manager noted that employees were taking longer and longer breaks, until they were consuming 30 minutes at each break. At that point she issued a memorandum forbidding coffee breaks. This was within her authority. Her reasoning: "Ten employees taking 60 minutes time per day adds up to 600 minutes. By abolishing coffee breaks I have added the equivalent of one staff member to my unit."

On paper it should work out that way; that is the way the formal organization tends to look at such problems. But the informal organization can defeat these objectives and projected results. In this example, the employees were angry. They could not take their breaks, but there was nothing that said they had to work or work hard. Therefore, they went to the restrooms more frequently; they had bull sessions. Some began to go out for coffee and soft drinks. Quality of work deteriorated. Employees were sullen, and morale dropped significantly. Eventually, the manager had to reinstitute the breaks. She learned a pointed lesson about the interrelationship of the formal and informal organizations.

Managers may say that this is a simple example. The same phenomenon, however, occurs when, for example, the manager makes the assumption, uses the formal approach, and assumes that if "X" number of products are currently being turned out by 50 employees, doubling the number of employees to 100 will also double the products turned out. But it never works that way. The problems and responses of the informal organization can never be fully determined, and the manager may find that 100 employees will turn out only one-half "X." Similarly, managers sometimes insist that work conferences or training activities be conducted on weekends, on the assumption that one or two work days will be saved. But if the informal organization resists this intrusion on what they consider to be "my" time, the manager may encounter personnel problems which will require five full work days to resolve.

Other phases of the informal organization studied by the behavioral scientists include a questioning of the financial carrot and stick as the best motivational model, the role of the supervisor as "the man in the middle," the conflict between employee and organizational goals, the impact of leadership style on morale and productivity, the influence wielded by informal groups and informal leaders within the organization, the staff-line conflict, the "distributive justice" implications for organizations, the role of trust and information on productivity, and the phenomenon and implications of "don't rock the boat." Other aspects were also explored, but this brief listing gives the flavor of the arenas of investigation.

Organization charts

One of the first areas of investigation was that of formal power, influence, authority, responsibility, and relationships. The organization chart presumably showed the relations of specialties, work units, and individuals to one another. It became evident, however, that this chart didn't reflect reality. The organization chart might describe a "wished for" state of affairs, but it seldom described relationships as they really existed and operated. For example, the organization chart, with its solid line, might indicate that Manager "A" closely related to and interacted with Manager "B." However, if Manager "A" hated Manager "B" 's guts, either no or extremely limited interaction existed. Even under the best of conditions, the organization chart could not reflect the totality of relationships. For example, a chart cannot show the varying degrees of experience and capabilities of those at a peer level; who actually interacts with whom; what other channels are being commonly used for interaction that may be more productive and useful than those indicated on the chart; the nature of the communication and interaction; what indicated responsibilities are being carried out, ignored, and what others have been added; who really has status; who is the informal leader; who is favored by management, etc.

About 15 years ago a number of attempts were made to redesign the traditional organization chart in order to more adequately reflect some of these relationships. Among the most frequently encountered attempts were the following.

1. *Decentralize the organization.* When the organization chart no longer fits on an 8½" × 14" sheet of paper, give thought to decentralization. Obviously, it was not this simple, but decentralization did offer a way to clarify relationships through the use of decentralized organizational charts.

2. *Flatten the organization.* One way relationships can be clarified and simplified is to "take out" echelons. A number of organizations followed this technique, which violated some of the principles of scientific management. One such principle was: "The span of effective control is about ten employees." Under the "flattened organization" technique, the manager might have as many as 35 employees reporting to him. This, in turn, changed the nature of what the manager could handle in supervision. It was also discovered that some managers could not operate effectively, since they could no longer closely control their operations. Further, the concept could, and often did, affect the kinds of persons recruited and supervised. The employee had to be able to work with a minimum of close supervision, take initiative, and exercise a great deal of self-control.

3. *Turn the organization on its side.* Simply give the organizational chart a 90° turn. Those who took this approach used this rationale: "The traditional organization chart calls for the use of terminology that gets in the way of effective staff relationships. For example, a manager who looks upward uses such terms as 'above me,' 'superordinate,' 'superior,' 'boss,' 'those over me,' 'top,' etc. A manager who looks downward uses terms such as 'subordinates,' 'staff under me,' 'inferiors,' 'those below me,' 'down there,' etc. The use of these terms subconsciously and unconsciously 'loads' the manager's perceptions of people and operates against effective relationships and perceptions. When the organization chart is turned on its side, the manager refers to 'my staff out there.' It makes a considerable difference in how the manager perceives the persons with whom he works."

4. *Turn the organization chart upside down.* A few organizations operate on the assumption that the real policy makers in an organization are not the president, the president's immediate staff, or any other group of planners; rather, actual organization policy is determined by the nonsupervisory workers at the very bottom of the organization

chart—those boxes below which no lines extend. These boxes are occupied by employees who interpret policy, give service, and engage in the interface with customers, clients, and consumers. One example is the clerk in a department store. It matters relatively little what the official company policy is about consumer relations. The customer's decision about shopping at that store again is determined by how the clerk treats the shopper. Thus, clerks can make or break a department store; they are the ultimate and real policy makers.

Another example comes from a police department. This department determined that what mattered was not the policies formulated by the Police Chief, his top staff, and the City Council, but rather the behavior of the patrolmen on foot or in patrol cars. How these low-level police officers treated the public, their public behavior and demeanor, how they responded to calls for help, and how they treated those arrested or affected by the police call—these were the behaviors that shaped the department's policies.

Those who subscribe to this point of view often state that organizations have reversed the proper monetary-rewards systems. These interfacing employees are critical, and they should be the highest paid.

5. *Place the organization boxes in a dome-shaped circle.* Those who utilize this technique claim that the treatment of the chart in circular- and dome-display form allows a more realistic portrayal of relationships in the organization. For example, such a display can show the reality of the manager encircled by staff rather than an erroneous picture of the manager.

6. Two other models are sometimes seen. These are not usually shared with either the staff concerned or the total organization. Rather, the charts are maintained within top management. The objective of both models is to help management understand more accurately the real relationships of peer employees, and presumably this knowledge will help management to better understand the dynamics at work and to predict some of the probable effects of any decision, planning, or operational matter.

In the usual organizational chart of the first model, peer-level boxes are all drawn the same size, and all the lines connecting the boxes to the next higher- or lower-level echelon are of the same diameter and length. This is supposed to transmit the idea that employees are peers and are equal. This, says management, is never true. "Some are more equal than others."

Some organizations keep the lines the same, but vary the sizes of the boxes, as shown in Fig. 11–1. Such a portrayal, says management, gives a more accurate "reading" on the relationship of these five "peers." "A" has a tremendous advantage—more experience, status, personality, influence, etc. "B" is the newest member and has little of these factors. "C," "D," and "E" are relatively equal among themselves, but not in their relationships to "A" and "B." Actually, of course, each of these five persons would or should have different-sized "boxes" to indicate their interrelationships and influence. Such "psychological size" is never identical, and since it is also continually changing, such a display needs to be reassessed from time to time.

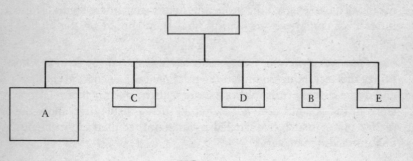

FIG. 11–1

The second similar model keeps the size of the boxes constant, but varies the length of the line connecting that box to the next higher echelon, as shown in Fig. 11–2. In amount of influence over the boss. Employees "B," "C," and "D" have about an average amount of influence, and their influence is about equal. Employee "A" has practically no influence and is either a new member of this group or one who will soon be leaving.

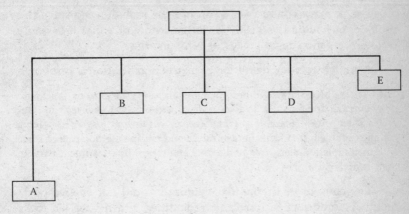

FIG. 11–2

THE MATRIX ORGANIZATION

Other techniques have been tried, but the ones discussed here are those most frequently encountered. Of course, there has been experimentation with getting away from the use of rectangular boxes—making them circles, triangles, no outline at all, etc. Increasingly, it has become evident that organization charts are quite limited in the information they can portray, and efforts to utilize such charts to communicate a great deal of information about functions and relationships have been largely abandoned. Two other factors have contributed to this development:

1. An increasing awareness that basically, an organization may well be thought of as a process or structure to solve problems, make decisions, and plan.

2. The emergence of a new form of organization—the matrix organization. Basically, the matrix form of organization concentrates on organizing people around a problem or task; those employees who have the best skills, knowledge, or experience that can contribute most directly to the solution of the problem or accomplishment of the task are assigned to it. These assignments, normally and ideally, are not overly concerned with such matters as tenure, grade, salary, title,

etc. The primary concern is: "Who has the knowhow to solve this problem or handle this task?" Such knowhow does not necessarily reside in organizational grades, tenure, or titles.

A straightforward definition of matrix organization is as follows:

The Matrix process draws from formal organizations the persons, machines, procedures and techniques of diverse social and physical sciences and integrates them into a temporary group (force) whose purpose is to solve a complex problem that formal organization and routine method cannot solve and on completion of its task to dissolve and return its constituent parts to their functional homes.[3]

The concept of the matrix organization did not emerge overnight. A number of factors can be identified which have led to its development. Among the most significant of these are:

- The changing meaning of work

- Changes in the motivational requirements and demands of employees

- The emergence of the concepts of job restructuring, job enrichment, and self-actualization

- The emergence of the concept that organizations exist for the satisfactions of employees and the development of people through work, as well as for the production of goods and services

- An affluent United States

- The impact of intensified research, computers, gaming, and models of all kinds. These, and similar techniques, such as operations research, have increased our knowledge of interrelationships. At the same time, we have experienced a burgeoning body of knowledge and technology, and this in turn has led to increased specialization and fragmentation of knowledge.

- The desire of "knowledge" workers to work as teams and to approach problems on an interdisciplinary basis

- The influx of knowledge workers—many of them professionals, with less regard for traditional symbols such as grade, title, and infinite gradations of status—coupled with the significant salary increases of "blue-collar" workers has contributed to a leveling of pay differentials within organizations and a lessening of obeisance to traditional authority and hierarchal influence.

- The entrace into management positions of a number of managers who are graduates of schools of business administration and who have a familiarity with concepts not available to earlier managers. Also, for the past 20 years there has been a pronounced increase in the training and development of managers through workshops, conferences, seminars, tuition programs, and sabbaticals for learning purposes.

- The size of organizations has increased, and the number of mergers and conglomerates has grown dramatically. Many of these superorganizations now have a worldwide base, and we now speak glibly and casually of "multinational organizations." The problems stemming from these operations are legion, and the skills needed to cope with them increasingly require the inputs of all kinds of disciplines.

- The rapid increase in technology. Some engineering specialists are fond of stating that the half-life of knowledge in their field is now 4½ years. Some dispute this claim. The fact still remains that technological growth is rapidly expanding.

- Far-reaching changes in the external environment of organizations, such as the new impact of minority groups, women's liberation, and governmental controls.

- The public's expectation that organizations have some concern for consumerism and social awareness and that they join with government and society in contributing to the solution of major national social concerns.

There is no single form of organization that represents the pure matrix form.[4] The generic term "matrix" can refer to a fairly large number of specific adaptations; in general, however, the matrix form of organization reflects the factors just identified. Indicative of the number of variations are the specific terms used. The term "project" form of organization, among the earliest developed, was made popular by NASA's Project Apollo. Other terms used are: "free-flow," "free-standing," "tactical action," "ad-hocracy," and "task force." This last term is the one most frequently used in governmental organizations, although it is also very frequently used in the private sector. The term must be placed into proper context when it is used by government. Often, when government uses the term "task force," it simply means a study group, but the government also uses the term to describe a matrix form of organization.

In many ways, the matrix system capitalizes on the work relationships and informal systems that were described as communication systems in Chapter 4. Normally, the formal system remains intact to handle ongoing, routine business and problems and as a place to which employees return after assignments on matrix-organized problems and tasks. The formal organization becomes to such employees what the "homeroom" is to high school and junior high school students (the place to which they return after class); in this instance, the place to which people return after an assignment to a project or problem.

Usually, one person heads the matrix organization working on a problem or task. If the matrix organization is called a "project" form of organization, the leader is called the "project leader." The term applied to this position will obviously vary, depending on the name given to the specific matrix organization. Often, one of the immediate areas of unclarity is the question of who will evaluate the employee assigned to the matrix organization—the leader of that task or problem group or the employee's superior back in the formal organization. There are a number of possibilities: sometimes, the superior in the formal organization takes the responsibility; sometimes, it is placed on the leader of the matrix organization; and sometimes, the peer-level employees on the task participate in evaluating the performance of one another. The general practice seems to be that the matrix-organization leader will evaluate the employee's performance on the task, and the formal leader will evaluate the employee's performance in all other aspects and will also take the primary responsibility for ensuring that the evaluation is prepared. The superior in the formal organization usually has two areas of responsibility: matters concerning wage and salary administration, and the professional development and supervision of the employee.

Initially, the matrix-organization leader worked directly with top management in the reporting function related to the task or problem and in the selection of "next problems and tasks" to be worked on. As organizations began to develop more and more matrix-organization groups, this practice created a heavy burden and time commitment for management. Increasingly, a new position has emerged, usually with the term "coordinator" in the title. The function of this person is to coordinate the activities of the various matrix groups; keep up with their progress; see that they have equitable access to personnel, materials, facilities, budget, and other applicable resources; make required or desired reports to top management; and work with management on the selection of the next tasks and problems to be given priority.

Early in the life of matrix groups, the assigned leader generally did not have the authority and power to directly requisition resources—personnel, facilities, budget, materials, equipment, etc.—needed to get the job done. The leader had to depend on personal influence, charisma, and persistence in order to obtain these needed elements. The trend today is to give the leader both the authority and power to requisition the needed resources.

Among the advantages of the matrix organization, in addition to the ones already mentioned, are three others:

1. It provides an ideal way to develop or test leadership skills of potential organizational leaders. Back in the formal organization, limited opportunities exist, but in the matrix group the potential leader is limited only by his or her own limitations. Leadership roles can be taken on, and the employee can demonstrate an ability to produce.

2. The concept of job enrichment is more easily attainable. Employees are working on problems which can utilize many of their skills and knowledge, and the job to be done can be accomplished by means not as traditionally oriented as those in the formal organization.

3. Generally, the job, task, or problem is one which "turned the employee on" and is directly related to the employee's interests and values. Therefore, employees can more readily attain job satisfaction and self-actualization goals.

The matrix form of organization is not without its problems and is not the easy panacea that many envisioned. Among the problems managers identify in their experience are the following.

1. Employees often get pay raises or promotions while assigned to the matrix organization. Upon completion of the task or problem, the employee reverts to the formal organization and also reverts to lower pay and a lower classification. Few employees can make this adjustment, even when they know the upward revisions are temporary, without some negative feelings and feelings of being downgraded.

2. Employee rewards tend to be given on an individual basis in the formal system; they tend more often to be given on a group basis in the matrix organization. Some employees find it difficult to accept group recognition.

3. If the matrix group successfully solves the assigned problem or completes the assigned task, group feelings of cohesion are quite high, and the group is well pleased with itself and does not want to break up. They communicate this to management, with the request that more problems or tasks of this nature be assigned to the well-functioning group. Management responds, "But there will not again be such a task or problem, and the composition of the next group will have to be changed. Besides, to keep the group intact will simply replicate the formal system under the guise of the matrix system." For this reason, many managers state that they attempt to limit the life of a matrix group to about two years. If the life extends much beyond this period, the organization tends to replicate the formal system.

4. If assignments to the matrix group are based on such considerations as tenure, seniority, title, grade, and other traditional trappings, the odds are quite high that the group will simply replicate a miniature formal organization pattern and will thereby defeat the purpose of the matrix organization. Attention will be given to "form" —not to function or task.

5. Working on projects and tasks requires that employees have the ability to quickly establish relationships with others and just as quickly break off those relationships. Some employees do not do this easily and prefer to have a given job title in a given organization with associates who are fairly constant and where the work to be done is highly predictable and routinized. It is recognized that some em-

ployees like the reverse of this set of preferences and work very well in the matrix organization.

6. Managers back in the formal organization complain that the matrix groups "bleed off" their best performers and that they are left with the inadequate and marginal performers to service the ongoing business of their unit.

7. There are some questions related to the territorial imperative. Can employees continue to work effectively on a succession of tasks and problems, or will they at some point get frustrated by not having—over an extended period of time—a specific piece of the action and a specific piece of organizational territory that is peculiarly theirs?

8. Often, government workers object to the matrix system because so few other government agencies have adopted the matrix organization as a major form of organization. If a matrix group is created, often it is not a full-time assignment, but may require only a few hours work a week or two to three days a week. Government employees report that often the assignment is given as "temporary additional duty"; employees are not relieved of formal organizational duties, responsibilities, and workload; and no credit or recognition is given on the employees' evaluation related to the work performed on the matrix group.

Practical, and frequently humerous, guides to using the matrix concept are related in Ivor Catt's book, *The Catt Concept: The New Industrial Darwinism.*[5] For example, he observes that the most desirable project with which to affiliate is the most successful project, which will establish a time limit for completing its task and will meet that time limit. On the other hand, the unsuccessful project will not meet the established time parameters. However, by then, management has so much time, money, and ego invested that the project can be milked for an additional two to three years.

Should the manager and/or the organization use the matrix system of organization? There is no right or wrong answer, nor is there always an easy answer. Some of the impelling forces which indicate that many organizations need to consider the matrix form of organization are to be found in such books as Alvin Toffler's *Future Shock*[6] and Peter F. Drucker's *Age of Discontinuity*.[7] The government, in particular, has been criticized for not employing the matrix organizational form more extensively, since many of the nation's problems do not lend themselves to being solved, or worked on, by a single division, agency, or even department. Problems such as unemployment, health, ecology, education, and consumer concerns are fragmented among many agencies and departments. The data and inputs to approach the solutions to these problems must be marshalled on an interagency and interdepartmental basis, and this goes far beyond mere data-sharing, fact-finding, and use of study groups.

On the other hand, the matrix type of organization does not suit every organization, nor is it the best type of organization for all organizational problem-solving. It is a popular concept, and there is danger that managers and organizations, in their desire to appear "mod" and to be progressive, may inappropriately adopt a matrix form of organization when the bureaucratic, hierarchal organizational approach may be best suited to their needs.

FINDING THE MOST APPROPRIATE ORGANIZATION STRUCTURE

The following guides may be useful to the manager and organization in considering the best organization structure to adopt. First, the dimensions of the process of organization must be recognized.

1. There is a task to be performed. This may be defined as a problem or task or a host of problems and tasks. It may be stated as generic organizational goals, objectives, or missions.

2. There are people who will be employed (or recruited in the instance of a voluntary organization) who will be relied upon to solve these problems or to work on these tasks. These employees have needs, feelings, and emotions and are capable of both rational and irrational behavior. Many are looking for self-fulfillment. They have a multitude of expectations from the organization.

3. The manager and organization are attempting to identify and create the best structure which can "mix" these two elements and come out with individual employee job satisfaction and

products or services that are competitively produced and meet stringent requirements of cost, quantity, quality, and innovativeness.

Second, each organization will vary in the kind of external environment and dynamics to which it must respond. The nature of the products and services will vary greatly. In some instances, the problems and tasks of the organization will be relatively orderly, stable, predictable, and lend themselves to a "standardized" approach to solution. In this instance, the bureaucratic, hierarchal type of organization may well be best suited to that organization. On the other hand, the organization's environment may be quite chaotic, disorderly, and unstable. The tasks and problems to be confronted and solved are not predictable and do not lend themselves to "standardized" solutions or problem-solving approaches. In this continually shifting milieu, the matrix-type organization may well be the best answer. Still other organizations will have a situated as clean-cut as we have described. They will have elements of both states of affairs. Some of their work is predictable and can be standardized; some of their work is not predictable and cannot be standardized. In this instance, the organization may be basically bureaucratically designed, but provision will need to be made for utilizing both types of organizations—matrix and traditional bureaucratic.

Third, the changing milieu, problems, and tasks may require a low, loose, flexible structure if an appropriate response is to be made. The more constant milieu, problems, and tasks may well allow for high structure and many levels of hierarchy.

Fourth, the kinds of persons to be recruited will vary considerably, depending on the nature of the organization's milieu, tasks, and structure. Employees who work best under the bureaucratic structure will tend to be quite loyal, have high security needs, be dependent, have a low intellectual and conceptual interest and capacity, have a high need for affiliation, be low-risk takers, and have a very low tolerance for ambiguity. Employees who work best under the matrix type of organization will tend to be high conceptualizers, have a high toleration for ambiguity, like to work independently, have a lower need for affiliation, be high-risk takers, be capable of exercising self-control, and will be self-starters. The manager should avoid placing value judgments on these different kinds of employees. In the work place, all kinds of people, talents, and psychological orientations are needed. There is a place for both kinds of personal orientations, and the in-between shadings. Organizations and society have both kinds of tasks, and the manager should be grateful that there are enough individual employee orientations so that both chaotic and predictable tasks and problems can be worked on effectively by different people. The manager may intensely dislike routine work. *The manager should be eternally grateful that there are people who love and thrive on this kind of work assignment.*

The implications of the matrix-type organization for our society and our time should not be dismissed lightly. There is ample evidence that employees may have to stay flexible and plan on two or three careers within a lifetime.[8] Vocations come and go with increasing speed. One has only to reflect on what has happened to blacksmiths, agricultural workers, aerospace workers, ship builders, railroaders, elevator operators, street vendors, and similar occupations to understand this phenomenon. Currently, teachers, psychologists, and engineers are being "ground out" in numbers that far exceed the supply of jobs. Further automation and revolutionary technologies will probably expedite this process—as will the concept of job enrichment and job restructuring.

Our entire economy is quite interrelated. At one time the country needs ship builders; at another time, aerospace engineers and related technical persons; at another time, agricultural expertise; at another time, welfare expertise; and at still another time, raw-material producers. How does a nation cope with these wide swings in occupations and expertise vitally needed? In one decade certain professions and technical expertise are critically needed; in another decade the demand drops off dramatically, and new needs emerge. Coping with this phenomenon has far-reaching implications on worker versatility, career-life expectations, and personnel practices on both an inter- and an intra-industry basis for such employee benefits as retirement plans, tenure rights, sick- and annual-leave benefits, etc. The nation has not yet begun to grapple with these questions and problems.

The government is increasingly putting the burden on industry and business to help it solve such major social problems as unemployment, hard-core unemployment, ecological and environmental concerns, safety, and employee health. Increasingly, the solutions to these problems, or at least the approach to such solutions, will require a matrix-organizational approach utilizing the capabilities of both government and the private sector.

One last consideration should be mentioned. Often, managers and organizations are concerned about how top management can best organize to give leadership to the organization. Several patterns have emerged. Once again, there is no one right or wrong pattern or approach. The answer can be found only by determining what, for the specific organization, seems to be the best approach and seems to work best. There are several major patterns that can be identified.

1. Having one head. Ideally, organizations like to see this person have two basic sets of skills: technical expertise, and human relations and administrative skills. Those who have been around organizations longer than a month know it is exceedingly difficult to find these skills equally balanced in any single person. Almost inevitably, the manager will be significantly better at one set of skills than at the other. However, in small organizations or small organizational subunits, the attempt is made to find the manager with the best balance of both skill sets.

2. For larger organizations or large subunits, the matter is frequently resolved by having two persons at the head of the organization. Generally, such titles as "Associate Manager" or "Associate Director" are used to indicate co-leadership. One will be good at technical expertise; the other, at human relations and administrations. The two leaders thus complement each other.

Organizations will bleed and die over the issue of whether the chief person should possess technical expertise or administrative/human relations skills. No one is going to change anyone's mind on this issue. Generally, scientific, engineering, and other highly professional-oriented organizations or subunits will adamantly insist that the top person have technical expertise. More generic organizations will vary in their preference, but usually they will prefer the person who has good management, administrative, and human relations skills. This pattern seems to be most frequently found in government. Some studies indicate that these two persons tend to be promoted in tandem, as if their complementary skills make them an entity to be dealt with as such.

3. Industry and business seem to follow the pattern of the chief executive and an associate—one good at technical expertise and the other at human relations/administration. However, industry and business tend to add a third person to create a triumvirate. This third person is the comptroller or the financial head.

4. A few organizations have experimented with the group concept of management. One person may have the major titular role, but sometimes even this is rotated. Each manager can "pinch-hit" for the others and make decisions in another manager's absence. In other instances, all major decisions are "team" or "group" decisions. This form of management seems to be more prevalent in Europe than in the United States, though some American organizations have experimented with the concept. This approach, which seems to work better in small organizations, is sometimes identified as "offices of the president" or "committee management."

5. Very limited studies are now being reported on submitting major policy decisions to *all* employees for voting and making comments before top-level or organization decision/plans are made. The experimentation is too limited and too recent for any trends or generalizations to be made. It is noted here as the most recently reported development.

Other management leadership patterns have been discussed and probably some others have been tried, but in the main, the ones described here appear to be the major ones in current American usage.

NOTES

1.
For a first-hand exploration of scientific-management concepts by the man who contributed most to this concept in the United States, see Frederick W. Taylor, *Principles of Scientific Management,* 1947; reprinted ed., New York: Norton, 1967.

2.

The Hawthorne studies are discussed in full in Henry Landsberger, *Hawthorne Revisited: Management and the Worker, Its Critics and Developments in Human Relations in Industry,* Ithaca, N.Y.: New York State School of Industrial and Labor Relations, Cornell University, 1967.

3.

This definition is from a prepublication paper by Gordon L. Lippitt and R. E. Stivers.

4.

A good explanation of the matrix organization will be found in Thomas L. Quick, *Your Role in Task Force Management: The Dynamics of Corporate Change,* New York: Doubleday, 1972. Another good explanation will be found in Fremont A. Shull, Jr., Andre L. Delbeco, and L. L. Cummings, *Organizational Decision-Making,* New York: McGraw-Hill, 1970. In this book the authors discuss the matrix organization and three other styles under the topics "group structures," "group process and roles," "group style," and "group norms."

5.

Ivor Catt, *The Catt Concept: The New Industrial Darwinism,* New York: Putnam, 1971.

6.

Alvin Toffler, *Future Shock,* New York: Random House, 1970.

7.

Peter F. Drucker, *Age of Discontinuity: Guidelines to Our Changing Society,* New York: Harper & Row, 1969.

8.

You can examine these facts and some of the projected implications in Warren Bennis and Philip E. Slater, *The Temporary Society,* New York: Harper & Row, 1969. Another excellent book is Donald R. Kingdon, *Matrix Organization: Managing Information Technologies,* New York: Harper & Row, Barnes & Noble Import Division, 1973.

Understanding and Using Conflict Creatively

12

In the past 15 years conflict and open confrontation—often aggressive, militant, and using illegal methods—have become a way of life. Many managers come from cultural backgrounds in which the values taught were quite different from those currently employed. The manager feels not only uncomfortable, but also relatively impotent in knowing how to deal with such conflict and confrontations. In this earlier culture, people were taught to "turn the other cheek"; today, people demonstrate militantly and "clobber" the proferred cheek. People were taught to hide feelings and emotions; today, people engage in all kinds of encounter experiences in which they are encouraged to "let it all hang out." People were taught to respect authority—as the military would put it, "You're not saluting the man or woman; you're saluting the uniform." Today, authority is questioned, challenged, and defied. The immediate response, when dealing with a lower-level employee and not getting your way, is to immediately scream for the manager or demand "to be taken to the top."

Most managers will recognize that even they are beginning to adopt such behavior; not to do so is to invite being trampled and abused. As someone commented, "The meek may inherit the earth, but who will want it after the aggressors get through with it?" It has been noted that organizational functioning is seriously threatened when lower levels are consistently by-passed. Part of the organization's response in dealing with this dynamic has been twofold:

1. To push the decision-making process lower in the organization, with attendant decentralization of power and authority, and to encourage flexibility in the application of policies.

2. To redefine authority and to recognize that traditional, blind acceptance of organizational authority is not likely to reappear. Authority must be defined in terms different from those used in the past.

THE NATURE OF CONFLICT

Conflict—actual or latent—seems to be a built-in proclivity in people. In the discussion about the territorial imperative, it was pointed out that no species seems to be able to tolerate boredom. To escape boredom, most species will engage in conflict—real or mock—simply to relieve monotony. Man probably has the same genetic inheritance. Our national preoccupation with the conflicts in sports may well support this research. If one doubts this statement, one need only review the sports page of any newspaper and note the nouns and adjectives employed to describe the scores and activities of the preceding day's sports events; teams "slaughter," "lay low," "cream," "wallop," "annihilate," "clobber," and "overpower" their opponents. No two persons or groups can be in close proximity without one asserting authority and domination over the other. This dynamic is consciously and heavily employed in organizations, particularly in the sales department. The use of competition is another extensively employed technique. If one will observe the placards, slogans, and write-ups of current standings, the implications of the territorial imperative become quite clear.

Each group which a person voluntarily joins, or automatically becomes a member of because of birth or organizational affiliation, differs somewhat in values and objectives from all other groups. Groups meet our affiliative needs; secure cohesion through mutual identification; have shared values, causes, beliefs, and miseries. Any other group will be perceived as being a threat to our own groups. True, this is often very subtle and quite dormant, but the threat is always there. When another group is seen as directly threatening our shared values, causes, beliefs, and values, or when the group's life itself is threatened, the conflict springs quickly into the open. One of the problems of international detente is how nations with widely different ideologies can coexist. The balance is always tenuous. Within the work organization, there is constant latent tension and awarenesss of differences in group goals between management and labor; the manager is aware of this even in periods of relatively stable and peaceful relationships. Any organizational action is consciously weighed against "*how they might react*" and upset the momentary equilibrium. The same phenomenon will be observed in the relationships of the manager to subordinates, customers to salesmen, personnel service to employees, production to sales and marketing, maintenance to production, engineering to production, etc.

Generally, we tend to identify conflict in a negative sense. If a group is asked to give synonyms or phrases for the word, most of the responses will be in an aggressive, destructful context: battle, combat, strife, fight, clash, collision, struggle, discord, antagonism, dissension, hostility, etc. Seldom will the word or phrase be in a positive vein, such as healthy, desirable, or opportunity to create.

Utility of Conflict

It is very doubtful whether any significant progress can be made without conflict. Man is a needs-satisfying animal. When all needs are met with little energy output, degeneration, atrophy, staleness, and satisfaction with status quo set in. Some very interesting research is now being conducted on what happens to rats when their every need is met and they are free to multiply at will and do not have to extend themselves for food, water, shelter, or protection against enemies. Early evidence indicates that they become sluggish, lose the will to live, and even cease reproduction activities. Some of the implications for families going into the third and fourth generation on welfare, crowded urban living, ghettos, and affluency among other groups are disturbing to contemplate.

It is often observed that "necessity is the mother of invention." There is much to support this view. Henry Ford believed that creativity could be commanded, and many of his company's breakthroughs seem to support this view. During the 1960s NASA often found the need for a nonexistent process or piece of hardware and proceeded to discover or invent it. It is doubtful if the automotive industry would have "discovered" or "utilized" new engine designs, pollution control devices, or improved bumpers without the necessity imposed by consumerism and environmental and ecological concerns. Brainstorming and value analysis are techniques which recognize that creativity and innovative answers can be supplied "on demand." From confrontation come creative solutions and answers.

Every annoyance encountered when one says, "Why don't they invent . . . ?" is an open invitation to an improvement in whatever is represented by the annoyance. Rather than view conflict as undesirable, the manager should fully understand that inherent in every conflict is the potential for a better plan, decision, or action than would be possible without the conflict. There is a role, as many managers have discovered, for the deliberate use of the "devil's advocate." An organizational decision or plan born out of conflict, disagreement, and differences of opinion will almost always be superior to the decision or plan born out of unanimity of opinion and the milieu of a contented status quo.

This is not to say that all conflict is desirable or that conflict cannot be destructive, immobilizing, and negative. It can. One of the skills a manager needs to cultivate is the ability to detect latent or emerging conflict and then not to deny or run from it, but to confront the conflict and utilize it for constructive decision-making and planning before it reaches the stage of a destructive force.[1] Most managers, because of their value system and culture, tend to avoid conflict and confronting it. Usually, however, the manager will find that the realities and consequences of confronting conflict are considerably less than anticipated and that facing the conflict results in a better resolution of the problem, with less employee emotional stress and strain. Most personnel directors dislike facing the reality of confronting an employee whose performance is unacceptable, as do most managers and supervisors. The usual procedure for handling such a situation is to either not admit its presence or assign the employee to another manager, hoping that the matter will resolve itself. It does not. Submarginal performance continues. However, when the problem is finally confronted (six managers and 20 years later) the employee's tenure has put him in line for the presidency. If the employee is confronted early, the interview is seldom as hostile or unpleasant as the manager or personnel director assumed it would be. Normally, the employee is not unaware of his or her performance. Often, the employee will say, "I've been expecting this. I am surprised it didn't happen sooner." If the matter cannot be resolved within a stated and specific time frame, the employee should be released—no passing the employee on to another manager, hoping that a different manager will be able to find the magical motivational key. It is surprising how many of these fired employees will later contact the personnel director or manager and state, "The best thing that ever happened to me was your making me face up to reality and firing me. I didn't like that job and was miserable in it. I now have a job I really like, and I was never happier. Thank you."

Conflict can be valuable in another context. There are real dangers to "group-think" (discussed in Chapter 3). One of the major problems managers must continually fight in their area of influence and responsibility is satisfaction with the status quo and the predictable channeling of staff energy to "nest-feathering," ensuring creature comforts, and blind, unthinking acceptance of "what is" with "what can, should, or needs to be." Some managers take the position that because of this factor, no person should be retained in the same job longer than five years. It might be well to deliberately bring an "outsider" into the work group to simply act as a catalyst and to challenge present operations. In brief, when the work group's major concerns are with group maintenance, the manager should suspect that that group is in imminent danger of becoming obsolete, sterile, noninnovative, nonrelevant, and nonproductive.

The manager should also be aware that the expenditure of energy is amoral. People generate energy, and they must get rid of it. Parents are painfully aware of this as they observe their children's efforts to find outlets for their vitality. It would appear that energy must be "discharged" and that it is not selective as to what object is selected—it can be a significant object or an insignificant one. Someone once commented that a slice of bread will create a given amount of energy; however, the eater has to decide whether to expend that energy on a significant cause such as planning, or whether the energy will be released in bickering or a family fight.

It would appear that energy, like lightning, selects as its target the closest object. This has frequently been observed among participants in a cultural-island training activity. Here are mature men and women with significant jobs in their organizations. Energy is produced. No really significant "objects of discharge" are readily identifiable. The energy is released on such matters as deciding whether to begin the morning's session at 8:30 or at 8:35, deciding on the lunch menu, agreeing on an arrangement for the tables and chairs, deciding whether or not to tape record the session, and determining the order in which five items should be recorded on the chart paper. At times, it is unbelievable that such emotions, feelings, and intensity of behavior could possibly be generated by such insignificant items. Managers will observe the same phenomenon in their own work groups and organizations. Employees generate a given amount of energy. This can be channeled and spent on attaining organizational objectives, productive work, planning, making sales calls, or self-improvement activities. It can also be spent on bickering, griping, personal fighting, bull sessions, horseplay, and countless trips to the cafeteria. Managers should understand this fact and provide appropriate, useful, and ready targets for the discharge of employee energy.

Conflict and Human Development

One aspect of handling conflict should be highlighted. Most managers assume that people are born into the world in a state of extreme dependence. Literally, the newborn baby's life depends on others. The process of maturation and development is considered to be the process of assisting this dependent baby to become independent. Hopefully, this process will be completed within 21 years, though legal interpretations define different aspects of independence at different ages—voting at 18, drinking hard liquor at 18 or 19, marrying at 16.

Managers and others have assumed that independence is the highest stage of development; independence, or maturity, is the stage at which the individual no longer depends on others for subsistence and is entirely capable of making all the decisions that go along with maturity. However, one does not proceed directly from dependence to independence. Usually, one goes through a stage identified as "counterdependency." Any parent is excruciatingly aware of this stage, which is the phenomenon associated with "teen-age." The increasingly independent child begins to turn on the very people who have assisted with the maturation process and says, in effect, "Who needs you, anyway? Get out of my way. I am capable of making decisions related to my welfare." As any parent knows, this hurts. But the stage seems to be inevitable.

Employees, too, go through this stage in their relationships with supervisors and managers. New employees are quite dependent on others, especially the manager. Managers or supervisors may perceive their major role as one of helping this new employee emerge from a state of dependence on the supervisor or manager to one in which the employee is independent and fully capable of independent operations. As this process unfolds, the employee will almost inevitably engage in the phenomenon of counterdependence and, just like the teen-ager, turn on the manager as if to say, "Who needs you? You're holding me back. Not only can I do what you do, but I can do your job just as well." The manager should not be hurt when this occurs; it is part of employee maturation. Instead, the real concern should come when an employee does not go through this stage. This is one of the earliest tip-offs that the employee is arrested at the stage of dependence and is not likely to mature into an effective employee capable of independent action.

Fortunately, the stage of counterdependence does not last forever; it may vary from a few months to several years. Ultimately, the child will say to the parent, "How did you ever stand me during those months or years?" At last, the parent is seen and treated by the child as a human being. The same is true in the relationship between the employee and the supervisor or manager. However, it should be emphasized that many employees never progress beyond the counterdependence stage. Their entire work life is spent arrested at this stage, and their whole work life is devoted to fighting the manager, thumbing their nose at the manager, acting like persons in revolt, fighting the "establishment," and finding immature ways to get around rules and regulations.

Only in recent years has it been emphasized that the stage of independence is not the most mature stage of growth. The most mature stage is that of "interdependence." No one is free to be entirely independent, and the manager would not want completely independent employees. Children have become interdependent when they can see their parents as humans—with feelings, emotions, ambitions, hurts, pains, frustations, and limitations of all kinds—and still love and accept them. "I, the child, need you, the parent, for some things. You, the parent, need me, the child, for some things also. We are interdependent." This is also the desired stage of relationship between a manager and subordinates, peers and superiors. "In some things I am perfectly capable of acting independently. In some things I am dependent on you. In some things you are dependent on me. We are interdependent."

MANAGING AGREEMENT

As strange as it may at first sound, the manager's most difficult job is often not how to manage conflict, but rather how to manage agreement.[2] It is surprising how much conflict can exist within an organization when in fact everyone concerned with the issue actually agrees on many things. They agree that there is a problem; they agree that the status quo is unsatisfactory; they agree that something ought to be done. But despite the surprisingly large amount of agreement, the parties continue to act and behave as if they were all at loggerheads over every single aspect of the issue. The role for the manager is not to concentrate on the conflict, but to focus attention on the areas of agreement and to decide how best to manage the agreement that exists.

Sometimes, staff people focus so sharply on what appear to be areas of conflict that they do not look at the other side of the coin. One organization was divided into opposing camps on an issue. Positions had become solidly polarized. Three meetings to resolve the issue got nowhere. Members of the group were nearly convinced that no possible solution could be found: "We disagree on *everything.*" An external consultant was brought in to the fourth meeting to observe the group's process and to help the group decide if there was any possible methodology that could be utilized. Before the group started to work, the consultant said, "Let's forget about the issue, so far as possible, and let's not think about a possible solution now. You know where you disagree. Instead, let's think about the areas where you agree, identify them on the chalkboard, and then explore whether, based on these areas of agreement, a possible solution can be found. Now, what are the areas upon which both sides agree?"

At first, the group sulked and was defiant. "We agree on nothing." Finally, one person ventured, "Well, I guess we agree that there is a problem." This got some laughter, and tension was reduced. Said another person, "We agree that a solution should be found." Still another added, "We agree that not finding an answer is hurting the organization." More specific areas of agreement began to emerge, some of which actually gave parameters within which a compromise could be found. Ultimately, the group agreed on 15 statements. The consultant then asked the group to think about finding part of the solution within the parameters of the agreements. This was done, and the group finally tackled aspects of the solution around the items on which there was significant disagreement. Actually, the group discovered that these were fewer than they had imagined, and although sharp and strong differences did exist, within two hours the group had hammered out a complete solution that both sides could accept. It is doubtful that this outcome could have occurred had the group continued to focus on their areas of disagreement and had not come to grips with the question "How can we manage our areas of agreement?"

Here is another common example. An employee is performing unsatisfactorily, is unhappy in the job, dislikes the job, does not believe that this attitude will ever change, and occasionally threatens to quit. The manager is unhappy with the employee's performance, does not believe the employee will ever come up to an acceptable level of performance, recognizes the adverse affect the employee's conversation and habits of work behavior are having on other employees, and threatens to fire the employee. The two have a meeting. There are many significant areas of agreement: the employee wants to quit, and the manager wants the employee to quit; both the employee and manager are unhappy with the employee's performance; and neither believes that the employee can ever be happy within the organization. But what happens? Frequently, the employee will begin the conversation like this: "I am unhappy with my job. I know I'm not doing well. I can learn the job; I know I can. But I don't know, I just can't get interested in it. I guess I have created some problems for you. I'm sorry." Too frequently, the manager then replies, "Oh, come on, Sue. It's not that bad. Sure, you've got problems, but I'm sure they can be overcome. Let's work on it, and I'll bet that in six months we'll both laugh over this episode. Maybe it would help if you took the next supervisory-development course. I'll see about getting you into it. Just try a little harder, huh?" And so both are stuck, and the organization is stuck, because the manager did not know how to handle the areas of agreement.

This approach, it will be recognized, has some elements and techniques similar to those used in behavior modification. Find areas of agreement that have positive connotations and in which movement is in the right direction of finding a solution. Acknowledge these through feedback and set targets for further movement toward the areas of mutual agreement. Of course, it is recognized that conflict of a significant, even unsoluble, nature does exist within organizations. However, these instances are far more rare than most managers realize.

Other clues to handling the management of agreement are set out in the film *Is it Always Right to be Right?*[3] Three major points made in this film indicate some of the assumptions that often must underlie acceptance by groups in conflict before compromise or an agreement can be reached. These are stated as:

All men are created equal, but each develops in a unique way.

All men are endowed with certain inalienable rights, but each must assume certain inevitable responsibilities.

The happiness of all depends on the commitment of each to support equality and difference, rights and responsibilities.

CHANGE EFFORTS IN ORGANIZATIONS TODAY

The last several years have witnessed a significant change in efforts directed toward changing organizations, the status quo, and the "establishment." Methods that in the past were generally not considered appropriate are increasingly being employed today—mass demonstrations, picketing of public persons and offices, sit-ins, lie-ins, occupying offices, and destruction of property. Just as the influence methods are changing, so, too, are the methods considered appropriate by various professions or levels of hierarchy. Teachers strike, government employees threaten to strike, nurses demonstrate, professors join students in protest groups and teach-ins, and business and industrial employees participate in demonstrations against their own organizations.

Many managers have been caught quite unprepared to cope with these trends. Their professional codes and prior organizational experience have not prepared them to deal effectively with these methods. Several observations about this situation deserve mention.

1. The methods employed range from traditional change efforts to extreme physical violence and property destruction. Traditional change efforts are such influence attempts as formal reports, organizational decision-making processes, staff meetings, study groups, etc. Change efforts, then, range on a continuum from relatively passive efforts to highly involving, aggressive, direct action methods, as shown in Fig. 12–1.

Traditional
methods;
relatively
passive

Direct
personal involve-
ment, action, and
confrontation methods

FIG. 12–1 Continuum of change efforts.

2. The closer one is to the power center of an organization, the more one will tend to use passive change methods to influence the organization. The farther one is removed from the power center, the more one will tend to use active or direct methods to influence the organization. Those at the extreme right of the involvement continuum, the disenfranchised (the poor, criminals, mentally disturbed, extreme ideologists), frequently will not hesitate to use the most violent means to bring about change. They have the least to risk and the most to gain. The more one has to gain by playing "the game," the more security the status quo offers; thus, the change efforts employed will be more passive and traditional. However, even this is changing. Methods once considered the province of those "far

removed from power and influence" are being increasingly employed by "closer-in" groups.

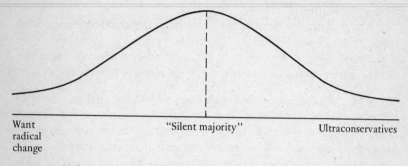

Want radical change   "Silent majority"   Ultraconservatives

FIG. 12–2 Normal distribution of those desiring change.

3. The distribution of those desiring change in organizational and societal systems follows a normal, bell-shaped curve distribution, as shown in Fig. 12–2. It is assumed that normally, one will find a small group pressing for radical change, a small group pressing for the status quo, and the great majority somewhere in the middle. In reality, it may be argued that there seldom is a silent majority, or a number of people occupying a middle position; the majority is "silent" because it lacks leaders, spokesmen, and "influence machinery." What often tends to occur is that the vocal, extreme minorities will force the majority to choose between them—to be presented with "win-lose," "either-or" choices. The curves can be skewed in either direction, as shown in Fig. 12–3.

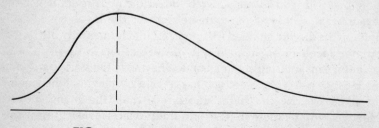

FIG. 12–3 Distribution (skewed to the left).

4. The concentric circles of power, influence, and feelings of being removed from the organization's power center can be portrayed in many ways and will vary by type of organization—public agency, voluntary, industrial, nonprofit, business, and city government. Three examples are illustrated in Fig. 12–4. Each manager can construct an accurate, specific "power circle" for his or her own organization.

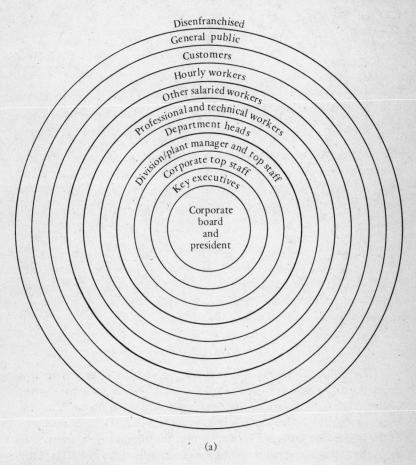

(a)

FIG. 12–4 Organizational circles of power, influence, and feelings: (a) industrial model.

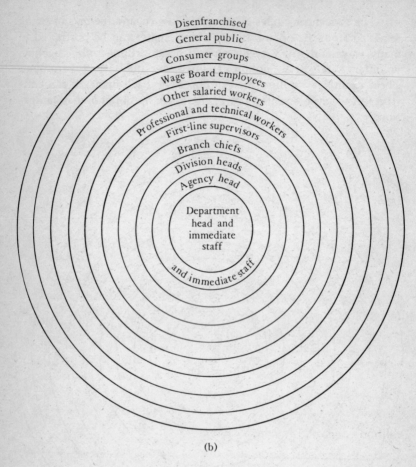

Disenfranchised
General public
Consumer groups
Wage Board employees
Other salaried workers
Professional and technical workers
First-line supervisors
Branch chiefs
Division heads
Agency head
Department head and immediate staff
and immediate staff

(b)

FIG. 12–4(b) Federal organization model.

5. The influence methods a manager regards as appropriate will depend on factors such as: the manager's distance from the power center of the organization; the manager's skills; the manager's feelings of security and how much is to be gained or lost; the importance of the issue; the manager's feelings about the organization; the manager's age and sex; the cultural and subgroup influences bearing on the manager; present economic conditions; the manager's value system; and the "psychological effect" at the moment in the nation, industry, or organization.

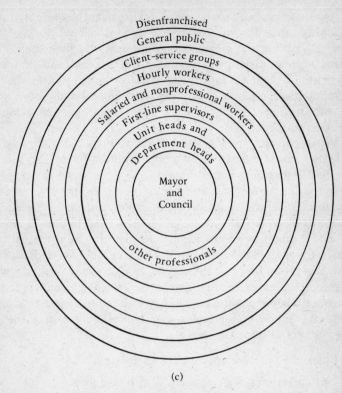

Disenfranchised

General public

Client-service groups

Hourly workers

Salaried and nonprofessional workers

First-line supervisors

Unit heads and

Department heads

Mayor
and
Council

other professionals

(c)

FIG. 12–4(c) City government model.

Methods of Bringing about Change

Among the influence methods used by various groups and occupants of the "concentric circles" are: participation in demonstrations or social action groups, sending letters to newspaper editors, using professional societies as a forum for protest, revealing confidential organizational information to the press or to politicians, pursuing personal interests on the organization's time, publishing articles critical of the organization, having less loyalty to the organization, winking at Hatch Act violations, using consumer groups or customers to force change, joining a union, participating in a slow-down, calling in sick or indulging in frequent absenteeism, using EEO machinery, working "strictly by the rules," demanding representation on policy-making/decision-making groups, refusing to carry out a policy, destroying the organization's property, taking over the office by force, petitioning, appealing to Nader-like groups, using stockholders' rights, boycotting the organization's products, "telling them off," starting a rumor, making a grievance of the smallest incident, taking legal action, violating company rules and/or policies, using the underground press, refusing to do a job, speaking up to the boss, quiting, encouraging others to make complaints, and engaging in malicious obedience.

When one or more of these confrontation methods are used by employees, many managers and organizations have been caught quite flat-footed. A manager should fully understand the range of possible influence methods and should never assume that "it can't happen here." Once confronted with these influence methods, the manager is often faced with the problem of what to do and how to respond. It might be useful for you to identify, from the list that follows, the response(s) you normally believe would be most appropriate. It is recognized that the specific response may well vary with the specific influence method employed. However, your responses may reveal a commonality, which may well require a questioning as to the maximum appropriateness and effectiveness of those responses. Typical responses are:

I kick the problem upstairs. It's their baby.

I go on leave (sick or annual) 'til it blows over.

I call the police. It's a community or social issue or problem.

It will pass. Wait it out.

I ignore it.

I may take over and give leadership to this protest.

I lay down the law; I let them know who is boss.

I make an example of key persons the first time the influence method is tried.

I make concessions as I am forced to. I give way only when defeated.

Maybe the thing called organization development/organizational renewal is the answer. I refer the solution to those people.

I get young people, minority groups, pressure groups, etc., on my boards, committees, policy-making groups, etc. I try to take a "proactive" stance.

I may join the protest.

I consider finding a less hectic job.

I continually pray that nothing will happen.

GUIDES FOR MANAGING CONFLICT

Generally, proactive managers have three questions they consciously and continually attempt to answer:

1. Where is my organization particularly vulnerable?

2. What action steps can I suggest be taken now to prevent or lessen the vulnerability of my organization?

3. Which methods should I, my peers, and top management encourage organizational groups to use to bring about organizational change?

There are also several other guides and techniques managers may find useful as they assist their organization to confront and cope more effectively with conflict. (You should also review the suggestions for dealing with change, which is often a central issue in confrontation, that were discussed in Chapter 9.)

In any confrontation that is highly charged with emotions, feelings, and polarized views, the *early* introduction of facts, data, and logic is relatively meaningless. In this situation, both polarized parties are usually present. Few are thinking. Feelings run rampant. The need for ventilation and "blowing one's stack" is paramount. The decibel level of the meeting will look like that shown in Fig. 12–5.

This phenomenon has been observed repeatedly in such settings. At the beginning of the meeting, there is an out-pouring of talk, shouts, accusations, curses, threats, and general ventilation of pent-up feelings and emotions. Some managers make the mistake of attempting at this point to introduce facts, logic, reasoning, and appeals for "civilized" behavior and possible solutions. Forget it. No one is thinking. No one cares about facts or data: "I want to vent my

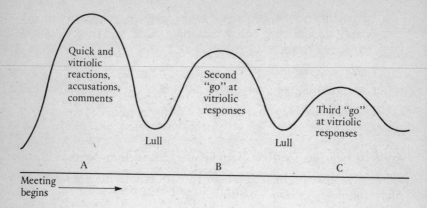

Quick and vitriolic reactions, accusations, comments

Second "go" at vitriolic responses

Third "go" at vitriolic responses

Lull

Lull

A

B

C

Meeting begins

FIG. 12–5

biases." The manager should understand this and simply let the ventilation take place.

Ultimately, people will spend themselves. One can shout just so long; then, exhaustion, fatigue, and energy expenditure take their toll. There will come a lull. This is not yet the point for the introduction of reasoning and facts. Be patient. The lull will be quite short. Everyone takes a second breath. Again, the tempo and decibels rise —only this time not as pronounced as before.

Now comes the second lull, but this is still not the time for inputs based on reason and facts—nor the time for proposed compromise or solutions. All energy has not yet been expended. A third rise in accusations and noise will take place, only this time it will be considerably more short-lived and less chaotic. One can shout only so long; fatigue really does take its toll. Vocal cords are hoarse. People have called one another all the names they can think to call them.

A third lull will ensue. Now is the first time the manager can begin to inject matters related to reason, logic, and facts. But don't shoot the whole wad initially. The crescendo of feelings will still come and go—but it is under control. Find simple, manageable ways to get some order and to introduce reason, facts, and data. Now you will have a fighting chance to have reason prevail—if indeed it is even possible for reason to prevail.

1. The technique of the force-field analysis is often an excellent technique to use. Identify the resisting forces and determine how they can best be dealt with.

2. It may be that a neutral, third party can best attempt to bring about a solution or comrpomise. This is the technique frequently employed in management/labor disputes and conflict.

3. When working with low-tolerance, anxious people, focus on the tasks; give emotional support and assume some of the responsibility for the results yourself. Many people find it much easier to deal with the external realities of the task than with their own feelings or with relationships with other persons or groups.

4. Do not make the mistake of believing, or accepting, the notion that because two parties in conflict cannot agree on all things, they cannot cooperate on some things. Many marriages do this admirably.

5. Search for win-win solutions, not win-lose solutions. How can each of the adversaries win something?

6. Remember the spindle theory. If conflict is difficult to manage, how can the environment be manipulated so that the two opposing groups do not directly interrelate and the desired objectives can be obtained? For example, one may forbid salesmen to contact the shipping dock, although providing other ways for necessary communications between the two to occur.

7. In conflict situations, it is often helpful to refuse to meet on the "turf" of either group, for turf gives its "owner" an advantage. Find a netural location for the discussion. For example, some social-welfare organizations have found that it is helpful to schedule the meeting place at the home of one of the group members. When one meets in another person's home, social customs will prevail, as will courtesy and common decencies. One will tend not to offend the host. One will think twice before loudly "cursing out" another group member when the host's children and wife or husband may overhear.

8. Try to depersonalize the issue. This is the objective that sensitivity-training groups attempt to teach: "how to reject the idea without rejecting the person."

9. Since conflict can easily expand to other issues and values, try to identify and contain it as early as possible. Have your antennae out. It is amazing how many early signals work-organization groups flash indicating latent, or impending, serious conflict which are entirely missed or misassessed by managers. This is the point at which it is highly desirable to check with other persons, or at least one other trusted person, to be sure one is not missing critical signals.

10. A person usually holds more values than the ones apparent in the conflict. Try through communication to find other mutual values that both sides hold as one key to finding a solution or a compromise.

11. Take a good look at your organization, functional statements, program statements, and job descriptions to be sure that overlap and duplication of effort are really under control.

12. When people are upset, do understand that they will assign greater meaning to what you say or do. Remember when, as a child, you stole a nickel or a cookie? The most innocent communication exchange between father and mother was interpreted by you as firm evidence that you had been found out.

13. Set up feedback techniques in the organization so employees can feed uninhibited data to management. Some organizations use tape recorders, scattered throughout the plant, for this purpose. Others use a "hot line" to management so that questions can be directed to specific managers for answers. Other organizations periodically conduct departmental dialogue sessions in which managers come to field workers' questions—no holds barred.

14. Place employees on decision-making and planning bodies.

15. Look at the organization's house organ and other similar employee media. Take active steps to ensure that they are less public relations focused and more issue-oriented. Employees are adults, and they are capable of handling organizational issues, concerns, and problems. Level with them. Give them facts—not "pap."

NOTES

1.

A very helpful booklet that looks at the phases of confrontation, search, and coping in difficult issues in which conflict is significant is Gordon L. Lippitt,

Quest for Dialogue, Philadelphia: Religious Education Committee, Friends General Conference, 1966.

2.

An entertaining and insightful look into this concept will be found in Jerry B. Harvey and D. Richard Albertson, "Neurotic Organizations: Symptoms, Causes and Treatment," *Personnel Journal,* Sept. and Oct. 1971.

3.

Is it Always Right to be Right? 16mm, 9 minutes, color, Stephen Bosustow Productions, Santa Monica, Calif.

For Further Managerial Insights ...

13

Most managers have two continuing interests and questions:

1. *"How can the manager stay abreast of developments within the field of management?"* The manager does not wish to either do extensive reading or read textbooks, "heavy" books and periodicals, or research-oriented materials. The manager's primary concern is with "what does it mean and how do I apply it?"

2. *"What are other insights into the process of management and the manager's job that would be helpful to me?"* Here, the manager has reference to oblique contributions that may not be well researched or scientific and that may even seem to violate professionally held managerial principles.

This chapter addresses itself to these questions. The resource materials are listed under three headings:

1. "Off-beat" books that cannot usually lay claim to being based in research. Many of them are the author's own personal insight.

2. Periodicals that contain articles on management and the manager and that are widely read by managers.

3. Books reported by managers to have had the greatest impact on them and which they have found most useful in their managerial practice.

OFF-BEAT BOOKS AND CONCEPTS

Some of the books listed below have a single concept that would have made a good article, but which have instead been expanded to book length. Almost all are humorous and poke fun at managers and the process of management. A fairly reliable indicator of maturity is the stage at which groups or professions can begin to take themselves less seriously, laugh at themselves, and understand that those in the group are, after all, human and are therefore vulnerable to all the foibles, mistakes, and stupidities to which all other humans fall heir. Although the content of these books often hurts and irritates, there is enough bite and truth to provide realism and useful insights into "managerial traps."

Although the listing that follows does not include all the possible candidates, the ones listed are the best known and have provided managers with valuable insights into their profession.

1. Murphy's law

This is not a book, but should be acknowledged here, since it was probably the forerunner of its category. Whether or not there was a real-life Murphy is unknown. Apparently, there was initially only one law, which was known as "Murphy's law." It was understood that Murphy was an engineer and that he held one primary axiom that became the axiom of all engineers and scientists:

"In any field of scientific endeavor, anything that can go wrong, will go wrong."

As time went on, a number of other laws were identified and added, and almost every profession has its own set of "Murphy's laws." The following examples give the flavor of these laws:

- Left to themselves, things will always go from bad to worse.
- A dropped tool will land where it will do the most damage.
- If there is a possibility of several things going wrong, the one that goes wrong is the one that will do the most damage.
- Nature always sides with the hidden flaw.
- Interchangeable parts won't.
- If everything seems to be going well, you have obviously overlooked something.

- If you play with anything long enough, it will break.
- In any miscalculation, if more than one person is involved, the fault will never be placed.
- Everything is more complicated than it looks.
- Almost anything is easier to get into than out of.
- If something can fail, it will. If it can be hooked up wrong, someone will do it that way. If it can be operated incorrectly, someone will operate it that way. All failures occur at the worst possible time and place (this is known as the missile engineer's Murphy's law).

(It should be noted that specific professions will modify these laws to fit their work. For example, salesmen will modify one of these laws to read: "If anything can go wrong, it will—during the demonstration.")

2. C. Northcote Parkinson, *Parkinson's Law,* New York: Ballantine Books, 1957.

Probably the principal law addressed by the author is: "Work expands to fill the time available for its completion." Many of Parkinson's examples come from government settings. A number of corollaries are abstracted from the major law, and a few other laws are formulated, such as the law of triviality, which states that "the time spent on any item of the agenda will be in inverse proportion to the sum involved." All in all, this is a delightful book, with points that are often too painful to be really funny.

3. C. Northcote Parkinson, *Mrs. Parkinson's Law,* New York: Avon Books, 1968.

It probably could have been predicted that a "Parkinson's law" series would develop. The idea for this book might have been related to women's liberation, but this movement is probably still too young to tolerate much humor. Therefore, most of the laws have to do with the home, family, and entertaining. The basic law expanded in the book is that: "Heat produced by pressure expands to fill the mind available from which it can pass only to a cooler mind." Although filled with pertinent and biting insights, the book does not "come off" quite as well as does *Parkinson's Law.*

4. Eric Berne, *Games People Play: The Psychology of Human Relation-ships*, New York: Grove Press, 1964.

The concepts behind this book are "for real," and many people probably would not list the book in this category. It is recognized that some well-validated research makes this a "serious" book. However, it is listed here because of the terminology employed and the general treatment of the subject. The basic assumption is that much of life consists of "playing games." The context of games is similar to that of "role playing" and the roles managers assume in their organization (discussed in Chapter 1). The approach can be sensed from the titles given to some of the games people play: "Kick me," "Now I've got you, you son of a bitch," and "Let's you and him fight."

5. Antony Jay, *Management and Machiavelli*, New York: Holt, Rinehart and Winston, 1968.

The subtitle to the book is "An Inquiry into the Politics of Corporate Life," which indicates the focus of the book. This, too, is a "serious" book, but with a "different" approach—particularly related to the name Machiavelli and all that Machiavelli's name has come to represent, usually in a negative vein. The introduction states the purpose of the book:

there is a simple framework ready to hand, into which all these diverse observations fit neatly and appropriately. But it means looking at the corporations in a new way: looking not through the eyes of the accountant and the systems analyst and economist and mathematician, but through those of the historian and political scientist. It [the book] does not attempt to supply more information about the corporations—heaven forbid. Its purpose is to make sense of the vast amount of information we already have.[1]

6. Robert C. Townsend, *Up The Organization*, New York: Alfred A. Knopf, 1970.

Robert Townsend, it will be recalled, was Chairman and Chief Executive Officer for Avis Rent-a-Car. Most of Mr. Townsend's insights into organizations, management, and managers are not humorous, but they are quite pungent, blunt, and "off-beat." He begins by asserting that "my last survey of the public, private and independent sectors shows that we have 6001 major institutions in the country. Six thousand of these are ineptly led. The other one is Nader's

Raiders. . . . Big, successful institutions aren't successful because of the way they operate, but in spite of it." Some of his suggestions indicate the tone of the approach:

- "Fire the whole advertising department and your old agency."
- "Firing people . . . is a neglected art in most organizations."
- "Don't hire Harvard Business School graduates."
- "Marketing departments . . . are usually camouflage designed to cover up for lazy or worn out chief executives."

7. Dr. Laurence J. Peter and Raymond Hull, *The Peter Principle,* New York: William Morrow, 1969.

The major principle is: "In a hierarchy every employee tends to rise to his level of incompetence." Corollaries drawn from this basic principle are: "In time, every post tends to be occupied by an employee who is incompetent to carry out its duties" and "Work is accomplished by those employees who have not yet reached their level of incompetence." The implications of the book for current operations, staff development, promotional systems, and organizational efficiency are enormous.

8. Ivor Catt, *The Catt Concept: The New Industrial Darwinism,* New York: Putnam, 1971.

The basic concept is that "firing people is fun and good for business." As is true of many of the other authors writing in a similar style, additional subconcepts and corollaries are drawn from this basic concept. The observations cover the entire organization, but some of the insights into matrix organizations are helpful to managers who are contemplating this form of organization, e.g., his comments about "lay-off fodder." "Once a year management demands a 10% lay-off for every department to get rid of deadwood and keep others on their toes. How do middle managers react? They hire lay-off fodder—as a reserve to use for the annual pruning."[2]

PERIODICALS AND MAGAZINES

The periodicals and magazines listed here are the ones most managers indicate they read in order to keep abreast of new trends and developments in the field of management. The listing was compiled on the basis of periodicals identified most frequently by managers in self-development discussions. Some exploration into managers' reading has been done on a limited scale.[3] This rank-ordered list does not in any way reflect on the quality of the publications. Rather, it reflects such considerations as whether the periodicals are well known and readily available, the frequency of publication, the number of management-related articles appearing in the publication, and current managerial reading habits. Some excellent reprints and original publications are made available by nationally known companies in the private sector. However, these sources are not listed here, since they are not generally available on a regular basis, and it is often difficult to ascertain whether or not the company wants to enlarge its mailing list. The following appear to be the primary periodicals and magazines utilized by managers (excluding directly related trade and industry-type periodicasl):

- *Harvard Business Review,* bimonthly, Boston.
- *The Wall Street Journal,* daily except Saturday and Sunday, New York City.
- *Fortune,* monthly, New York City.
- *Administrative Management,* monthly, New York City.
- *Dun's Review,* monthly, New York City.
- *Business Week,* weekly, New York City.
- *Nation's Business,* monthly, Washington, D.C.
- *Newsweek,* weekly, New York City.
- *Time,* weekly, New York City.
- *California Management Review,* quarterly, Berkeley, Calif.
- *Michigan Business Review,* five times a year, Ann Arbor, Mich.
- *Personnel Journal,* monthly, Swarthmore, Pa.
- *Training and Development Journal,* monthly, Madison, Wisc.
- *Psychology Today,* monthly, Del Mar, Calif.

BOOKS MANAGERS READ

Managers sometimes ask, "What are the books, published since 1900, which managers, organizations, and management scholars believe have most influenced management and managers in the United States?" This is a very difficult question to answer, but a number of attempts have been made to respond to this natural question.[4] Obviously, the replies will vary, depending on the category of persons who are queried. One would expect to receive differing answers from company presidents, training directors, middle managers, supervisors, behavioral scientists, researchers, authors, etc. These anticipated differences are reflected in the several studies.

What managers read may not be the books and concepts which have most influenced management practice since 1900. For example, it is extremely doubtful whether many of today's managers read the works of Max Weber, Frederic W. Taylor, Henry L. Gantt, Mary Parker Follett, Kurt Lewin, Abraham Maslow, or Frank B. Gilbreth, although these persons have made a most significant contribution to modern-day management. And, of course, the moment in time when such a study is made makes a good deal of difference in the results. For example, which author is currently being widely quoted, even if the author's material is froth and of momentary interest or impact?

The list below indicates the books of the 21 writers, researchers, practitioners, and scholars who have probably made the most impact on managers, management, and organizations since 1900. The list is, of course, highly subjective and was highly influenced by the studies referred to earlier; inclusion in this listing was, in large part, accounted for by the book's appearing in two or more of those studies. It is not intended to be an authoritative list; rather, it is an attempt to begin the process of identifying those concepts and authors who have most significantly influenced the modern-day manager, organization, and management thought. (It should be understood that these books exclude those mentioned as "Off-beat Books and Concepts.")

Argyris, Chris, *Integrating the Individual and the Organization,* New York: McGraw-Hill, 1961.

Barnard, Chester I., *Organization and Management,* Cambridge, Mass.: Harvard University Press, 1948.

Blake, Robert R. and Jane S. Mouton, *Managerial Grid,* Houston, Texas: Gulf Publishing, 1964.

Drucker, Peter F., *The Practice of Management,* New York: Harper Trade Books, 1954; and *Age of Discontinuity: Guidelines to Our Changing Society,* Cambridge, Mass.: Harvard University Press, 1969.

Follett, Mary Parker, *Dynamic Administration,* ed. Metcalf and Urwick, 1941, no longer in print.

Gantt, Henry L., *Organizing For Work,* 1919, no longer in print.

Gilbreth, Frank B., *Motion Study,* Clifton, N.J.: Augustus M. Kelley, 1911, reprinted in 1972.

Herzberg, Frederick, *Work and the Nature of Man,* New York: World Publishing, 1966.

Leavitt, Harold J., *Managerial Psychology,* 3d ed., Chicago: University of Chicago Press, 1972.

Lewin, Kurt, *Field Theory in Social Sciences,* 1951, no longer in print; and *Resolving Social Conflicts,* New York: Harper Trade Books, 1948.

Likert, Rensis, *New Patterns of Management,* New York: McGraw-Hill, 1961.

McGregor, Douglas, *The Human Side of Enterprise,* New York: McGraw-Hill, 1960.

Maslow, Abraham, *Motivation and Personality,* 2nd ed., New York: Harper College Books, 1970.

Mayo, Elton C., *The Human Problems of an Industrial Civilization,* New York: Viking Press, 1960.

Roethlisberger, F. J., *Management and the Worker,* Cambridge, Mass.: Harvard University Press, 1939

Simon, Herbert A., *Administrative Behavior: A Study of Decision-Making Processes in Administrative Organizations,* New York: Free Press, 1965.

Skinner, B. F., *Beyond Freedom and Dignity*, New York: Bantam Books, 1972.

Taylor, Frederic W., *The Principles of Scientific Management*, New York: Norton, 1947, reprinted 1967.

Toffler, Alvin, *Future Shock.* New York: Bantam Books, 1970.

Weber, Max, *The Theory of Social and Economic Organization*, trans. Parsons and Talcott, New York: Free Press, 1947.

Whyte, William F., *Man and Organization*, Homewood, Ill.: Richard D. Irwin, 1959.

It will be noted that no attempt has been made to reference the articles which have most significantly affected the manager, management, and organizations; this is because an article seldom packs the influence and wallop of a book, and the data are generally much less clear. With the multitude of articles that appear annually, it would be almost impossible to identify the most impactful ones, though some of the studies mentioned earlier in this chapter have attempted to do so on a very limited scale.

One indicator, fairly heavily relied on by managers, is the "HBR Classic" series of the *Harvard Business Review.* From time to time HBR reprints an article which has been in fairly heavy demand as a reprint since its initial publication. Usually, the author or authors are asked to indicate how they would now change the article, its concepts, and its implications. In a limited way, referring only to those articles published by HBR, this is viewed as an indicator of articles which have significantly affected managers—or, perhaps more accurately, have been read by them.

CONCLUSION

One cannot deny the power and influence of printed words and concepts. Earlier in their development and to a fair degree even today, some of the concepts and generalizations about their application in the work place had a very limited research base, and sometimes the studies were conducted on persons not in the work place. However, the thesis of this book is that managers are applied behavioral scientists, that the work place is the most proper arena in which to test out behavioral findings that relate to work, and that the experience and observations of the practicing manager have tended to be both downgraded and ignored.

The lot of leaders (managers, supervisors) in today's organizations is not an easy one. Their life is frantic and is etched in their faces. Their world has little orderliness or predictability—as witnessed by energy crises, chaotic markets, unstable political leadership, rapid technological changes, and a kaleidoscope of public moods. Forces from the outside world intrude on the organization and are brought into the organization by its employees. In recent years the leader has looked to the behavioral scientist for clues and found a few. However, behavioral scientists tend to deal with an ideal world, and many of their remedial proposals are designed for this fantasy world.

The leader deals with the real world—like it really is. Perhaps it is time to listen more attentively as the leader describes this world and attempts to cope with it—with whatever degree of success. The leader needs the fantasy view of the behavioral scientist, and the behavioral scientist needs the real-world input of the organizational leader.

The leader is human, and the price exacted by organizations, employees, followers, and the public is frequently outrageous. More and more supervisors are looking at unionization as the answer, just as more and more managers are looking for escape into other, less demanding, more humanized pursuits. According to one unknown wag, "The successful business man is a man who was born in the country, where he worked like hell so he could move to the city, where he worked like hell so he could move back to the country." Perhaps, as this book has attempted to do, we can come closer to understanding the managerial job, and helping the manager humanistically perform in it, by drawing on the best counsel of both the behavioral scientist and the practitioner.

NOTES

1.
Reprinted by permission from *Management and Machiavelli* by Antony Jay. Holt, Rinehart and Winston, Inc. as Publishers.

2.

This quote is from the column "Your Money's Worth" by Sylvia Porter, February 12, 1970.

3.

One such study was conducted by the Bureau of National Affairs Communications, Inc., and was reported in their publication *The Projector* March 1970, BNA Communications, Inc., Rockville, Maryland.

4.

Several attempts have been made to answer the question "What books, published since 1900, have probably most influenced management in the United States and are most widely read by managers?" This, of course, is a two-pronged question, and those who have sought to find the answer have approached the problem in two different ways: (1) which books are read by managers, and (2) which books have most influenced management in the United States. The following studies attempted to answer these two questions:

- Joseph L. Massie, *Essentials of Management*, 2d ed., Englewood Cliffs, N.J.: Prentice-Hall, 1970. Massie has a table (Table 2–1) entitled "Pioneers in Management and their Contributions" which lists the contributors to management thought and gives a brief synopsis of their contribution.

- BNA Communications, Inc., Rockville, Md. The November 1970 issue of its publication *The Projector* has an article entitled "What Do Businessmen Read?" BNA has an Executive Library Service—a subscription service of about 150 management books, most of which have been published in recent years. This study reported on the 15 books most frequently requested by subscribers over a two-year period.

- Ferdinand F. Mauser wrote an article, "What Books Do Presidents Read?" which appeared in the March-April 1968 issue of the *Harvard Business Review*. The presidents referred to are 200 company presidents.

- Marvin D. Dunnette and Zita Marie Brown, "Behavioral Science Research and the Conduct of Business," *The Academy of Management Journal*, June 1968. Data from 119 executives are exhibited on p. 181 in Exhibit 1, "Articles and Books Examined by 119 Executives and Frequencies of Executive Votes on the 'Visibility' and 'Significance' of each Contribution Along With Mean Ratings on Six Dimensions Given by Panel of Twelve Judges."

- Harold M. F. Rush, *Behavioral Science: Concepts and Management Application*, Personnel Policy Study No. 216, New York: National Industrial Conference Board, 1969. This publication gives data on a questionnaire mailed to 500 companies (302 replies) which requested information about which behavioral scientists the respondents felt were most influential to them and on their organizations.

Index